A Short History of Asia

A Short History of Asia

Second Edition

Colin Mason

First edition published 2000
Second edition published 2005 by
PALGRAVE MACMILLAN
Houndmills, Basingstoke, Hampshire RG21 6XS and
175 Fifth Avenue, New York, N.Y. 10010
Companies and representatives throughout the world

PALGRAVE MACMILLAN is the global academic imprint of the Palgrave Macmillan division of St. Martin's Press, LLC and of Palgrave Macmillan Ltd. Macmillan® is a registered trademark in the United States, United Kingdom and other countries. Palgrave is a registered trademark in the European Union and other countries.

ISBN-13: 978–1–4039–3611–0 hardback
ISBN 10: 1–4039–3611–0   hardback
ISBN-13: 978–1–4039–3612–7 paperback
ISBN 10: 1–4039–3612–9   paperback

This book is printed on paper suitable for recycling and made from fully managed and sustained forest sources.

A catalogue record for this book is available from the British Library.

Library of Congress Cataloging-in-Publication Data

Mason, Colin, 1926–
    A short history of Asia / Colin Mason.—2nd ed.
       p. cm.
    Includes bibliographical references (p.) and index.
    ISBN 1–4039–3611–0—ISBN 1–4039–3612–9 (pbk.)
    1. Asia—History. I. Title
    DS33.M29 2005
    950—dc22   2005050865

10   9   8   7   6   5   4   3   2   1
14   13   12   11   10   09   08   07   06   05

Printed in China

Contents

Part III The Modern Nations

List of Maps

List of Figures

The author has taken and supplied all the photographs used in this book.

History is a mirror for the future.
Jiang Zemin

1 *Introduction*

Asia, making up more than half of all humans, is rapidly becoming more productive and influential. In 2003 China achieved its fastest rate of growth in six years with a gross domestic product increase of 9.6 per cent. Its development of new infrastructure, probably the largest and fastest in world history, consumed in that year more than half of total global cement production and one-third of the world's steel. Some economists claim that in real terms China can be considered the world's second economy after the United States. In 2003 five Asian central banks, in Japan, China, Hong Kong, Taiwan and South Korea, held almost half the world's financial reserves, around $1.3 trillion, most of these in United States dollars.

This movement of Asia away from vestigial 'colonial' economies is now a major current of history, which 'the West' might ignore at its peril. The most developed of the Asian nations now have levels of prosperity and industry that strongly challenge those of the West. China's steady growth and wealth and Japan's affluence are the most obvious, but India, South Korea, Taiwan, Malaysia and Singapore all have educated and relatively well-off middle classes, and market their products and expertise worldwide. Already multinational corporations are shifting expert work to Asian countries to take advantage of generally lower wages there – the fast-growing information technology sector in India is an example. As electronic technology, especially the Internet, becomes universal, this participation of Asians in world business must increase. Quite apart from the economic effect, rapid means of global communication will bring greater numbers of Asians and non-Asians into a close working relationship.

A second major element in almost all the Asian societies is the economic gulf between their islands of the educated and modestly affluent and the surrounding sea of the poor, the disease-afflicted and uneducated. If one considers the region as a whole, as many as three-quarters of its people are disadvantaged in at least one of these ways. Can at least a modest level of prosperity be extended to this huge segment – almost one-half – of the human race? At present Japan and Singapore are the only Asian countries that provide most of their people with standards of living and affluence at high levels. China, South Korea and Taiwan have made considerable progress. But in the nations of south Asia – India, Pakistan, Bangladesh, Sri . Lanka, Afghanistan – and south-east Asia, especially Indonesia, the Philippines, Burma, Cambodia and Laos, poverty and ignorance are, if anything, increasing.

And these poor and ignorant are the most vulnerable – they made up the large majority of the 280,000 (conservatively estimated) killed by the December 2004 tsunami in south and south-east Asia. More than perhaps a quarter of a million of those dead were from the beachfront regions of west Sumatra and Sri Lanka, and of these almost half were children too small and weak to struggle with the huge waves that came up from the sea. There are, of course, reasons for the continuance of poverty in the world. A billion dollars a day given as subsidies to agriculture in the developed world is effectively money taken from farmers in the undeveloped world. Unsubsidized agriculture cannot compete on the export market nor, often even more disastrously, in its own. And Asian governments since independence have persistently favoured urban elites. Typically, the average income in an Asian capital is as much as three times that in the surrounding countryside. Natural resources like forests are exploited without regard to the people living in them; smallholdings are compounded into large agribusinesses as peasants are driven off their land by compulsion or by debt. In some cases unjustifiably high taxes are levied on farmers, such as the 25 per cent export tax on rice imposed in Thailand in 1955. The Philippines, Java and Thailand lost more than half their forests in the first two decades after the end of the Second World War, and with a few exceptions, that depredation continues unchecked today. This poverty of the undeveloped world is, of course, so horrendous in its consequences as to be of importance not only to the Asian region but to the world at large. If it continues it must be associated with growing populations, global pollution, lawlessness and 'terror'. The developed nations might then be hard put to insulate themselves from the consequences.

A third major thread in this pattern is occidentalism – in the words of Ian Buruma and Avishai Margalit, the authors of a 2004 book with that name – a view of the West, and especially the United States, as 'a mass of soulless, decadent, money-grubbing, rootless, faithless, unfeeling parasites'. This is the background to what Western leaders call 'terrorism', the response to which by late 2004 had caused fear, foreboding and the expenditure of many billions of dollars in counter-measures. The authors' arguments relate mainly to the social and economic reasons for Islamic extremist terrorism. They conclude that the West's worst mistake would be to simply try and protect itself, rather than making active efforts to understand the economic and social reasons for occidentalism. In this context it is worth noting that the large majority of Muslims live not in the Middle East, but in Asia.

A struggle between traditional and modern values compounds this problem. The large peasant majority are not unaware of the way they are being exploited by their rulers – this leads to a general mistrust of the machinery of government, especially evident in today's Indonesia. Modern education is often seen as eroding traditional values. However, the availability and use of cheap radios and television sets does mean that the underprivileged of Asia are only too aware of the differences between their lives and those of affluent Westerners. It would be naïve indeed not to see that this must drive discontent at the very least – at worst terrorism and war.

Finally, a new pattern of politics, which might best be described as 'controlled democracy', is emerging in many nations of Asia. The government of Singapore was perhaps the earliest experiment along these lines. Controlled democracy amounts to retention of the forms of representative government – general elections, houses of parliament – but restriction of their powers, as well as the political and human rights of the population, so that not only is government effectively exercised by an elite, but its actions and its right to rule are asserted as beyond question.

Controlled democracy is almost always associated with a strong charismatic leader, as Lee Kuan Yew has been in Singapore, and Mohamad Mahathir was in Malaysia. Thailand under Prime Minister Thaksin is following a similar path, with indications that Indonesia may also take it. The Communist states of the former French Indo-China, Vietnam, Laos and Cambodia, are effectively run by elites. It is significant that the Association of South-east Asian States has recently become more tolerant of direct and enforced military rule in Burma, which also has economic support from China.

Possibly because of the persistence of this elitism of the wealthy, and in spite of the abject poverty of millions, Asia has built and is building an extraordinary array of multi-storey skyscrapers, presenting a bizarre contrast to the villages and urban slums. Expensive to build and requiring huge amounts of energy to maintain, this proliferation of more than 20,000 commercial towers seems the result more of a desire to compete in sheer 'face' terms than of intrinsic value to the communities in which they are built. Hong Kong, with more than 7000 buildings over 12 storeys high, now has more skyscrapers than New York. Twelve of the 15 tallest buildings in the world are in Asia. Kuala Lumpur's Petronas Towers, from 1998 the highest building in the world, gave place in 2004 to a dramatic 101-storey pagoda-like structure in Taipei, while this will be outstripped in 2007 by the even taller World Trade Centre in Shanghai.

Most Western people, even those who consider themselves educated, seem largely uninformed about Asia's history, especially that before the colonial era, and often have inaccurate perceptions even at the most fundamental levels, views coloured by the opinions of the colonial period, with assumptions of white supremacy, and vague, shocking concepts like the well at Cawnpore and 'the black hole of Calcutta'. Others visualize a picture of 'Asian tigers', vast communities almost magically transforming themselves into clones of Western consumerist societies, or, equally mysteriously, visited by economic catastrophe. These Asian people sometimes say and do things which seem not to make sense. Just what are the influences on them of religion, most frequently categorized as violent and fundamentalist? Many of them seem 'westernized', but are they really? All this, like anything else not understood, prompts disquiet and, unhappily, often ill-judged action.

Most inappropriate of all is to visualize 'Asia' as a homogeneous unit, when in fact it is a term of convenience embracing widely varying peoples and cultures. But it is also necessary to recognize a certain commonality of problems and social and economic attitudes which is increasingly coming to overlie that variety. Many of these problems – underdevelopment, extreme poverty, ugly and unhealthy urbanization, difficulties of government, internal civil war and overpopulation among them – can be traced back to the colonial era.

Greater economic co-operation between the Asian nations is a third major trend. China, early in the third millennium, will probably lead a loose zonal union of developing nations in Asia, which were former colonies of European, Japanese and American imperialists, into enhanced power and world status, in spite of – and possibly because of – the region's economic downturn from 1997. The increasing difficulty smaller nations, such as South Korea, are finding in competing with Chinese manufacture must eventually prompt them into greater economic accommodation with China. Chinese influence in mainland south-east Asia is increasing steadily in places like Laos and Cambodia. The Asian mainland states, in the past largely isolated from each other and the West, are building one of the world's most ambitious and expensive engineering projects – the 80,000 mile network of roads, bridges and ferries which will make up the Asian super-highway. Co-ordinated by the UN Economic and Social Commission for Asia and the Pacific, this immense project will involve 31 countries. One of the first routes will be Asian Highway One, the modern equivalent of the ancient Silk Road, linking Tokyo and Istanbul. The Asian Development Bank and China are lending Laos $900 million to build its section of a highway between Kunming and Bangkok that will permit major overland trade between China and mainland south-east Asia for the first time.

Five Asian nations, including India and China, were initial members of the G22 bloc of developing nations within the World Trade Organization (WTO) that resulted from the failure of the WTO meeting at Cancun, Mexico, in 2003. The G22 group, formed to counterbalance the influence of the United States and Japan in world trade matters, represents more than 51 per cent of world population.

The Asian nations have shouldered their way into virtually every area of modern technology; they typically have an active and able middle class; at least four have nuclear weapons or the means to make them; and they influence regions outside Asia, like Africa and the Middle East. The products of their industry now feature prominently in the lives of almost every Westerner. This new power bloc must increasingly affect, and even challenge, the rest of the world. An East Asian Community was proposed by Malaysian prime minister, Badawi, late in 2004. He called for a summit to lay the groundwork for an EAC, which would be a free trade area, and co-operate on finance and security. A reported statement of the then Chinese Premier, Li Peng, in August 1997 is relevant. It attacked 'the Western world order', supported a call from Indonesia for a review of the UN Human Rights Charter to place less stress on individual rights, and promised Chinese support to an east Asian economic union. However, this rhetoric had become less strident by 2003, following Chinese entry into membership of the World Trade Organization; China, rather, seemed anxious to placate a bellicose United States, intent on a worldwide crusade against 'terror', and to concentrate on domestic development rather than foreign affairs.

China's growth has been due substantially to a remarkable reversion to private enterprise in recent decades. That transition has been driven by powerful motivations, themselves rooted millennia-deep in the traditions of the past: hard work, familial connections, respect for learning, a distancing between business and government, a passion for money and material success, acceptance of authoritarian government are among them. These are all elements of a Chinese ethic that can be traced back thousands of years, and which made China through most of her history the world's largest, wealthiest and most literate society. Always evident, this ethic was suppressed by a rigid authoritarianism during the first decades of the Communist mainland state, although it prospered in Hong Kong, Taiwan and Singapore.

These 'Asian values' are not exclusively Chinese. They are shared by other Asian peoples. Again, it is ridiculous to regard 'Asia' as a monolith ethnically or culturally, but it is equally important to recognize these common qualities, and that there is an Asian point of view – perhaps more accurately Asian points of view – which the Asian nations themselves see as different from Western ones. The fact that educated Asian people often wear Western clothing, speak English, use the same technologies, can easily lead to the assumption that they are becoming 'Westernized'. This surface appearance is misleading. The Japanese, Indian or Thai in his office at his computer, wearing a Western business suit, speaking English, will be a very different man at home in the evening, in his religious observances, when he contemplates marriage, in his relationship with his family, in his view of the world.

China's move towards world supremacy – and that without doubt is her intention – is unlikely to be military, although military strength will be there to back it. It will be economic and social, and its front-line forces will be the influential network of Chinese businessmen and women in most Asian countries, and the emerging Chinese multinational corporations, substantially based on Hong Kong and Shanghai. This is not to forecast the development of a vast Chinese territorial empire in Asia. The world's other powers would be unlikely to permit such a thing, in the first place. In the second place, China has had opportunities for that before, as far back as the fifteenth century, and rejected them. Her traditional attitude has been to maintain a loose authority among peripheral states – not unlike the position the United States has in the Americas.

These general statements may serve to introduce two important and basic contentions: the first, that the Asian region, occupied by more than half of all humans, is rapidly becoming an economic and social zone of great significance, unable to be ignored by the rest of the planet; the second, that, whatever the outward appearances, the modern states are powerfully influenced by their past history and traditions.

In the year 1407, 2000 Chinese scholars compiled an encyclopaedia of the thought and writing of their nation's past. When completed it occupied over 11,000 volumes, and so was too large to print. Any single volume of reasonable proportions that seeks to encompass the history of the Asian nations requires ruthless selection, and special care in priority of material. This has led to the omission of many interesting and important facts from this book, and the inclusion of more general statements than the writer would have liked.

The reader needs to know the basis on which selection has been made. The first objective has been to follow broad trends – constants, as it were – especially where these still have effect today. A common quality of Asian societies is this importance of the past, of tradition. Why is it that the Tamil Tigers have pursued their rebellion against the central government in Sri

Lanka with such dedication and ferocity? Why was it seen by modern Indonesians as natural that their first president ceremonially contacted the earth with his bare feet, exposed himself to electrical storms, hugged trees? Why has Western-style representative government generally not succeeded in the Asian nations? Why might Indonesian schoolchildren reasonably think their nation has a historic right to all of New Guinea, parts of the Philippines, possibly even some of northern Australia? The answers to these questions and many others emerge from a knowledge of Asian history, especially that before the colonial era.

Links to the past become all the more important because the new nations of Asia look back beyond the colonial era to their own often legendary and shadowy past for a sense of national identity. And sometimes they identify what was probably not real, exaggerate something quite minor, in theories which have more to do with present-day political ideology than the facts of history.

A second priority is to sketch the enormous variety of cultures and peoples in Asia, and to give due credit to the achievements and greatness of its societies, which are by no means properly understood or appreciated. It is, for instance, extraordinary that many Western children are still taught that Johann Gutenberg invented printing with movable type in Germany around 1450, when movable type had been developed in China 300 years earlier; and that European mariners 'discovered' Asia.

Most people would know that fireworks and the wheelbarrow were invented in China, but it may come as news to them that the twelfth-century Song society used credit banking and cheques, and could inoculate against smallpox, and that there were Indian cities with mass-produced standard housing and efficient urban sewerage systems as early as 2500 BCE. Too often Asian histories by Europeans have been unduly preoccupied with the activities of European colonizers. This book tries, among other things, to redress that balance.

Asia's past is often obscure, with much of the story of its great civilizations buried beneath the ruins of later and inferior cultures. During this past, such records as existed were not informed by any precise sense of history. In most cases the earliest written records, and many later ones, have little historic value because they did not record reliable fact, but were intended to flatter the aristocracy and justify the actions of kings. In other cases no written record exists, because there was no writing. Of the enigmatic Harappa civilization of Pakistan and north India, records of a kind exist, but have not been deciphered.

The present nations of south and south-east Asia substantially follow the boundaries of convenience and expediency set by the colonizing powers. Here again, the past can hint at future possibilities. In time, shared problems, shared faiths and languages crossing borders are almost certain to alter national boundaries. This process has begun in India, where state boundaries have been greatly changed since independence. Civil war and regional conflict on a major scale have resulted from boundaries at odds with the traditions in Sri Lanka, Vietnam, Korea, Burma, Thailand and the Philippines.

Transplanted Western concepts of nationhood and government, especially 'democracy', which grew in Europe with painful slowness and have had varied fortunes, have generally not prospered in Asia. It is not an Asian tradition that individual freedoms should extend as far as national politics. Typically the rule of the past has been authoritarian and individuals have been obliged to conform to it. Around this central authority, usually one man arrayed not only with the honours but the disadvantages of near-divinity, has been grouped an aristocracy whose duties, rights and obligations have also been rigidly defined by tradition. Terminology may have changed, but to a considerable extent this situation continues today. Yet the Asian peoples now seem more inclined to support the machinery of representative government, with relatively high voter turnouts in elections in India, Indonesia, Taiwan and the Philippines in 2004. Whether these will substantially alter the nature of governments remains to be seen.

The perceptive reader will notice another constant, common to virtually all Asian history – a pattern of economic and social elites exploiting the majority of the people ruthlessly and with often self-defeating avarice, using the backing of armed force. This less than admirable tradition can readily be observed in several Asian nations today, and has much to do with their problems.

Asia contains the mightiest mountains on the planet, a series of ranges, rocky escarpments and bleak uplands, from which rise the Himalayas. Among this wild and lightly-peopled mountain country the big rivers find their source in the perpetual snow and glaciers. As they flow south, east and west, these rivers broaden, meander, and slow down into great, turbid, discoloured streams. Some of them, like the Mekong and the Ganges, reach the sea in the midst of delta regions with miles of backwaters, low marshy swamps and almost impenetrable mangroves. Above these swamps are flat, fertile plains which are regularly flooded and enriched by fresh deposits of alluvial silt. These plains have been for thousands of years the regions best suited for growing food crops. They have become both the centres of successive civilizations and a temptation for less well-endowed marauders from outside.

As one proceeds north from India, progressively higher mountain ranges block the way, giving the few possible roads, like the Khyber Pass, great strategic and political importance. Once across Afghanistan, Kashmir, Nepal and the southern valleys of Tibet, civilization peters out into a region of desolate, high plateaux, swept perpetually by snow-laden winds. These plateaux, the Pamirs and northern Tibet, give place in the east to the shifting sands and dun-coloured parched soils of Xinjiang in China.

Thence, across Mongolia through the loose dunes of the Gobi, the terrain changes to the fertile loess soils of north-west China and the grasslands of Manchuria. This is east Asia, a second major concentration of population and culture. Once again, in China it is the fertile river valleys that make up the heartland. The valley of the Yangzi River downstream from its celebrated gorges, now flooded, is the most fertile and populous.

The high, arid deserts of central Asia, with their cold, thin air and perpetual requirement of constant struggle to maintain a bare existence, have bred a group of toughened races who, for thousands of years, invaded and conquered the plains below. Good horsemen, bred from childhood to the saddle and the sword, they were typical nomads, who moved constantly from one grassy valley to the next, living in felt tents, driving their herds with them. The names of these nomad people and their leaders ring through history, the very epitome of battle and conquest – the Huns, the Vandals, the Mongols, Timur, Genghis Khan.

To the south the picture is different. Tropical Asia consists of two big promontories and thousands of islands. India projects nearly a thousand miles into the ocean that bears her name. On the other side of the Bay of Bengal is another peninsula nearly as large, shared by the mainland south-east Asian states: Burma, Thailand, Malaysia, and the three Indo-Chinese nations, Vietnam, Cambodia and Laos.

Finally, in a great arc, swinging from west to east and then northwards, lies an almost continuous chain of islands. Some, like Borneo and Sumatra, are among the major islands of the world, but the rest range down to tiny specks of land with only enough soil to support a few palm trees a foot or so above the heave of the sea. One of the smaller of these islands, linked to the Malayan mainland by a causeway, contains a dynamic, mostly Chinese, city-state, Singapore. Thousands more, running across 3000 miles of equatorial sea to the south of Malaysia, make up Indonesia, the world's fourth most populous nation. To the north, across the atoll-studded Sulu Sea, the archipelago merges with the islands of the Philippines. Less than 200 miles north from the principal Filipino island of Luzon is the southern promontory of Taiwan; once again to the north the Ryukyus lead to Japan.

The traveller has passed from the tropics to the temperate zone, then through the Japanese islands to the northernmost, Hokkaido, into a region of ice, snow and fiery volcanoes. The craggy and inhospitable Kuriles lead to the last peninsula, Kamchatka, pointing out into the Pacific, south-west from the Arctic Circle.

PART I

Before Imperialism

2 Prehistory and the First Indian Civilizations

The Asia of remote prehistory was very different from the teeming continent and islands of today. Its population was tiny and dispersed, living mostly on the seacoasts and the plains of the big rivers, each small group of humanity separated from the others by virgin forest, full of wild animals. Families stayed together, developed into clans for mutual protection. Life was precarious, death came early and was often sudden and violent.

This time of prehistory can be traced back at least a million years, when the humanoid species *Homo erectus* is presumed to have moved out of east Africa into Europe, China and parts of south-east Asia. In 1891 the skull of a *Homo erectus* individual, now thought to date back 1.8 million years, was found in central Java. Stone implements dating as far back as half a million years indicate a proto-human presence in India, while the remains of 'Peking man' found in China are estimated at half a million years ago. The bones of perhaps 50 people, including five almost complete skulls, were found at Dragon Bone Hill, 25 miles from the Chinese capital. Earlier conclusions that this ancient community used fire, made crude stone tools, and may have been capable of speech seem unlikely following the reports in 2004 of a Chinese/American research team at the site. These hominids were primitive creatures, and probably survived, as did other *Homo erectus*, on what they could scavenge from the kills of large predators.

The most recent glacials of the quaternary ice age had major effects on the development and distribution of humans. Rigorous conditions caused by the extension of the ice shifted the areas of population. People, still in insignificant numbers, were forced towards the central belt of the planet, or were trapped behind barriers of ice, to adapt as best they could to the centuries of bitter cold.

These glacials lowered the level of the seas by as much as 300 feet, so that much of what was water became dry land. Australia was linked through Indonesia, except for two straits, to the Asian mainland. People could cross land bridges over much of what is now sea, and there is abundant evidence

Map 1 Asia

they did so. The Sunda Shelf, now the shallow seas of Indonesia and Malaysia, was dry land some 18,000 years ago. While the glaciation associated with this lowered temperatures and rainfall, what is now the tropical zone was not covered in ice, as was so much of the world to the north and south. Temperatures on the huge Sunda Shelf – a region of almost two million square miles – would have been four to eight degrees Celsius cooler. Many of the racial patterns of the region were set by this pattern of rising and falling sea levels. In the interglacial periods the sea submerged what must have been huge areas of fertile plainland. An east Asian mountain range became the islands of Japan.

The nature of the earliest proto-humans is conjectural at best. However, to modern eyes these creatures would seem ape-like. Skulls recovered show them to have had low, slanting brows and small though developing brains. They are classed as hominids mainly because they stood upright and showed signs of significant development of the frontal lobe of the brain. This human evolution in Asia was not very different from that elsewhere in the world. Differing racial types began to emerge. It is believed the Mongolian type, that of the Chinese and other east Asian peoples, had its origins on the northern steppes of Siberia. One theory considers that the distinctive features of these people are due to the effects of the extreme cold on their ancestors, trapped for many generations in Siberia during the last glacial age. It is claimed that under these extreme conditions humans evolved protective features – the flat brow to protect the sinuses, deep-set eyes and high cheekbones.

Whether or not *Homo erectus* evolved into later populations of *Homo sapiens* is controversial. Modern man appears to have spread through southeast Asia about 40,000 years ago, during an interglacial. Sea levels were high, and the islands of the region were not joined to each other and the mainland as they would later be. Granted this, the movement of humans by island-hopping is both interesting and important. These people must have used some kind of boat, so this could well have been the very beginning of human maritime history. From the end of the most recent glaciation about 10,000 years ago human evolution in the region becomes more coherent, with evidence of toolmaking, domestication of livestock and agricultural societies leading on to the village communities of the immediate past and present.

The Mongoloid people who now make up most of the south-east Asian populations appear to have migrated from southern China, displacing earlier Australoid peoples from about 7000 years ago onwards. From that time a relatively advanced agricultural society evolved in the fertile Yangzi valley of China and along much of the southern coast. These were probably the first people in the world to grow rice and to make woven matting and ropes. When migrants from this area moved into mainland south-east Asia they settled first in low-lying swampy areas where the soil proved fertile. Even at that time malaria was probably a great killer, due to the prevalence of its vector, the *Anopheles* mosquito – one reason why populations remained low.

About 4000 BCE small, primitive mud-brick villages developed in what is now India and Pakistan. In some, in the valleys and foothills of Baluchistan, their inhabitants may have domesticated cattle, sheep and goats. Some Indian scholars have speculated that a rather more developed society existed in western Rajasthan along the Sarasvati River, mentioned in ancient Indian texts, but now long since dry, as early as 6000 BCE. Villages like Amri, close to the Indus River in Sind, developed perhaps 2000 years later. Copper implements and decorated pottery have been found in this region, and some houses had stone walls or stone foundations.

The past of Egypt and Mesopotamia is fairly generally known, but it is less appreciated that a more extensive and developed civilization than either of these existed in Asia almost 5000 years ago, with the biggest cities and the most sophisticated society the world had yet seen. This society, still largely enigmatic, was utterly forgotten for more than 3000 years from the time of its demise until its ruins were investigated from 1922 onward. It is called Harappa, from the name of one of its major cities, although there was also a second and similar city, Mohenjodaro.

Over almost 1000 miles along the Indus River and its tributaries are the remains of hundreds of other towns and villages with common characteristics. Their grid pattern of streets and lanes would have given them a strikingly modern, planned appearance. Their use of standardized materials and efficient sewerage and drainage systems was paralleled in Europe only in quite recent times. Inscriptions on fragments of pottery found in Harappa in 1999 are considered by some archaeologists to be the world's first writing.

The Harappa site alone covered almost 400 acres and probably housed 40,000 people. The location of this culture on the floodplain of a big river is no accident, since the earliest cities were generally so situated. In most regions the soil became exhausted quickly from cropping and people had to move on to new fields. Only on the river plains, where annual floods deposited rich, new layers of silt on the land, were they able to stay long in one place. The city civilizations of Mesopotamia depended in this way on the Tigris and Euphrates rivers, and those of Egypt on the Nile.

The ruins of Mohenjodaro are in Sind, in what is now hot, forbidding desert. Those of Harappa are 350 miles north-east in the Punjab. However, distinctive Harappan artefacts have been found over an area larger than present-day Pakistan, indicating that at its height this society was considerably larger than either Egypt or the Sumerian empire at that time. The Harappa civilization had a flair for standardization unusual in the ancient world. Its kiln-baked salmon-coloured mud bricks were of uniform size everywhere and this has made it possible to identify Harappa remains with relative ease. These were the world's first planned urban centres, with grid-planned, straight streets and lanes orientated north and south, east and west, dividing the cities into 12 blocks. Corners were rounded off to allow carts and other traffic to turn easily.

This society was innovative and versatile, engaging in a wide range of art and manufacture and trading with other parts of the civilized world. These were probably the first people to grow cotton, spin it and weave it into cloth, which became a major export. Harappa traded with Sumer in Mesopotamia – its soapstone seals have been found in the excavation at Ur. Lapis lazuli, tin, turquoise and silver were imported from Afghanistan, jadeite from Tibet, and made into ornaments. Trading was by sea, from the Arabian Sea port of Lothal.

Most Harappan architecture is strikingly similar. The buildings were plain and in the same style, the layout of streets and lanes geometrical. Individual houses were built with the rooms facing on to a central courtyard, with few openings to the street frontages. These houses were well-adapted to the hot, probably humid, climate of the time. They were provided with efficient covered drainage from the bathrooms to main sewers in the street outside, which carried waste water well away from the city. Every house had a bathing platform and a latrine. Some of the tiled bathroom floors still show signs of polish from the repeated contact of the bare feet of their users. The largest buildings seem to have been public ones – in Mohenjo-daro a granary and a large pool, probably designed more for ritual washing than for bathing.

The cities had internal fortifications – the postulated 'citadels' – but lacked any apparent defences against outside enemies, which suggests a small privileged class in control of the mass of the people rather than any need for protection against an outside invader. There is other evidence to support this: the ruins include long monotonous rows of small barrack-like structures which were probably workers' tenements.

It was once thought that the Harappa civilization emerged fully fledged about 2500 BCE, existed for 1000 years, and was then destroyed just as mysteriously. However, later archaeology indicates a continuous agrarian society from perhaps 7000 years ago, which was probably the authentic beginning of Indian civilization. Excavations at the Mehrgarh site indicate a farming society that grew wheat and barley and had domesticated sheep and goats and the typical Indian hump-backed cow. There is evidence of a considerable pottery manufacture, using the potter's wheel, by 3500 BCE.

Although the Harappa cities are presumed to have developed from this earlier society, they had distinctive and unusual features that still pose unanswered questions. Harappa had a written language, found on some 2000 soapstone seals recovered throughout the cities and villages, but this has not been deciphered. The Harappa showed considerable artistry in small objects. Among the ruins small figures in soapstone, alabaster and marble have been found depicting people, often in a sophisticated and lively style. There was a well-developed, distinctive system of weights and measures. Copper and bronze were used for weapons, tools and ornaments.

The nature of the religion is unclear, but there are strong indications of a connection with gods of the later, Hindu, period, with evidence particularly of worship of a mother-goddess concerned with the fertility of the earth and the creation of life. This is interesting because it is traditional Indian belief that a light-skinned people, who much later infiltrated into India from the north-west, were the first to evolve an ordered civilization there. The early Indian epics assert that when these people came they found only a simple village culture in north India. This was indeed the commonly held historical view until the Harappa ruins were investigated.

A mysterious catastrophe brought the Harappa civilization to an end about 1750 BCE. It must have been huge in its scope, because Mohenjodaro had been damaged many times before, probably by floods, and had been rebuilt regularly. There is evidence that the final blow was very sudden and very damaging. It might have been a combination of major earthquakes and flooding. Remnants of the society continued in some villages, but at a much lower and more primitive level. This was presumably what the pastoral people who are thought to have come into India from the north about 200 years later would have found.

This second influx of people, who, according to the epics, began to enter India from about 1500 BCE, had leaders who called themselves *aryas*, which means noble. The modern name of Persia, Iran, is significantly derived from it, and so is the term 'Aryan', applied to the language group to which these people belonged. This language group is now more commonly called Indo-European because of close links between the north Indian written language, Sanskrit, and some early European languages, including Greek, Celtic and High German. Hence a single ethnic group has been postulated, which spilled over into Europe as well as the north Indian plain.

At one stage, notably in Nazi Germany, it was romanticized into ideas of a super-race with almost divine rights to ascendancy over other humans, and a duty to maintain its genetic purity. However, India's new settlers appear to have been a simple people, much less sophisticated than the Harappa – herdsmen and hunters who worshipped deities that were mani- festations of the elemental forces of nature. Their art was unspectacular and their architecture, in particular, suffers in comparison with Harappa. Since they used only wood, none of their buildings survive, but accounts in the Sanskrit classic, the *Rigveda*, describe small hut-like houses, grouped together inside earth and wooden palisades.

The *Rigveda* makes it quite clear than the newcomers disliked and despised the people they found already in north India. While there was, no doubt, more intermarriage and cultural exchange with the existing popula- tion than the classics admit, the people from the north seem to have been much concerned with their racial purity. They were light-skinned, and placed much store on colour. It was regarded as good to be light-skinned and shameful to be dark – a prejudice still strong in India, and elsewhere, today. When my family lived in a north-east Thai market town people asked if they might simply touch my children, who were fair-haired with blue eyes, to bring good fortune.

By the eighth century BCE the former nomads, almost certainly mingled with the residual population from Harappa after its decline, had spread eastward across north India to the banks of the Ganges River. By 600 BCE they were using iron and planting rice, strengthening their agri- cultural society and expanding over the Ganges plain. Since the only verbal information we have about this stage is a bewildering assortment of myths, these must be approached with caution. A major point of inter- est was the gradual accumulation of this vast mass of religious strictures and legends which were committed to memory and carried on by word of mouth, and which are a basis of several major religions, and especially of Hinduism.

The extent to which these reflect the times in which they originated is doubtful. They must have been added to and modified extensively over the period – perhaps 1000 years – before they were written down. Out of the obscurity of this early period one can still make some deductions. The nomadic herdsmen who had come in from the north learned to be farmers and town-dwellers. A need for established law and order led to the selection of kings, who benefited from taxation – this much is evident from the myth describing how Manu, an early king, laid down quite specific percentages of produce and livestock as his own stipend.

The extensive co-operative work involved in developing agriculture led on to ordered villages and eventually to towns and cities, with hints of some communities that governed themselves by consensus consultation. There can be no question of an Indian 'nation' at this time. But there did evolve on the north Indian plain tribal groups and eventually states who fought each other ceaselessly in a struggle for land and power, but who nevertheless shared a common cultural heritage.

3 The Development of Indian Culture: Hinduism and Buddhism

One of the major aspects of the culture that evolved during this expansion was a class system of such vigour that it still exists today, although it is now infinitely more complex. This culture and religion – for it is both – is generally called Hinduism by Europeans, by Indians *sanatan dharma*.

Ancient India had four major classes. The highest, the priest-teachers, or *brahmins*, soon came to hold authority, even over nobles, by virtue of the roles they assumed as interpreters of religion. The old gods changed, and worship became more complex. Rituals and formality clouded what must once have been fundamentally a simple faith.

The second important class were the *kshatriyas*, the soldier-nobles, whose duty it was to fight for the state. Some historians believe that the many successful invasions of India, often by quite small armies, were effective because it was believed that only kshatriyas could or should fight back – in contrast with Korea, for instance, where peasant and even slave guerrilla forces attacked invaders from Manchuria and Japan ferociously. A third Indian caste of less importance were the *vaishyas*, the merchants. These three main classes, of lighter skin colour, had important privileges. They were described as 'twice-born' for, during late childhood, they were initiated into the rites of their high position. This was regarded as a mystic second birth.

The fourth main caste, the *shudras*, living on the fringes of society, were servants, forbidden to read, or even hear, the sacred scriptures. Even in the centuries before the Christian era, there existed a fifth caste, corresponding to the present *dalits*, formerly known as 'untouchables'. Most of these were the dark-skinned descendants of slaves and aborigines and were restricted to filthy and menial tasks. Once born into their class, death was the only escape from it. Generation after generation were compelled to carry out lowly and unpleasant work, nor could they marry outside their caste.

At the very bottom of the social heap are the *chandals*, the caste who carry out the actual work of cremations – cremation over a wood fire is the usual way of disposing of the bodies of adult Indians. Children's bodies are

Figure 1   Acute poverty in many parts of the Indian plain has perpetuated this kind of traditional village housing, with its low mud walls and thatched roofing

simply placed in rivers. The *chandals* use long iron rods to stir the ashes and remains, and to smash the skull and other larger bones so they will be totally consumed – this might take seven or eight hours. Although they no longer have to shout or ring bells to announce their presence, to avoid the ritual contamination of any other Indian, they are effectively cut off from the rest of society. Higher-caste persons would be contaminated even if the shadow of a *chandal* should fall on them. There are caste divisions even among the *dalits*, a present-day minority of 160 million people. In ascending order on the social scale are leatherworkers, lavatory cleaners and sweepers, laundrymen.

This set pattern of privilege inevitably resulted in discrimination, oppression and harsh laws. The mass of the people, living in villages similar to those of today, were heavily taxed to support their masters. A complex legal code provided sweeping discriminatory provisions covering virtually every aspect of life for the lower orders. Often taxation reached such ruinous levels as to leave the peasants destitute, and even minor weather fluctuations resulted in major famines. The death penalty was imposed for a multitude of offences.

However, social inequality and art often flourish together, and such was the case in ancient India. This era produced the great Indian classics – the *Mahabharata* and the *Ramayana*. These writings stress the basic lesson that everyone must maintain his or her due place in society, that 'it is better to do one's own duty badly than another's well' – thus guaranteeing the privileged position of the twice-born. The *Mahabharata*, which is a collection of poems rather than a single story, is largely based on the fortunes of two rival ruling families, but its major significance is its statement of the duty of the religious, law-abiding man.

The other great epic is the story of Rama, a legendary prince who, although he is the legal heir, accepts banishment for 12 years. While in exile his wife Sita is kidnapped by Ravana, the devil king of Lanka, sometimes identified as Ceylon, now Sri Lanka. Rama, going to her rescue, enlists the aid of the monkey king, who provides an army of monkeys to tear up rocks, earth and trees to build a bridge between the Indian mainland and the island. Rama crosses the causeway, kills Ravana, and rescues his wife. He is then said to have created a virtually Utopian society, of unprecedented peace and prosperity, based on his capital city of Ayudhya.

These epics must not be thought of as antiques without any present or future significance. Rama's Ayudhya, granted attributes far beyond what the historic record seems to justify, is regarded as an ideal to emulate in today's Hindu politics. The epics also play a much greater part in the lives of ordinary people in at least six Asian countries than their equivalents do among Westerners. Few people in most of mainland south-east Asia and in many parts of Indonesia, as well as the Indian continent itself, would fail to hear stories from these epics from early childhood. Ceremonies and carnivals, which often involve whole communities, annually celebrate the victory of Rama over Ravana. Art, especially painting, sculpture and the shadow theatre, uses themes from the epics extensively, as also do much of literature and drama. Although Indonesia is predominantly a Muslim country, Islam is the top layer of a succession of faiths, and Arjuna, one of the heroes of the *Mahabharata*, is a widely revered and loved figure.

The growing complexity of Hinduism resulted in a huge variety of schools and shades of thought. The present state of the Christian religion is comparable. Basic to all systems, however, was the feeling that life is evil, that all material things are deceptive if not downright illusory, and that man's objective is a purification of the spirit achieved by renouncing carnal desires in a succession of lives. This belief in reincarnation became, and remains, a major theme. Perhaps its most important implication is that the present condition of an individual is not a matter of chance, but a consequence of their good or evil actions in previous lives.

The caste system is intended to regulate this process of slow advancement through a series of lives. The whole religious concept would be meaningless if individuals could be allowed to move from the station in life to which they were born, since the Hindu faith has it they were not born into that life by accident, but by the dictate of a divine plan. The caste system then, is much more than a social order; it is deeply involved with the religious beliefs of the people – it has an inevitability that reinforces its acceptance by those who believe in it. It also has strong associations with occupation, castes often resembling the medieval trade guilds of Europe.

As the centuries passed, castes split into sub-castes, and these again into even more complicated categories. That remains the case in India today, even though caste discrimination is technically illegal. I had Indian friends in Singapore, both well educated, a doctor of medicine and a journalist, of differing castes. When this couple married they found it expedient to live outside India.

Meanwhile in the India of today, *dalits* – untouchables – continue to be sweepers, leatherworkers, rubbish collectors, in spite of attempts by the central government to change things. Even within the small but growing educated middle class, caste still strongly influences basic matters such as marriage alliances.

Implementing national policies, especially on a matter so fundamental as caste, is all the more difficult because of an effective regionalism resulting from India's multiplicity of languages and dialects. The print media, radio and television generally operate in their own area, rather than as national networks. Political forces have the same constraints, thus perpetuating the strong regional influences already defined by history and tradition. India's recent political predicament, forcing frequent general elections because of a lack of a dominant unifying force, is a likely consequence. Its inability to impose reform of the caste system is another.

In the sixth century BCE the son of an affluent *kshatriya* family with the clan name of Gautama wearied of the straitjacket of Hinduism, and renounced his wife, home and family to become a wanderer. After six years of meditation and study he is believed to have achieved perfection in the spiritual sense and so has become known as 'the enlightened one' – the Buddha. The philosophy he has left is by no means the only heresy of this period, although it became the most pervasive and important.

Buddhism, originally an offshoot and an interpretation of 'Hindu' principles, has become immensely diverse and malleable. Even though its practice varies widely from region to region in Asia, it is basically a guide to conduct oneself rather than a religious belief. It is largely based on tolerance, gentleness and moderation. Indeed, what it calls 'the middle way' is its essential. It seeks the abandonment of hatred, envy and anger. Its aim is the cultivation of purity and kindness.

While these sentiments are commonplace enough now, it must be recalled that Buddhism preceded Christianity by more than 500 years, and was a tremendous step forward in a world which had, until then, generally accepted without question the principle of an eye for an eye and a tooth for a tooth; a world in which cruelty and injustice were simply to be taken for granted. This new philosophy, born in the foothills of the Himalayas, was to become a profound influence throughout Asia. This became evident perhaps more forcibly in Tibet than anywhere else. When Buddhism reached this arid plateau four miles above sea level in the seventh century CE its message of peace and tolerance strongly modified the warlike violence and savagery of Tibet at that time.

A second major religion from this time, still important in India, is Jainism, which asserts non-violence as a major principle. It was probably an influence on Gandhi when he advocated non-violence during the Indian struggle for independence more than 2000 years later. Jains believe everything in nature has a soul. Jains, who are mainly concentrated in Gujarat State, have always been merchants and are relatively wealthy and influential.

Important things were also happening in the political sense. For almost 200 years the Punjab was a province of the great Persian empire until, in the fourth century BCE, the Persian King Darius the Third was defeated by the Macedonian soldier-adventurer Alexander the Great. Alexander's elephants pushed over the high passes of the Hindu Kush mountains and crossed the Indus River in 326 BCE. Alexander's death soon afterwards brought his short-lived empire to an end, but one of his generals, Seleucus Nicator, was able to take control of the Asian part, including the Indian province. Towards the end of the century Seleucus Nicator traded the Indian province for 500 elephants to a vigorous administrator of Indian birth named Chandragupta.

This man welded much of north India into a single state for the first time. There is a great deal of information available about him from the fragments remaining from the written account of the Greek Megasthenes, sent by Seleucus Nicator as his envoy to Chandragupta's capital, on the site of the present city of Patna. The dynasty founded by Chandragupta is called Mauryan and was based on a city which, Megasthenes tells us, was sprawled along nine miles of the banks of the Ganges and as much as a mile and a half inland. He regarded it as a pleasant, well-ordered place, and his account is of a people – or rather an upper class – accustomed to grace and beauty. There were large and pleasant gardens, in which jasmine, hibiscus, the water-lily and the lotus were already cultivated for their beauty and perfume; lakes and bathing pools, where the air was cooled by fountains; and contrived grottos for relaxation.

There was an organized civil service, whose officers specialized in the collection of taxes, inspection of irrigation works, road building and similar activities run and paid for by the state, almost entirely, it must be said, for its own financial benefit. This elaborate bureaucracy even had a war office with specialist sections dealing with such matters as elephants, cavalry and naval activities.

In spite of the luxury with which he was surrounded, Chandragupta's own regime was strictly ordered; we are told he was left only four and a half hours out of 24 for sleep. Administering his empire kept him fully occupied and much of his time was devoted to intrigue and receiving the reports of the elaborate network of spies he maintained. He went in constant fear of his life, regularly shifted his abode for fear of assassins, and never went out in public without an armed escort. He travelled in a gold palanquin carried by elephants, accompanied by his guards, fan, pitcher and umbrella bearers, who seem invariably to have been women. The route of his progress was marked off with ropes, and Megasthenes recorded that it was instant death for anyone who set foot inside them.

The Mauryan empire reached its zenith under Chandragupta's grandson Ashoka. Ashoka was a great builder, but where his forebears had used wood, he built in stone. So for the first time since Harappa, building and sculpture were constructed that have lasted into our time. Of the numerous stone columns Ashoka set up, the capital of one, with its figures of four lions, is used as the emblem of the present government of India.

However, Ashoka is remembered mostly because he turned from cruel and amoral absolutism to institute quite revolutionary and remarkable reforms, unique in the world of their time. Ashoka's conversion to the ways of peace are said to have resulted from an experience of the realities of war during an expedition against the neighbouring kingdom of Kalinga. In this war it is said 100,000 people died, with as many more captives taken. Ashoka was deeply influenced by this episode of violence and loss, and by Buddhism, which spread as a result of his missionary efforts as far as Burma and Sri Lanka. An embassy was even sent to Egypt.

Ashoka was much given to setting up inscriptions of moral precepts. Thirty-five of these still exist in caves and on the monoliths previously mentioned. A system of law and order hitherto unparalleled is attributed to him, aimed at the protection of the sick, the unarmed and the helpless and the convenience of travellers. Staged resthouses for travellers along roads –

still a feature of several Asian countries – were one of the public services he instituted. He devoted a great deal of attention to the highways, planting groves of shade trees and digging wells. He also built hospitals for the care of the sick and infirm, who, until then, had died unless they were succoured by a casual charity. There was even a corps of circuit magistrates who travelled the kingdom resolving disputes. At this time Buddhism developed its most significant divergence from Hinduism, its rejection of the caste system (except in Sri Lanka). Classic accounts of Ashoka's life from Buddhist publicists present him as a saintlike figure. Whatever the truth of that there seems little doubt he was a man of some personal force of character, with a sense of humanitarianism rare in his time. The Mauryan empire declined rapidly after his death.

Five centuries of small regional states ensued, briefly illuminated by a Bactrian Greek empire in north India under a king called Menander. Coins and statuary from this Gandharan school show unmistakable Mediterranean influence and have permanently influenced Buddhist art.

From the fourth to the seventh centuries much of the distinction and order of Ashoka's empire reappeared under the Guptas. This period is notable for exquisite paintings, like those in the Ajanta caves, its sophisticated sculpture and its Sanskrit drama, especially the plays of Kalidasa, a poet and dramatist who is regarded by some as comparable with Shakespeare. Kalidasa's *Sakuntala*, based on part of the *Mahabharata*, has been translated into many other languages and has taken its place in world literature. So prolific and varied was this literary output there is strong evidence that it was the work of a school of writers, possibly three people. The *Kama Sutra*, which has remained popular around the world to this day because of its explicit expression of erotic elements of the Hindu religion, also dates from this period.

This was the heyday of Buddhism in India, the time of the great teaching monasteries and universities that became famed throughout Asia. One of the great universities, Nalanda, is said to have had 4000 students in the seventh century. Pilgrims came from as far away as China to study in them. One of these, Faxian, who spent ten years in India in the fifth century, has described a peaceful, well-organized and prosperous society with moderate laws and taxation. Although Hinduism was again the faith of the ruling house, the powerful and influential Buddhist community co-existed peaceably with them.

Standards of education were high among the small lettered class and important developments in algebra and arithmetic (including the decimal system of nine numbers and the zero) occurred in India in the seventh century. These innovations, so long known as 'Arabic' in the West, seem, in fact, to have been learned by the Arabs from India. There is also evidence that the concept of the zero, which appeared in India at this time, might have originated even farther east, perhaps in Indo-China.

Buddhism entered something of a decline towards the end of the era – instead there was a renewal of the influence and authority of the *brahmin* Hindu caste. Invaders from the north – the same Huns who were such a cause of concern to the Chinese – successfully attacked the Gupta state, which had fragmented into a number of smaller units by the middle of the sixth century.

Meanwhile Hindu power and culture had permeated only slowly to the south of India. This area of dense tropical jungle, steamy heat, and dangerous wildlife such as tigers and giant snakes, had little appeal to the predatory invaders from the hills. However, independent societies were evolving in the south. Two of these were located on the island of Sri Lanka (Ceylon).

Basic to an understanding of Sri Lanka is the fact that two separate migrations from the mainland occurred: the first of people who called themselves the Sinhalese – People of the Lion – in the sixth century BCE; and a second, smaller one, of Indian Tamils, from about 300 years later. The Sinhalese displaced an aboriginal, hunting people called the Vedda, who have now virtually disappeared as a separate identity due to displacement and extensive intermarriage – which also had a major ethnic influence on the invaders. Recent research has also indicated a migration, which must have been by sea, of south-east Asian people, well before the entry of the Sinhalese and Tamils. The Sinhalese appear to have come not from neighbouring south India, but from the north-west, and their migration southwards may have coincided with the Aryan occupation of northern India. Little more is known about their origins, but they knew and worked iron, used advanced irrigation techniques to grow rice, and quite quickly developed a sophisticated urban society based on their first capital, Anuradhapura.

It was important as early as the third century BCE when, according to legend, Prince Mahinda, either a brother or a son of Ashoka, visited Sri Lanka and converted its king to Buddhism. Certain sacred relics are said to have been transported to Sri Lanka, including the Buddha's alms bowl and part of his collarbone, and, most celebrated of all, one of his eye-teeth. Possession of this tooth became important to establish the legitimacy of kings. Now it is kept in the pink Temple of the Tooth in Kandy, where a replica of the tooth is ceremonially carried about on elephant-back each August. This procession, the Perahera, takes place every night for two weeks.

The advent of a line of kings over the next thousand years who at times resembled Ashoka in their attitudes and achievements is an indication of the power of Buddhism to influence societies at that time. This was the era of Sri Lanka's glory – moderate well-regulated societies with their own art, notably sculpture and painting, that derives from India but has its own individuality. Taxation, set at ten per cent of production, was moderate by later standards in south Asia, although the peasants were also subject to a corvée, which provided labour for the irrigation works, canals and roads. There was a strong accent on efficient agriculture and huge irrigation works, among the largest and most technically-advanced in the world. These were based on stone-walled dams and artificial lakes, which made two and sometimes three rice crops a year possible. Some of these 'tanks' still exist, irrigating thousands of acres.

Meanwhile the Tamils in the north became stronger as a result of a steady trickle of migrants from the mainland over the centuries. By the twelfth century they had evolved a separate northern state on the dry, flat Jaffna Peninsula. The Tamils have important racial and language differences from the Sinhalese. They are traditionally enterprising and energetic – qualities forced on them by centuries of farming the arid north of the island.

In the tenth century the south Indian Chola empire invaded Sri Lanka, occupying much of the north and central plains. Thousands of Tamil migrants came in at that time, and as many more in the fourteenth century, when a disastrous and extended civil war developed between rival generals and claimants for the Sinhalese throne. These Sinhalese factions recruited large numbers of Tamil mercenaries.

The Tamils gained control of more territory in the north, including the valuable and world-renowned pearl fishery. The decaying Sinhalese state was pushed southwards to a new capital at Kotte, near Colombo. The great irrigation works in the centre of the country were destroyed by rival armies or fell into disrepair, leaving an arid zone between the Tamil and Sinhalese kingdoms. Huge tracts of previously cultivated country reverted to dense jungle. It may have been *Anopheles* mosquitoes breeding in the reservoirs and subsequent epidemics of malaria that hastened this process. Lavish pagoda building, at huge public cost, impoverished the Sinhalese kingdom, forcing it further into decline. A new kingdom grew up at Kandy, resulting in three rival authorities controlling the island.

Such was the situation when the Portuguese arrived in Colombo in 1505, attracted by the trade in cinnamon and pepper, which were Sinhalese royal monopolies. The lack of any central authority over the island gave the Portuguese the opportunity for intrigue, and eventually conquest. They had taken over the country by the end of the century, except for the fabled kingdom of Kandy deep in the jungle-clad hills of central Sri Lanka, jungles that were later to give place to tea plantations. Spirited resistance came from the Tamils of the north, who were not subdued until 1591. As elsewhere in Asia, the Portuguese intermarried freely with the local people. There is a profusion of Portuguese names in Sri Lanka.

Sri Lanka was occupied by British forces during the Napoleonic Wars and became a British colony in 1802, largely on the insistence of the East India Company. The ancient kingdom of Kandy, involved in a series of rebellions, was subdued in 1818. Thereafter the colony faced considerable economic difficulties. When coffee was planted there the Sinhalese refused to carry out the hard and ill-paid work involved. The planters brought in Tamil labourers from India, and with them a further cause of the communal problems to come. Later in the century tea and rubber proved to be more viable industries.

The early twentieth century saw the establishment of state schools and a university college. Hence, when the country was granted independence as a single state in 1948, an educated middle class existed to carry out the tasks of government. However, the largely Sinhalese government refused citizenship to almost a million Tamils, and later attempted to impose Sinhalese as the national language. This, and severe communal disturbances in 1983, exacerbated traditional tensions between the Tamils and the Sinhalese, leading to the bitter and protracted armed struggle that has continued until the present time. During two decades of civil war more than 50,000 people have been killed.

The Sri Lankan political scene has alternated between government by the socialist Freedom Party, which has nationalized major industries, such as the tea, coffee and rubber plantations and banks, and the conservative National Party, which favours foreign investment and close relations with the United States. Following nationalization of the petroleum industry in 1963 and the subsequent cessation of US aid, Sri Lanka came close to bankruptcy. After the most recent elections in 2004 the Freedom Party formed government, winning 45 per cent of the vote as against 37 per cent for the National Party.

Sri Lanka is a poor country, with a per capita GDP (Gross Domestic Product) of about $950. It is still highly dependent on foreign aid, but the economy has improved modestly in the new millennium with a considerable growth in service industries, which account for 54 per cent of GDP. There is a significant export of plantation products – rice, tea, rubber and spices – garments and leather goods, and a growing income from tourism. However, a major setback came when the 2004 tsunami devastated the east coast, killing 30,000 people and destroying the infrastructure in areas controlled by the Colombo government and the Tamil Tigers.

Early south Indian mainland communities were based on seacoast cities and a thriving maritime trade. It seems likely that as early as 500 BCE fishing boats had evolved into small ocean-going ships, engaged in trade as far afield as Burma and Malaysia. Kingdoms of consequence arose, like that of the Tamil Cholas, which dominated much of peninsular India in the eleventh century, and which became a maritime power with considerable influence in south-east Asia. The Chola state appears to have been relatively enlightened and advanced, with a system of village self-government, efficient revenue-raising, major irrigation works, and a distinctive Tamil literature and architecture.

The huge pyramidal temple they built in honour of the god Shiva is still a major landmark in the city of Tanjore, and inscriptions on its walls are a major source of information – or probable information – about the Cholas. Chola certainly seems to have been the largest and most influential state in India around the end of the first millennium, especially during the long eleventh-century reign of King Rajendra. Much of its extravagant wealth, a great deal of which was devoted to ornamenting and maintaining the Tanjore temple, was obtained from marauding expeditions against Chola's neighbours.

This region's exports – among them ivory, cotton cloth, pepper and other spices, diamonds, pearls, apes and peacocks – included a considerable trade with Rome, evidenced by numerous Roman coins found in south India. But the most consequential export was the Indian cultural and architectural influence still so evident in much of south-east Asia.

4 Early South-east Asia: the Ships from India

The Indian merchant-adventurers' first journeys were probably slow passages hugging the Bay of Bengal coast, always in sight of land. Their early acquaintance with south-east Asia must have been due not so much to enterprise as the facts of geography. The art of sailing was elementary indeed, and it was not until relatively recently that one of the most important of man's inventions – how to sail efficiently into the wind – evolved.

When the first Indian argosies left the coast, they were forced to go where the wind took them. On the outward passage, between the months of June and November, that wind is the south-west monsoon, which blows with remarkable steadiness, day after day, week after week. It still propels many a sailing craft across those waters. Simply by proceeding before and slightly off the wind, a ship would naturally make her landfall on the tip of Sumatra or the Malaysian peninsula. Having arrived, the earliest Indian adventurers found it difficult to get back, since the wind persists from the south-west until the months December to May, when it blows with equal steadiness from the north-east. Hence the Indian merchant-adventurers went prepared to stay wherever they made a landfall until the monsoon changed. It was probably in this way that their customs, religion and art began to spread eastward, as far as the China Sea coast of Vietnam.

It would be seriously to underrate the south-east Asian peoples to make the simple assumption that Indian ways were grafted on to primitive societies. The point probably was that rulers or would-be rulers saw advantage in a religion and culture that would advance their own interests, and which possessed an efficient, if Machiavellian, statecraft. The Indian merchants and priest-missionaries were in fact providing ambitious rajahs with a blueprint for societies in which elites could control and use the ordinary people. These, characteristically, were wet rice farmers or fishermen – and very good ones at that, who already had quite advanced systems of local self-government.

Archaeological sites in north-east Thailand give evidence of agricultural bronze-using societies as advanced as those in other parts of the world as early as 3000 BCE. A six-acre mound rising from ricefields at Non Nok Tha has revealed evidence of rice-growing and bronze-casting – a factory making adzes in split sandstone moulds – from around that date. Iron objects have been dated back to 500 BCE. Three hundred years later beautifully worked bronze ceremonial drums made at Dong-son, in what is now Vietnam, were in use in many parts of south-east Asia. The archaeology of south-east Asia is still in its early stages, so there can be little doubt that eventually more discoveries will be made there which will reveal a clearer picture.

The wide dispersal of the Dong-son drums indicates a thriving maritime trade before the Christian era. There is evidence of Malay shipping trading as far as China as early as 300 BCE, and engaged in the cinnamon trade by 100 BCE. From this early maritime experience quite large trading vessels evolved – up to 400 tons, with two to four masts and carvel hulls built without nails or screws. I have seen new ships very much along these lines, using wooden dowels to edge-fasten each plank, under construction along the Pattaya coast of the Gulf of Thailand, as recently as 1965. Indonesian handcrafts, like the complex creation of *batik* fabrics, are also believed to have predated Indian influence.

Hence in the discussion which follows of 'kings' and 'states' it is important not to overrate the importance of their total effect on the majority of society, or that of the 'cultural grafts', for that matter. Since what written sources there are almost always deal with those kings and states, and are more concerned with eulogy than fact, it is difficult indeed to trace the development and history of the ordinary people. Nevertheless, it is worth trying to do so.

This can be attempted through a study of the south-east Asian village societies as they are today – their legends, beliefs and customs, and the evidence of archaeological remains. Deduction from these is assisted by a reasonable assumption that these societies show all the signs of having been stable and largely unchanging for very long periods of time, possibly thousands of years. They are also societies in which a complex and formal pattern of personal relationships seems to have existed for a long time. This in itself would have tended to make the Indian cultural influence acceptable, and even welcome. The extraordinary profusion of carved scenes on the massive Javanese temple-mountain, the Borobadur, created more than 1300 years ago, depict fishing, market, craft, and agricultural scenes very similar to what can be seen in daily life today.

Prehistoric south-east Asia gives evidence of a considerable diversity of occupation by tool-using primitive societies going back at least 30,000 years. It could be assumed that these were ancestors of indigenous

Figure 2 These thatched houses, with their high-peaked roofs, are much the same as those going back many thousands of years throughout tropical Asia. However, the local materials in them are now often being replaced by concrete blocks and corrugated iron

Australoid peoples, the remnants of whom may be the short-statured, shy, hunting peoples, classed as negritos, who are still found in remote jungle areas of Malaysia, Thailand and the Philippines. Others moved on to New Guinea and Australia.

By the time of the first contacts with India, however, the islands and coastlines had long been settled by people who are Malay in type. Basically Mongoloid, they came from south-western China, through a gradual process of cultural osmosis that must have occupied many centuries. The first Indian contacts were probably with Malay villagers close to the sea on estuaries or creeks. They made beautifully finished and polished tools from very hard stone, were excellent navigators with some knowledge of astronomy and then (as now) sailed long, narrow and graceful sailing-craft with considerable skill. This maritime tradition is still very important. To today's Malaysian or Indonesian sailors, their craft is more a way of life than simply work – as one can see along the mudflats of coastal Singapore where the racing of light, very fast outrigger models called *jukongs* is a major Malay sport, and their construction an art.

In places such as Brunei and Palembang their way of life persists, in many respects unchanged. Some, like the Bugis, spend their entire life on their ships. People living in villages often build their houses on stilts on mudflats, so they are completely surrounded by water at high tide. Most are fishermen. Otherwise for food they depend very much on the coconut, which thrives along the beaches and on the many islands of this region. This estuary culture is found particularly in places where the soil is poor, like much of the Malaysian peninsula and Kalimantan (Borneo).

Loosely organized principalities at the river mouths were regarded as the personal bailiwicks, and the tax revenues the personal property, of the ruler and the clique supporting him. Pre-colonial Malay history is mostly a tedious and repetitive chronicle of the feuds, wars and disputes of these petty princelings. Often these principalities resulted from pirate alliances which preyed on passing merchant shipping – something that has persisted into modern times.

Rich soils, found on plainlands, drained swamps or hillsides where water is available, have from the earliest times been devoted to the growing of 'wet' or *padi* rice. Indeed, so old is this cultivation of irrigated rice that in some parts of south-east Asia the most suitable land was devoted to it, and expanding populations seem to have been forced into hilly regions, as much as 3000 years ago. In the mountains of northern Luzon, the main island of the Philippines, is an engineered complex of terraced ricefields and irrigation canals that is intricate in design and so large it has transformed whole mountainsides. Its construction, which is thought to have commenced more than 2000 years ago, occupied many generations. It is not known why these people, the Ifugao, decided to leave the plains and commence the staggering task of terracing such huge areas of mountains. It is possible they did it to escape malaria, since the sluggish *Anopheles* mosquito which carries that fever is seldom found higher than 2000 feet above sea level. However, the cultural history of the Ifugao in recent times indicates that building the terraces and growing rice in them is central to the social structure and religion. It seems likely that building the terraces was to the Ifugao what temple or pyramid construction was to other peoples.

But whatever the reason, the Ifugao were remarkably determined and resourceful people. If these terraces were laid end to end, they would extend 12,000 miles. First, a stone wall was built as high as 50 feet and the land behind it excavated. The trench so made was lined with impervious clay so that it would hold water, then levelled with sand and soil. Another such terrace was built above and below this, until entire hillsides were covered with parallel terraces like giant flights of steps, engineered to follow the contour lines. Coupled with this skilful engineering the Ifugao showed a considerable knowledge of hydraulics. The waterfalls and torrents of the hillsides were harnessed, bamboo pipes being used to provide a water supply to the rice terraces. Forest growth was controlled on the divides to prevent flash flooding and erosion.

While these Ifugao structures are of special interest because of their age and their extent, terraced ricefields like them can be found almost everywhere in south-east Asia, and are indicative of highly skilled and co-operative societies. The culture of *padi* rice is in itself an expert and demanding business. Without doubt the art of selecting the best-producing varieties must have begun a long time ago, and the custom of growing first in seedbeds and then transplanting the young plants must be almost as old.

There is evidence that this work was in some cases carried out under the supervision of a central authority. This was the case in the great Khmer empire of Cambodia. But in most cases it appears to have been undertaken by villagers for their own benefit. This required a considerable degree of co-operation between families, especially in negotiating the allocation of water resources, and indeed in building the elaborate irrigation systems so often used. It is also how complex systems of relationships must have developed, providing a stable, continuing ethical framework necessary for harmony in close-settled societies. There were definite social hierarchies, favouring the old and presumably wise. Decisions, when necessary, were made by these councils of elders on a basis of discussion until consensus was reached – not on a majority vote, which would be regarded as socially crude.

There has always been a strong tradition of joint responsibility for all members of a group. People who are ill are looked after by their neighbours. If a family's house is burned down, the whole village will help build another. Care of children extends outside nuclear families to many other people and especially to the extended family, in which the bonds are very close.

All this is of much more than academic interest, not only because it is still the way things generally are outside the cities, but also because consensus is an important part of national consciousness, and of politics. It is a major reason why Western-style democracy has not succeeded in Asia, indeed in many places it is politely condemned as being government 'by half plus one'.

How far such ideas go back is not known. It has even been postulated that the cradle of human civilization was south-east Asia, or rather Sunda, the shallow seas linking the islands to the mainland that were dry land during the ice ages. Stephen Oppenheimer, in his *Eden in the East* (1998), argues persuasively, though by no means conclusively, that when Sunda was flooded at the end of the last glacial, a civilization which grew rice, perhaps even worked bronze, was displaced in several directions to create, or influence, those regions such as Mesopotamia and the Indus valley, which are conventionally regarded as the earliest civilizations.

The methods of growing *padi* rice are closely interwoven with animist religions – that is, worship of gods corresponding to and controlling the elemental forces of nature, together with a belief that virtually everything contains a life-force, a 'soul'. Later religions, coming from India, have not generally displaced these, but have simply added a top layer. Even in Thailand, where Buddhism is virtually universal and the state religion, the old animist beliefs are widespread. One such concerns a rice mother without whose approval the crops cannot succeed. Thai children are told about Mae Phra Phosop, and warned that if they don't eat all the rice given to them she may be offended, and refuse the life-giving rains for the next planting.

And this is not only the case in remote villages. Towards the end of the Second World War the Thai Electric Corporation in Bangkok reached the stage where it could no longer get the usual firewood and rice husks to keep its generators going. So it was decided to use surplus rice grain itself. Before this could be done a Buddhist religious ceremony, attended by two cabinet ministers and other dignitaries, was held. The chief Buddhist official speaking at this function asked the permission of Mae Phra Phosop to use some of the bountiful grain for fuel. He begged her not to be angry and visit them with her wrath. 'Mae Phra Phosop has always provided us with food,' he said. 'Now may she give us further blessings by supplying heat, wherewith we may get light, and power to drive the trams.'

The *Ramayana*, originating from the sixth century BCE, makes references to what seems to be south-east Asia, but these could have been later additions, perhaps in the second century CE. The point indicates the vagueness of the evidence on which assumptions about this period have to be made.

The first detailed description of an Indianized state comes from a third-century Chinese account. The state was Funan, located in the great delta of the Mekong River in what is now southern Vietnam, strategically on the trade route between India and China. Funan's capital, Vyadhapura, was a pirate base and an entrepôt port in flat, marshy country suitable for growing rice. It sprawled along the banks of mangrove-lined creeks, and here its many ships were moored. The Chinese record says the capital was a mud-walled city of considerable size, with dark, curly-haired people who were skilled artisans, exporting jewellery of wrought gold and silver, sandalwood and pearls. Funan seems to have been regarded as relatively sophisticated for its time, but to the Chinese it was a mixed blessing – often their merchant junks, which sailed as far west as Sri Lanka, were attacked by its fast pirate ships. However, its musicians, who visited China in the third century, were highly regarded there. Its rulers used Sanskrit and imposed trial by ordeal, such as carrying a red-hot chain or plunging the hands into boiling water.

Funan, which was probably a loose alliance of villages near the coast south-east of the present Phnom Penh, seems to have extended its influence beyond Vietnam into parts of what are now Cambodia and Thailand. Excavations there have revealed Roman-style medallions and ornaments. From a cultural and religious point of view its most important legacy was a belief in a line of rulers called the Kings of the Mountain, which persisted into later civilizations in several parts of south-east Asia.

Following its decline by the sixth century, its commercial monopoly was usurped by another estuary town called Shrivijaya, probably on the site of the present Palembang in Sumatra. Like Funan, it was close to fertile rice-fields and was thus able to provision visiting ships. Shrivijaya prospered under the patronage of China, which needed a strong 'tributary' state in this key area. A Chinese pilgrim named Yiqing who visited there in the seventh century said more than 1000 Buddhist monks lived there, and its rulers – once again, Kings of the Mountain – had links with the Buddhist university at Nalanda, in India.

Shrivijaya has prompted much speculation as a major Indonesian naval empire, but this is based on very slender evidence. However, it does seem to have been a central point for trade in nutmeg, cloves and other spices, scented wood, especially sandalwood, and pearls, and a major intermediate port in the traffic, actually quite small, between Persia, India and China. It appears to have prospered largely because it was able to unite the *orang laut*, the sea pirates of the surrounding waters, and so guarantee they would not attack trading ships. Shrivijaya was attacked in 1025 CE by the south Indian Chola empire, possibly because it made too exorbitant demands on Chola ships. Although it recovered from this, it finally faded into obscurity in the fourteenth century.

Another major kingdom flourished in central Java in the seventh century, and must have been appreciable because it built the tremendous monument called the Borobadur. This huge Buddhist shrine is a series of almost three miles of terraces built over a natural hill. The galleries of these terraces are flanked with stones on which thousands of bas-reliefs are carved with wonderful skill. There are some 400 statues of the Buddha, and the structure is crowned by a temple on the flattened top of the hill.

Other temples not far away, at Prambanan, show scenes from the *Ramayana* and were Hindu rather than Buddhist. However, these ancient

Figure 3 The giant Borobadur temple, built over an existing hill in central Java, is one of Indonesia's most impressive monuments. This detail is one of thousands of carvings there

Javanese societies are shadowy indeed, and on present available evidence are likely to remain so. They could scarcely have been 'empires' in the usual sense – they were more likely to have been loose regional alliances based on existing village structures.

In northern Cambodia, not far from the Thai border, are the ruins of vast buildings, painstakingly fashioned from intricately carved and jointed pieces of greenish sandstone, some of which weigh many tons. This city, Angkor Thom, was the capital of the Khmer kings, and is the remnant of what was south-east Asia's most impressive yet forbidding civilization.

It is relevant that when the ageing king of Cambodia, Norodom Sihanouk, returned to his country in 1997 from a stay in Beijing, he flew directly to Angkor rather than to the capital Phnom Penh, to pray for peace between the warring factions in Cambodia. He did this because Angkor was the city of his ancestors – this is also the reason for the remarkable personal influence he maintained in his country over many decades. There is a continuing presence about these ruins which still seems to have the power to stir even the most unimaginative person, although more than 500 years have passed since the builders deserted it.

Over those centuries it has been locked in a losing fight with the jungle. Season by season, after the city was abandoned, the jungle advanced across highly developed ricefields served by one of the finest irrigation systems ever built. Birds dropped seeds on the crumbling walls. Now great fig and belan trees, with broad, buttressed roots, perch fantastically over gateways, their roots grappling with carved faces. This whole fabric of slow decay is bathed in a green light of submarine aspect, filtering down through the canopy of leaves overhead. Yet the ruins convey a sense of futility. The narrow, forbidding galleries lead nowhere. Only a slave state of the grimmest kind could have forced men to shape and raise these huge blocks of stone. Teams of prisoners and slaves, impelled by the sword and the whip, built these.

A Chinese visitor to the Khmer court at the end of the thirteenth century, Zhou Dakuan, said that the tribesmen from the nearby hills were often caught and sold as slaves. He remarks that they were regarded as animals and that many families had more than a hundred of them. 'If they commit a fault, they are beaten,' Zhou wrote. 'They bow the head and dare not make the least movement.' His account describes the wonderfully developed rice-growing areas based on the two great artificial lakes, the East and West Baray, which flank Angkor, and an intricate system of canals using the water of the Siem Reap River.

Khmer society was based on a highly organized aristocracy and a savage law. Often trial was by ordeal, and punishment of prisoners was summary and severe. The beautifully carved friezes of the Bayon and Angkor Wat are still well-preserved and present a vivid picture of the life of Khmer society. They show cockfighting, men playing chess, slaves cutting stone, dancing girls, scenes of intimate family life, processions, and battle scenes with warships, archers and elephants.

The Khmer people became the masters of much of what is now mainland south-east Asia. Their influence extended east to the China Sea, westward through what is now Thailand to the Burmese border, and as far south as the Isthmus of Kra. The names of the Khmer kings, like those of certain Hinduized monarchs in Java, all end with the suffix *varman*, which means protector. This gives an insight into their role, which was perceived as offering spiritual and physical protection to the rice-growing majority who served them.

Construction of Angkor began during the eighth-century reign of Jayavarman II, who is thought to have been educated for kingship at the court of the Shailendra in Central Java. In the Angkor culture, then, there is again evidence of the pervasive tradition of the Kings of the Mountain, enshrining the belief that the prosperity of the people is directly linked with the sacred personality of the king. Each king was required to create a temple-mountain, a building with terraces and towers in which he would be buried after death – a custom which is among the oldest known of the human race, also seen in the ancient kingdoms of Mesopotamia.

This belief resulted in the staggering assembly of huge buildings in the Cambodian jungles which are now regarded as one of the chief wonders of the world. The most famous is the vast Angkor Wat, a mile square, the largest religious building in the world. So well was it built in the twelfth century that it remains virtually intact. Although the city itself was abandoned, Angkor Wat remained in use, and was a sizeable Buddhist monastery at the time the French became aware of it in 1850. The pictorial frieze along the inner sanctuary wall is carved with a remarkable artistry. Such things, of course, exist elsewhere. But the frieze at Angkor Wat, eight feet high, extends continuously for more than half a mile.

Few things here are life-size. Even the carved hands of figures are so massive they are often more than a man could lift. It is probable that this mania for building finally weakened the kingdom so much it could no longer control its enemies. Here again, it is also possible that the *Anopheles* mosquito, breeding on the great irrigation lakes, brought catastrophic plagues of malaria. Since only the stone temples survive, where the people of this city actually lived was unclear until imaging radar from NASA (the US National Aeronautics and Space Administration) in 1994 and 2000 revealed the remnants of a considerable network of canals and streets to the north of the temple complex, which must once have been lined with timber houses. These radar images indicated the huge size of Angkor for a city of its time – it covered more than 400 square miles, and could have had as many as a million people.

In 1431 a vassal people, one of the group called the Thais, who had come down into south-east Asia from south-west China, sacked Angkor after a seven-month siege. In 1434 the capital was moved and finally established 150 miles south on the banks of the Mekong River at Phnom Penh, which is still the Cambodian capital. Military pressure from the Thais, who had built up a considerable empire based on the city of Ayudhya, and economic factors related to trade with China, seem to have influenced the decision to abandon Angkor. This was probably a considered, relatively gradual process, rather than the sudden dramatic catastrophe conjectured by some historians. There is a theory that the sheer size of Angkor so disturbed the ecology of the surrounding area that it ceased to be viable.

North Vietnam has had strong connections with China, which it borders, from at least the second century BCE. Neolithic remains indicate a population of Indonesian type, but later bronze artefacts of considerable artistry are associated with a migration of Mongoloid people south from China into the Red River delta. The population grew steadily as the swamps of the delta were engineered to grow wet rice. In 111 BCE the region became a province of China called Annam, which means 'southern kingdom'. Direct Chinese influence continued to shape north Vietnamese society for a thousand years; then the Red River delta region became independent after the demise of the Chinese Tang Dynasty. Like China, north Vietnam was Confucian, with all the attendant mechanisms of tax systems, filial piety and respect for established rites.

A glance at a map shows at once the geographic features which have several times resulted in Vietnam being divided into two, or even three, countries. The narrow coastal 'waist' bordering the mountains of Laos is as little as 40 miles wide, and separates two regions with marked historic, ethnic and cultural differences.

The south, consisting substantially of the plains and great delta of the Mekong River, was part of the empire of Angkor. The coastline north, along the narrow waist, was the considerable empire of a seafaring people, racially Malay. These were the Chams, whose society had acquired an Indian cultural influence as early as the second century CE, and which persisted for 1300 years. This was not an empire, but again a loose federation of river-mouth towns.

Champa traded in spices and ivory, but it was chiefly known and feared for its piracy directed at the passing coastal trade. This attracted considerable annoyance from the Chinese, whose ships were nearly always those attacked, and led to a number of punitive expeditions. Champa was also noted as a slave-trading centre. Records of continual Cham wars with their neighbours were probably more often than not references to raids against neighbouring communities to obtain prisoners of war for resale. The point can be noted that, as with other south-east Asian kingdoms, power was linked to the possession of large numbers of people, rather than large amounts of land.

Judging from its architecture, Champa had considerable cultural links with Angkor with which, however, it was almost constantly at war. Constant military pressure came from China, too, after the Chams renounced Chinese overlordship in the sixth century. However, it was the Vietnamese advancing from the north who finally brought Cham influence to an end. They were virtually destroyed as a political force by persistent war with the north Vietnamese from the eleventh century onwards and a Mongol invasion in 1283. However, their descendants remain a distinct ethnic group in Vietnam and in Cambodia.

The Tran Dynasty in North Vietnam not only attacked Champa, it was successful in turning back the Mongol invasion directed by Kublai Khan. Several centuries of intermittent wars with China followed, then with the fifteenth century came perhaps the most successful and the first genuinely Vietnamese Dynasty. This was the Le, who, after inflicting a final defeat on the Chams in 1471, began to extend slowly into the Mekong delta.

At the time of the first contacts with Europeans, however, the Le emperors had become figureheads and the natural tendency of the country to divide had again asserted itself. Two families, the Trinh in the north and the Nguyen in the south, became the real centres of power. Cambodia, meanwhile, had dwindled both in population and influence, and had become a mere dependency of Vietnam.

5 China: the Eternal Nation

China's story is among the most remarkable of humankind; her river valleys have been the location of a society that has not only shown continuity and consistency for perhaps 4000 years, but was also the inventor of paper, printing, firearms, credit banking and paper money, rudder steering and watertight compartments for ships, blast furnace steel production, lock systems for canals, among many other foundations and tribulations of the modern world. The transfer of such things and the ideas that prompted them to Europe was slow but nevertheless consequential.

China's status as the most populous country in the world is nothing new. She has been so for millennia. All Chinese, including those living far from their homeland, are aware of this sense of continuity, of a culture that has withstood time and adversity as no other human institution has done, and are deeply influenced by it. China's Communist leaders are no exception. At the time of the new state's greatest financial need, when it had been deserted by the Soviet Union, an option would have been to sell the immensely valuable solid gold and gem-encrusted artefacts in the Ming tombs near Beijing. But this was not done. Instead the tombs were carefully restored and maintained, all their treasures still in place.

The durability and individuality of Chinese culture are due to a number of factors, of which geography is among the more important. China, to the east of the mountain spine of central Asia, does not have the immediate vulnerability of the north Indian plain. These great mountains, together with the deserts to their north and the Pacific Ocean to the east, were a formidable barrier between China and the rest of the world, insulating her until the relatively recent development of efficient shipping. Trade contacts with the West before the nineteenth century were slight and the effects of them, especially on China, are often overemphasized. Her mercantile contacts with other parts of Asia were much more important.

North of the mountains are arid, lightly populated plains and formidable deserts. These make overland travel and trade difficult. These outer regions were not, however, completely empty. Tribes of nomads moved through them, maintaining a constant pressure on China's borders and

Map 2 China and Korea

often invading her. The Great Wall was built and rebuilt or extended many times to keep them out. Yet unlike some of those who invaded India, the 'barbarians' who successfully occupied China had no great effect on her culture. Chinese civilization was able to absorb them, even when they were conquerors.

This cultural resilience was assisted by the fact that Chinese civilization has a powerful binding force – a common written language and a body of literature of great antiquity that can be read anywhere in China, regardless of the many differences of spoken dialect. Much of this literature is concerned with the way people should live and behave. It has had a remarkable influence, which has extended beyond China, notably to Japan, Korea, Vietnam and Singapore, and is the background to what have come to be called 'Asian values'.

The tenacity of Chinese civilization also has much to do with its basic religion, ancestor worship. This ancient belief stresses the duty of sons to care for parents, both before and after death, when they are considered to have the same needs as in life. The welfare of the two human souls, a lower soul existing from conception, a higher one from birth, depends on the making of sacrifices, which can only be carried out by sons. If the souls are not tended, they can exert malign or unlucky influences on the living. An effect of ancestor worship was to make Chinese families strong, united forces, capable of great mutual effort towards common objectives. This clan and family resilience remains a significant quality of modern Chinese people.

From about 10,000 BCE human societies developed relatively quickly in China under the warmer climate conditions, as they did elsewhere in the world. The archaeological record has revealed traces of developed agricultural societies by 5000 BCE. Those in the Wei and Yellow River valleys in the north grew millet on the light, friable windborne soil called loess, which can be cropped for many years before it becomes exhausted. Those in the south grew rice in irrigated fields. There is evidence of early villages located on the bays and lagoons of the south coast, dependent on fish and other seafoods. Hamlets gradually grew into towns, typically surrounded by fortified walls of rammed earth. In the lower Yangzi timber houses were far from crude, using skilled wooden joinery, including the mortise and tenon.

Remnants of silk going back almost 4000 years have been found, but the considerable cost and effort of producing it would have restricted it to luxury use. Hemp was used generally for everyday fabrics, since cotton was not introduced from India until perhaps 600 CE. Hemp is now being grown again in large quantities in China. The earliest weaving shuttles also date

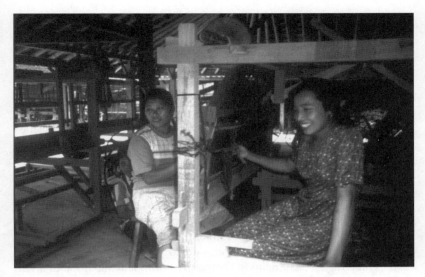

Figure 4   Remnants of woven silk have been found in several parts of Asia
going back almost 4000 years – women are still handweaving it today

from this early time. Pottery from 2500 BCE found in north China has graceful proportions, with geometric decorations in several colours of considerable artistry. At this time jade was already being worked into ornaments.

Chinese culture, then, had diverse origins, rather than developing exclusively in the north, as the classics suggest. In the Red Basin of the far western Sichuan Province, close to the uplands of Tibet and surrounded by
mountains and high plateaux, are the ruins of an enigmatic but plainly brilliant society for its time, even by world standards, since it dates back to
2500 BCE. Sanxingdui, near Chengdu, in the upper Yangzi region, has
revealed burial sites and house foundations that testify to an advanced and
sophisticated city covering more than a square mile – possibly the largest
city in the world for that time. By 1250 BCE it was more than four times that
size, with buildings suggesting specialized trades using workshops and
pottery kilns.

However, it is the more than one ton of extraordinary artefacts – of
bronze, gold, jade and ivory – found in two burial pits that have made
Sanxingdui an archaeological site of international interest, and indicated
the unique nature of its arts. The humanoid heads and masks, sometimes
made of gold, are of such bizarre and unusual design that they might be

from another planet. Its sophisticated bronze trees, in which small birds perch, and flowers bloom, and its ornamented ritual vessels are at technical and artistic standards as high as any known in the world of that time. This society seems not to have left any written records. It has only been studied with care since 1985.

However, other sites have been discovered near Chengdu, like that at the village of Jinsha 25 miles south in 2000, revealing artefacts showing they are clearly of the same culture. Along lower reaches of the Yangzi societies known as the Shue and Ba, also the ancient and consequential state of Chu, appear in the Chinese records.

The traditional division of Chinese history into 'dynasties' is convenient, but it needs to be regarded with caution. The fall of dynasties sometimes, but not always, caused nationwide social chaos. There were generally islands of prosperity and order in which Chinese culture progressed – even flourished. Nevertheless formal Chinese history postulates three early dynasties, the Xia, Shang and Zhou, said to have commenced during a vague 'golden age'. Xia remains in the realm of abundant and hopeful myth, such as the reign of the Yellow Emperor, when the world was considered to be perfect. However, grey pottery found in Shaanxi Province is evidence of a pre-bronze society that could correspond with the Xia. With the Shang a somewhat clearer view is possible.

The achievements of that time suggest a brilliant and quite sudden advance in art, technology and social order. Whether these have anything to do with contact with Sanxingdui is conjectural. Early in the twentieth century, inscribed bones and tortoise shells sold in Beijing for medicinal purposes were recognized as being very old. The inscriptions on them were of a strange and archaic pattern. These 'oracle bones', originally used for the prediction of future events, bore characters – and decimal numbering – so related to present Chinese writing they could be considered its antecedents. As in contemporary Chinese writing, this text did not use an alphabet representing sounds, but instead individual characters – pictures – for ideas, events, objects capable of description by words. Indeed, it was writing already highly developed. It was possible to establish the meaning of many characters, although some inscriptions are only partly decipherable. They supplied evidence of the existence of many rulers said in the traditional histories to have been of the Shang Dynasty.

Shang culture has left a number of sophisticated and beautifully worked bronzes, which indicate that northern Chinese culture made a major advance in this era. When this became fully appreciated, a search for their origins began. Between 1928 and 1937 excavations at Anyang, in northern Henan Province, identified the later Shang capital of Yin, probably founded about 1300 BCE. From 1951 onwards further work in this region revealed an even earlier Shang city at Zhengzhou, probably dating to about 1500 BCE. It had massive rammed earth walls, up to 55 feet thick, surrounding an area about a mile square. In the pottery kilns inside were found clay stamps for decorating jars in patterns, like the dragon, trellis and square spiral, which would persist in future Chinese ceramics. There were also ox bones and tortoise shells with incised written characters.

There is evidence of a wealthy and powerful ruling class, with impressive tombs, probably for the kings, containing bronze weapons and ceremonial urns – also pits with the beheaded bodies of horses, dogs and humans, perhaps prisoners. Human skulls appear to have been used as drinking vessels. Shang religious beliefs were animist, with gods representing the moon, sun, wind and other natural phenomena, but the beginnings of ancestor worship were already discernible. The king's role of conducting rites to guarantee agricultural prosperity was another Shang attribute to be carried forward into the future. The Shang army used bows and arrows with bronze heads, and horse-drawn chariots. Silk was used as a fabric, the silkworms being fed on mulberry leaves, as they still are.

The historical records have it that the last Shang king ended his reign in 1122 BCE. The Shang were followed by a less distinguished line, the Zhou, who had been rulers of a border kingdom. They were feudal lords, maintaining only a formal authority over the families that had assisted the establishment of the dynasty. During the nine centuries of nominal Zhou rule, the feudal families grew more powerful and the role of the kings nominal and ritualistic. Alliances and conquests led to the emergence of half a dozen major principalities, giving north China a political organization not unlike feudal Europe.

It was a time of tremendous growth, during which the Chinese states emerged from the primitive. Shang culture had been that of a small aristocracy, but now education and art became the preoccupation of a wider section of the community. A wealthy merchant class emerged in what must have been among the world's largest cities of their time, with populations of over a quarter of a million. Huge irrigation works, involving hundreds of canals, were built. The first coinage came into use. At first metal tools – hoes, knives, spades – were a means of exchange. These were soon replaced by small bronze replicas, which became China's first money. The use of iron from about 600 BCE must have given a considerable impetus to Chinese society. It was cast and forged into scythes, axes, saws, needles and weapons, much sharper and harder than the bronze in use up to that time. Craftsmen working in jade used wire saws and diamond drills.

Writing flourished, and for the first time became more than flattery of royal houses. Textbooks, poetry, treatises on medicine, the arts, mathematics, political theory, were all part of a major intellectual flowering. The scholar, able to write and read, became, as he would continue to be thereafter, an object of respect and authority. This was the time of Confucius, said to have lived between 551 and 479 BCE. His name was actually Kong Fuzi, of which Confucius is a Latinized version.

Many people know Confucius, if only because of his frequently quoted *Analects* (actually compiled after his death), of which these are typical:

> The man who makes a mistake, and doesn't correct it, makes another mistake.

> The mind of a superior man is conversant with righteousness; the mind of a mean man is conversant with gain.

As with many great figures of history, the facts of Confucius' life are unclear. However, if the scholar-teacher lived today he would probably have been considered a dangerous radical, because of his basic admonition that the welfare of the people was more important than the privileges of a ruling class. The rulers of the small state of Lu, in which he lived, disliked such ideas, nor could Confucius, during many years of wandering, persuade any other leader to accept them. He insisted on his students studying poetry, music and history to broaden their minds, a tradition continued almost into modern times in the great Chinese civil service, the mandarinate. The fact that he was a dissenter, yet was held in reverence by his students, indicates that he was probably a man of considerable personal force of character, with an innovative, revolutionary mind.

It is ironic that later Chinese Confucianism was anything but these things. Of its enormous body of writing, remarkably little came from Confucius himself. Confucianism, so long the ethical system guiding China, was developed in the work and thought of a mass of subsequent commentators.

Mengzi, who was active during the first quarter of the fourth century BCE, was such a commentator. His view was based on faith in the ultimate goodness of human nature. To him is attributed a practical Chinese political device of some importance – the 'mandate of Heaven' concept – although there are hints of its development much earlier. This idea is one of qualification of the absolute power of the ruler. It is regarded as morally justifiable, even laudable, to revolt against a cruel, unjust or even unlucky regime. In other words, a government is finally justified by its success, its ability to maintain a reasonably prosperous and equable society; an emperor by his probity, his high moral character, since only such a man would be able to intercede with the forces of Heaven to ensure prosperity.

Rather than voting at elections, this became a means of bending governments to the will of the people. The recent concessions of the Chinese Communist Party, especially its economic ones, are not inconsistent with this tradition. The habit of the Chinese Communist government of describing itself as 'correct' – that is, morally sound – may also have a connection. Contrasting with Mengzi, a second important early commentator, Xunzi, regarded human nature as fundamentally bad, in need of improvement through good government, the establishment of set rules of conduct, and the high moral example of rulers. China's formal stylized social patterns, maintained into modern times, owe much to him.

The Chinese world of this time consisted of a dozen or so large and small states grouped along the Yellow and Wei Rivers, which constituted Zhongguo – the Middle Country – plus a number of others, on the western and southern fringes, which were regarded as having a lower culture. Beyond this lay the world of the 'barbarians'. Of the fringe states the most significant was Qin, in the far north-west. Qin was traditionally a bastion against the hordes farther west that were a perpetual threat to the settled Chinese countryside and wealthy cities. Not for nothing were strong walls and defence outworks the most striking feature of Chinese cities.

The ideals attributed to Confucius were suspect in his own time by those who held and influenced power, the energetic pragmatists who really decided the policy of states. Far from regarding humanity as noble and susceptible to an elevated moral example, they believed that a rigidly enforced system of law was the best means of government. This 'legalist' school reached its greatest influence in the state of Qin, which is not surprising. In Qin military effectiveness was considered of paramount importance. The entire population was subject to conscription without notice: the men to fight, and the women and old people to carry supplies and to labour at the fortifications. The army was equipped with elaborate siege machinery: tall, wooden towers on wheels, battering rams, mangonels and similar engines designed to hurl huge stones at the mud walls of beleaguered cities.

By the third century BCE Qin had the 'barbarians' on its frontiers under control, and was able to use its efficient military machine against its more cultured but less martial neighbours to the east. Under the joint rule of its young king and his chief counsellor, Li Si, it won every campaign. Not all were military, for Li Si was an intriguer of ability. His negotiating was a major factor in a series of victories that led to no less than the unification of China for the first time. The king of Qin now restyled himself Shi Huangdi – the First Emperor – in 221 BCE.

His administrators had at least the virtue of energy, devoting themselves to a stream of reforms that transformed China – a name which, incidentally, derives from Qin. The width of carriage axles was standardized, a system of uniform weights and measures and coinage introduced, and – immensely important – Chinese writing reformed to make it more concise and practical and, moreover, standardized. The empire was linked by roads which must have been major engineering works even by today's standards. Qin also cut across the old feudal lines of authority, and established an efficient, if despotic, system of administration, based on division into 36 provinces, each controlled by three specialized officials responsible to the emperor.

Efficient communications and a rigid discipline became the basis of unity. To further reduce the power of the great families the emperor called in all their weapons. The huge pile of bronze was melted down and cast into 12 statues, each reputed to weigh 70 tons, which were set up at the summer palace, Afang. The building of Afang is said to have involved a labour force of three-quarters of a million.

Li Si persuaded the emperor to issue an edict that books from the past, except a few specialist texts, should be destroyed. Anyone who failed to burn his books within 30 days would be branded and sent to forced labour. The case Li Si put to the king was not, however, altogether unreasonable. Pointing out that the feudal princes were continually at war, he argued 'Why should we follow them? The empire has been pacified, law comes from a single authority, the people have work, but the scholars continue to study the past, causing doubt and trouble.' The books of the classics, compiled with great labour and almost irreplaceable, were bulky and difficult to conceal. Paper was not yet in use, and the books were mostly inscribed on ivory tablets, lengths of bamboo, and slabs of wood. At first some scholars defied the edict. More severe penalties were introduced. A huge pit is said to have been dug, and 460 scholars buried alive in it.

So Shi Huangdi earned the hatred of succeeding generations of Chinese scholars as 'he who burned the books and buried the scholars'. The story of this villainy has, no doubt, lost nothing in the telling, but the extent to which the First Emperor's reputation has been embroidered by later writers is not really known. Certainly a vast mass of stories, many fanciful, has grown up around his name. Myth has it that self-firing crossbows guard the underground passages into his tomb, and that rivers and lakes of mercury surround it.

While it is sometimes asserted that Shi Huangdi built the Great Wall, much of it already existed before his time. However, he recognized its importance as a defence against barbarians, and greatly improved the older fabric. This involved forced labour by vast hordes of people over 12 years, during which it is said a million workers died. Labour on the Great Wall was a common and greatly feared punishment. The existing wall is of later, Ming Dynasty, construction.

An elaborate signalling system was used by the garrisons on the wall, to bring reinforcements to any point of attack. As soon as the fast-moving horsemen appeared out of a cloud of dust to the west, signal fires were lit. During the day bundles of damp straw were used to send up columns of smoke, and at night the fires were coloured using metallic salts – the basis of the Chinese invention of fireworks.

The harshness of Qin rule and the extent of the revolution it had visited on China foredoomed it. Long before his death the emperor lived constantly in fear and told no one in which of his network of palaces he would spend the night. His fear of death led him into a deep preoccupation with immortality and a search for a potion said to procure it. He died in 210 BCE while on a tour of his empire. Such was the fear that the fact of his death would lead to a revolt, it was concealed until his body – with a load of rotting fish – could be returned to the capital.

The extraordinary scope and power of this regime was confirmed by the discovery in 1974 near the city of Xian of the Entombed Warriors – a half-buried army of almost 8000 life-sized archers, infantrymen and cavalry made from terracotta and located in several huge pits which had been roofed with pine logs subsequently destroyed by fire. Bronze chariots and many other artefacts still being unearthed here confirm that this is part of the mausoleum of Shi Huangdi, on which three-quarters of a million artisans are said to have worked. Seven human skeletons also recovered may be those of Shi Huangdi's children, murdered in the palace coup after his death, further weakening the dynasty.

Although the Chinese government has decided the substantial hill believed to house the actual burial place of the First Emperor will not yet be excavated, other archaeological work around the complex has revealed a very advanced technology for the world of its time, especially metallurgy. Bronze swords were made with a high tin content, resulting in blades of considerable sharpness and hardness. Some are uncorroded after more than 2000 years, and appear to have been coated for this purpose, probably with chrome. Blast furnaces were in use to make high-quality steel. Steel-making of this kind would not occur for another thousand years in Europe.

Here, too, appear to have been the origins of the alchemy which was to fascinate Europe a millennium later, and using much the same methods and materials. Like the alchemists, Chinese investigators of this time too often met an untimely end, either from poisoning by mercury, with which they were fascinated, or eating powdered jade, or mushrooms and fungi growing on high mountains.

Shi Huangdi's heirs and supporters were not able to maintain the empire, and in the end his family was murdered to the last child. Li Si was executed publicly by cutting in two. A period of confusion and civil war followed during which a general of peasant origins, Liu Bang, founded the dynasty called the Han, which was to institute much of the pattern China would follow almost up to modern times. Liu Bang negotiated patiently to win the feudal lords to Han allegiance, but nevertheless he maintained the basic principles of the Qin state, most importantly its ability to raise immense revenues through efficient taxation. A poll tax which had to be paid in coins was imposed on every Chinese, even small children, and adults were also liable to corvée duties and military conscription. The bureaucracy with clearly defined responsibilities was maintained, but its recruitment came to recognize the values of education and ability in officials. They were often appointed in pairs to limit their power. These traditions would be a continuing thread in Chinese history.

In spite of these efforts for peace and conciliation, at first the Han state had to struggle desperately to survive. To the north and north-west, 'barbarian' armies of more than half a million men were waiting outside the Great Wall. Liu Bang met this threat with a degree of success by diplomacy and bribery rather than war. It was not until the half-century-long reign of the Emperor Wudi, which began 60 years later, that China's enemies were subdued and she became, for the first time, an empire of proportions and power significant in global terms. The Chinese call themselves the men of Han to distinguish themselves from minority groups in the outer areas. It is a dynasty particularly favoured as an historic model by the Communist government, perhaps because of the similarities between its origins and their own.

The Confucian classics reappeared and copies were made from odd fragments that had been secretly buried, concealed in chinks of walls or under roofbeams, or retained in the memories of old men. In spite of such painstaking efforts to recreate the past, much had changed. The persistent effort to centralize power had all but destroyed the old families, and the long wars during the early Han impoverished China. The early Han emperors retained the provincial system and regularly interfered in the affairs of – and supervised – the former feudal states. It was largely this genius of the Han administration to divide and rule that allowed China the centuries of peace necessary to grow into a great power.

The population grew quickly and spread farther to the south. The increased use of irrigation, and the building of canals and fleets of river boats, made possible the growth and distribution of more rice than was needed for bare subsistence. Yet most of this additional wealth went to provide a luxurious lifestyle for the scholar-officials, most of whom came from the old feudal families. Records of the time indicate that life was generally desperate and precarious for the peasants, who were frequently in debt. Interest rates were rapaciously high and they were often forced to sell their land, and even their children into slavery, to survive. As a last resort men fled into the forests, compelled to robbery, joining one of the bands of brigands greatly feared by travellers. As well as a month's labour a year required of the peasants to work on public enterprises, they were also liable to conscription for two years in the army. They were provided with the necessities of life during this service, but were otherwise unpaid.

It was within the walled cities that the arts and graces flourished, based on an overall surplus there of commodities over demand. The first-century historian Ban Gu claimed for the capital, Changan (the present Chinese city of Xian), that a wall a hundred miles long surrounded its offices, palaces and suburbs, with water gardens and parks featuring rhinoceroses from Kanji (south-east India), birds from Chaldea, and unicorns from Annam!

The Han empire controlled the barbarians not only at the Great Wall, but far beyond it, pushing into the Tarim Basin and Tibet almost to the boundaries of India. It used armed cavalry, with long spears, to devastating effect. Probably the world's first large-scale mass production industry equipped this army. Iron or bronze arrowheads were manufactured in millions, since individual soldiers would have at least 100 arrows for their crossbows. These weapons were highly developed instruments, and remained more deadly and effective than firearms as late as the nineteenth century. Of particular interest was the standardized trigger-and-string release device, mass-produced in bronze to efficient and precise specifications.

However, these military expeditions were not designed to carve out an empire but to subdue the nomad tribes, driving them far to the west so they would not be a threat to China. It became a confirmed Chinese attitude that control of neighbouring states was a prerequisite to the security of China.

As the Christian era dawned, China had its effect on the world of the West, even though both scarcely knew it. The world now had two great empires, those of the Han and of Imperial Rome, which was probably slightly the smaller. The Chinese census of CE 2 estimates 58 million people. There were trade contacts between the two empires, including an expensive and widespread fashion in Rome for Chinese silk, which at one time threatened to deplete bullion reserves. More significant was the displacement of the nomad tribes westwards, eventually to have disruptive effects in both Europe and India.

Major contributions to the Chinese tradition were developed during Han times. One of the most important was a trend towards merit and education rather than birth as a qualification for high office. This was associated with the increasing power of the central government. Unlike in Europe, feudalism would virtually disappear at this early stage. There was also a major revival of Confucianism. These two factors, organized national government, increasingly by an intelligentsia, and the use of the Confucian classics to justify – even sanctify – the system of government, led on to the development of that great public service known as the mandarinate, the longest-lived and perhaps the most successful instrument of administration mankind has seen. Its influence and traditions are still apparent in the China of today, and may well become more so in the future.

In Han times the mandarinate had already developed many of its enduring characteristics, including examinations in the classics, and adoption of the Confucian idea that the educated man was to be guided by the force of example rather than driven by the fear of punishment. It had also developed a contempt for trade and what the West calls 'private enterprise'. To the Confucian scholars this seemed opposed to true moral values. Filial piety – the respect and support of sons towards fathers, the duties of wives to their mother-in-law – was a major Confucian idea, which was to permeate all levels of the society in time.

In spite of scholarly disapproval, there was at times almost unfettered capitalism and the accumulation of great fortunes by merchants. However, these caused such convulsions of the economy, due to 'cornering' and speculation in food, and illicit coining of currency, that the Han state eventually curbed them. Large public works and much of the significant domestic industry and distribution systems came under state control. Before controls were reimposed, capitalists in the iron and salt industries were making huge fortunes. The government nationalized these industries and ordered their former owners to run them on behalf of the state. The association of capitalism and state control emerging in China now is, then, a recurring theme in Chinese history, and ought not to occasion surprise. Indeed, some of the economic problems with which the Han state wrestled were not too far removed from those emerging in China today.

The invention of paper in the second century was a major step forward. Writing became an almost universal occupation among educated men in Han times, and special attention was given to history. The art of paper-making spread slowly west, reaching Europe 1000 years later. Han Confucianism developed its preoccupation with systems of complex rites and relationships in almost every area of life, a desire for an ordered harmonious universe, which, once established, would go on unchanged for ever. The idea of the ruler as a civilized, virtuous example to his subjects, a sort of moral pace-setter, became firmly developed. Already Confucianism was far from Confucius. It owed much not only to the horde of commentators after his death, but even to other sources; even to the seemingly antithetic Daoism, a philosophy from Zhou times which saw men as simply part of nature, to whose mysterious forces they must adjust, changing what was about them as little as possible – forerunners of modern conservationists, among some of whom Daoism is again popular.

Music and philosophy were thought to be so closely associated that proper calculation of the degrees of pitch in the musical scale was considered essential to the proper functioning of government. Hence mathematicians and philosophers were assigned to the task of calculating them. This suggests the importance attributed to an overall harmony of the universe in human affairs. The movements of the moon, planets and constellations were also carefully studied for similar reasons. Mathematics was developed to a high degree, Zhang Heng calculating the value of pi to be 3.1622 in the second century CE. He also invented the world's first known seismograph at that time. It is not without interest that in 2000 the Chinese government announced the discovery of a Han water closet said to be 2000 years old, complete with running water, a stone seat and a comfortable armrest, thus challenging the claim of English plumber Thomas Crapper to have invented this device in the nineteenth century.

Han government became so closely associated with Confucianism that the decay of one involved the collapse of the other. There was a massive revulsion from the formalism of Confucianism, and from the extensive corruption at the imperial court as the corps of eunuchs ostensibly enlisted to guard the harem became a major influence on the emperors. Many people turned to the newly arrived Buddhism and even more to the anarchic Daoism. Daoism lay behind the great second-century peasant revolt of the Yellow Turbans, in which millions were said to have been killed and which hastened the decline of the Han. Flood, famine and poverty increasingly weakened the Chinese nation. The 'barbarian' tribesmen took their opportunity, occupying much of north China. The Chinese fled to the alien, still lightly settled south.

Meanwhile Buddhism, which reached China via the trade routes in the first century CE, had been rapidly gaining adherents. The form of Buddhism that came to China was the *mahayana* school, which is very different from the more orthodox *theravada* of Burma and Thailand. *Mahayana* Buddhism was a religion, already equipped with magic, gods and saints known as *bodhisattvas*, who deferred their translation to a state of divine perfection so they could intercede in Heaven on man's behalf. It postulated a paradise in which humans were given hope of a far better life. A universally revered and characteristic Chinese *bodhisattva* is Kuan Yin, the goddess of mercy and examplar of feminine virtues. Certain aspects of Confucianism, such as ancestor worship and the cult of the family, were incorporated into Chinese Buddhism, which, as it has moved eastwards, has shown itself to be one of the more flexible and malleable human philosophies. It was in this sinified form that it began its further movement eastwards across the narrow seas to the islands of Japan.

6 Early Japan and the Tang Dynasty in China

The original inhabitants of this small, sunny but cool group of mountainous islands off the coast of China were not the people now known as the Japanese. Recent archaeological evidence indicates occupancy as early as 10,000 BCE by primitive hunter-gatherers who, by perhaps 5000 BCE, had established small farming settlements, and whose very simple round- or pointed-bottomed pottery, radio-carbon-dated back to around 10,000 BCE, is regarded by some as the world's earliest-dated utilitarian ceramics. During the preceding ice age the Japanese islands, part of a mountain range skirting the Asian mainland coast, were joined to that mainland, allowing free passage to animals and humans.

The ancestors of today's Japanese were quite late entrants to the country. They found a people in the islands quite unlike themselves – short in stature, with heavy body hair, light skin colour and a language different from any other in the world. These people, the Ainu, were considered to be of Caucasian origin because of these characteristics. Recent genetic comparisons indicate links with the peoples of Russian Siberia. The Ainus, who led a primitive hunting, fishing existence, nevertheless resisted the intruders ferociously. However, the Japanese, originally settled in the southernmost island, Kyushu, eventually pushed these earlier inhabitants northward. Now only a small Ainu community of around 20,000 remains on the northernmost island, Hokkaido.

Since the early Japanese were not literate and had no historical tradition, there is very little reliable information about this early period. When they arrived and just where they came from, remain conjecture. They were, however, Mongoloid, almost certainly coming to Japan from China via the Korean peninsula – although there are also intriguing signs of an ethnic connection with south-east Asia. There are links with Indonesian languages in Japanese, but the most striking resemblance is in the form of construction of Japan's oldest and most sacred shrine, that at Ise of the sun goddess Amaterasu, the chief deity of the Shinto religion.

For a temple that attracts such veneration the Ise shrine is unassuming – no more than a small wooden hut of post and beam construction holding up a heavy, thatched, single gable, and mounted on about 50 timber piles. The shrine is believed to be an exact copy of the kind of house built by the Japanese when they first came to their islands. Every 21 years it has been pulled down and rebuilt in new, specially selected cypress, so the copy and the original are identical. It is very similar to buildings still found in parts of south-east Asia, especially in the east Indonesian island of Sulawesi and in Sumatra.

This early Japanese society is called the *yamato*, named for the region inland from the big port city of Osaka on the island of Honshu. However, it probably originated in western Kyushu and then moved gradually north-east around the shores of the Inland Sea. It built large underground tombs in a variety of shapes, in which small terracotta figures called *haniwa* have been found. These figurines indicate that *yamato* warriors used the horse and armour. Their religion, which appears to have postulated gods based on the forces of nature – in particular the sun – came to be known as Shinto, which means 'the way of the gods'.

The earliest contacts with Chinese civilization were hostile. However, trade followed and a pact of friendship was concluded with two south Korean states, Paekche and Silla, in the fourth century. There was also considerable migration of whole extended families, and of craftsmen and scholars from war-torn Korea. Their clan loyalties were maintained in the new country and three or four of these families became powerful enough to manipulate the imperial line. Indeed, at least one early emperor appears to have been Korean. Written records appear only in the fifth century, when Chinese writing began to be used, hence the chronicles of earlier times cannot be taken as a reliable record. However, there can be little doubt that Koreans, themselves greatly influenced by Chinese culture, were a major factor forming early Japanese society.

The briefest of summaries will serve to indicate all that is of any importance in the area of myth. The goddess Amaterasu emerges as the most important deity and her grandson, Ninigi, is said to have descended from the High Plain of Heaven to rule among men. Ninigi's great-grandson, Jimmu, is revered as the first of a continuous line of 125 Japanese emperors considered to be of the same semi-divine blood. Hence, while Chinese emperors were mortal and ruled only while they held the mandate of Heaven, Japanese emperors rule by divine right, which they pass on automatically to their descendants. To preserve this continuity, Japanese emperors must be 'above the clouds', aloof from day-to-day politics, on which they accordingly have no influence.

The issue of the divinity of the emperor is not quite as simple as it seems. He is not regarded as a god in the Western sense, so much as a human figure possessing, more than any other person or object, the quality the Japanese call *kami*, the crude meaning of which is elevation or superiority. *Kami* is a spiritual quality which persons and objects – even the islands of Japan – possess in differing amounts. This concept is important because it represents a distinctive quality of the Japanese people – a belief that the main value of the individual is as a unit in the totality of Japan. It came to be expressed in the extraordinary loyalty, often tested to the death, of Japanese retainers to their lords, the willingness of Japanese *kamikaze* pilots to crash their bomb-laden aircraft on the decks of American ships during the Second World War and, in recent times, the almost feudal relationships between the huge Japanese industrial complexes and their workers.

The official Japanese religion, Shinto, is essentially animist, although it has characteristics which play a major part in the thought and life of Japan today. One is an insistence on personal cleanliness as the necessary companion of holiness. Worship at a Shinto shrine involves purification in both the physical and spiritual sense. The first is achieved by washing in running water and the second simply by passing under a number of large ceremonial arches called *torii*, which span the paths leading to shrines.

Another manifestation of Shinto that has become part of the Japanese character is a refreshing preference for simplicity and restraint. Its shrines are usually small structures of natural wood, deliberately left unpainted, a key to the Japanese fondness for this material. There are no images or statues, the deity being represented by a symbol, often a polished bronze mirror but sometimes a sword or the *magatama* jewel, which represent the regalia believed to have been handed to Ninigi by Amaterasu. Only the emperor, certain members of his family, or his special emissary, may pass the silken curtain over the entrance to the Ise shrine, for its sacred symbols must always be screened from the sight of ordinary men. Some Shinto shrines are not buildings at all. Among them are a waterfall, a rock and a mountain.

The Shinto ideal of simplicity, at the same time shunning the direct, the obvious or ostentatious, is the mainspring of all its forms of art. Where Westerners see beauty in massed displays of flowers, the Japanese purist would admire a single blossom. There are other aspects of Shinto which are not so appealing, such as a disregard for individual life and suffering, and a martial attitude involving great cruelty, much in evidence many times in Japanese history.

Japan is a mountainous country, with few large areas of flat land. Only 13 per cent is arable. Hence from the earliest times a remarkable intensity has had to be applied to cultivating the land, so that the last possible ounce of food can be grown. The traveller through Japan sees at every turn, in the elaborate cultivated terraces on so many hillsides, the results of many generations of devoted labour. Early Japan did not have to face this constraint. It was a simple clan society, still quite small in numbers, when it turned to China for its first civilized model.

Although the first millennium of the Christian era saw most of Europe asleep in the Dark Ages, these were centuries of light in Asia, and nowhere more so than in China. Under the rule of the Sui and Tang Dynasties China became the strongest, most populous and advanced society the world had yet seen. However, it would be quite wrong to conclude that the centuries between the decline of the Han and the accession of the Sui were some kind of interregnum – this was a period of tremendous growth both economically and culturally, with strong and in many ways quite different societies developing in the north-west and in the Yangzi valley. Indeed the spread of Chinese influence through south-east Asia at this time came from southern China.

A second major theme was the displacement of Confucianism by a complex amalgam of Buddhism and Daoism. China was to be a Buddhist society for 400 years from the fourth century. It could even be said that a dualism still apparent in China today, evidenced by the resistance of the Falung Gong movement to state suppression, is part of the millennia-long contest between the formal behaviourism of Confucianism and the desire for the mysterious, magical, individual and contemplative so distinctive of the other two great religions. Indeed, it would not be too much to describe this era as 'green' in the contemporary sense, or indeed its poets – like the Seven Sages of the Forest of Bamboo – as 'bohemian' in their aversion to rites, politics and conventions. The world's first landscape painting, more than a thousand years before it evolved in Europe, derived directly from the Daoist view of nature as remarkable, even holy, and a place of liberation of the human spirit.

The centuries of independent states gave place, in 589, to a brief preparatory dynasty, the Sui, which again united China. As with the Qin, Sui achievements were largely due to the qualities of the dynasty's founder, the Emperor Wendi. His successor, Yangdi, laid an important economic foundation for the future by building a huge network of irrigation and transport canals, among them completion of the 1300 -mile Grand Canal, linking the Yangzi and Yellow rivers. This, considered by some to have been the largest engineering project in the world at that time, was nevertheless achieved at a huge human cost among the peasants conscripted to the work. There was nothing small about this network for waterborne transport. The canals were typically 40 metres wide, with well-constructed highways running alongside them. But Yangdi is perhaps more reasonably criticized for his despatch of huge, disastrous expeditions to Korea. The emperor was murdered in 618 by his own courtiers, and a general of the north-west command succeeded him, commencing the Tang Dynasty.

Tang saw a pattern of administration in China which endured almost without change into the early twentieth century, and in which the system of recruiting the mandarinate through very difficult public examinations became established. China had at various times during her long past experimented with codified law, and was aware of its deficiencies. The alternative was seen as entrusting decisions on legal and administrative matters to a corps of highly qualified, broadly educated men, then controlling them rigorously with a system of inspectorates and by shifting them regularly from one post to another far away. This administrative elite were the mandarins, never numerous for a country of China's size but with immense powers in their regional bailiwicks. The 'law' they administered was based on custom and precedent. Reference to any Chinese Dynasty as a government invites misunderstanding. Modern governments exist mainly to make and amend laws. The Chinese dynasties and their bureaucrats maintained law and order but their main purpose otherwise was to raise revenues.

More than ever the art of graceful and elegant writing was required of the scholar-administrator. The chief examination, for the *jinshi* degree, which maintained its position into the twentieth century, tested administrative ability, but also literary skills – especially the composition of poetry. This tradition has not disappeared. Mao Zedong wrote poetry, as anyone who passed through Beijing airport in the 1970s would know – a translation of his poem 'The Snow' featured prominently on a wall.

Tang was the age of perhaps the best-known Chinese poets. Its two more celebrated, Li Bo and Du Fu, were contemporaries. Du Fu was a scholarly poet, well regarded by the intelligentsia of the time, but the impetuous, rebellious Li Bo has had the greater international appeal over time. A rebel against constituted authority and one who could not be bothered with study, Li Bo was a womanizer and a regular drunk, along with his companions, the Eight Immortals of the Winecup. Nevertheless the power and passion of his verse impressed even the emperor, although its Daoist, nature-worshipping philosophy was directly antithetic to the Confucian ideal. Li Bo is said to have drowned when, leaning from a boat, he tried to embrace the reflection of the moon in the Yangzi River.

China again became powerful militarily. All of Tibet, the Tarim River Basin, and even parts of Afghanistan, came under Chinese influence. While the Tang army did use conscripted peasant foot soldiers, its cutting edge was the cavalry, very much in the tradition of the steppes, using bowmen who could effectively fire arrows at the full gallop. Even though this expansion of influence was precarious, due to long supply lines and skirmishes with growing Arab power, the overall result was to pacify Central Asia so thoroughly that traders could use the overland routes without undue fear of robberies or delays. This was the heyday of the Silk Road. A steady stream of horse and camel trains carried, among other things, paper, silk, gunpowder, spices, condiments and tea to the West. The journey was a long and perilous one, during which it was necessary to pass the dreaded 1000-mile stretch of the Taklamakan Desert. Without the bad-tempered double-humped Bactrian camel, able to survive without water for two weeks at a time, this trade would scarcely have been possible. Beautifully worked Persian gold and silver, myrrh, precious stones, Turkish carpets, glassware came from the West into China. There were also the beginnings of sea trade, particularly from the southern port of Guangzhou. It was then regarded as uncouth, dangerous and unpleasantly hot, but it was a convenient point of entry into China for Persian ships, also large vessels, as much as 200 feet long, from Sri Lanka. Silk and china were the main exports.

This was a time of major cultural transfer to the Middle East and thence to Europe, both from China and the Buddhist universities in India. This transfer was not only one way. The capital, Zhangan, became the principal metropolis in the world of the eighth century, and probably also the most important repository of knowledge. It was certainly the largest, with more than a million inhabitants. There were many libraries in Zhangan, and there is evidence of a knowledge of, and a lively interest in, other parts of the world and their thought – the cult of Zarathustra from Persia and Nestorian Christianity among them. Neither of these took hold in China but Islam, at the height of its missionary phase, eventually attracted millions of adherents among China's border peoples, many of whom are still Muslims today.

The world's first books were printed, using wooden blocks on which all the characters for a complete page were engraved. The world's oldest known surviving printed book, a copy of the Buddhist Diamond Sutra, discovered in 2004, is dated 864 CE. The Chinese experimented with moveable type in the eleventh century, but abandoned it as impractical because of the large number of Chinese characters. (In the Kangxi dictionary of 1716, there are 40,545 characters.) However, the Koreans later persisted for some decades with moveable type.

Tang China had its rebels, its eccentrics and its non-conformists, which it was well able to accommodate, but generally it was an orderly, regulated society, based on state control of the economy and good communications. In more ways than one the old China was disappearing. The emphasis was going more and more to the south where the rich ricelands of the Yangzi valley were creating a new prosperity. Although enormous efforts were devoted to building canals and roads to take this new wealth northward, Zhangan's days were already numbered.

The Chinese belief that it was a religious duty to have many sons provided an almost inexhaustible pool of manpower for public works. Every ten miles along the road system radiating out from Changan post stations were built, which provided horses and other facilities for couriers of the government.

Intrigue and dissension within the imperial court itself – famously involving a courtesan, Yang Guifei – resulted in a major civil war for eight years from 755, the Rebellion of An Lushan. The Tang state was severely weakened by this conflict, from which it never really recovered. A steady deterioration, associated with an increasing shift of power to regional lords and a weakening of China's foreign policy, ended with the eclipse of the dynasty in 907. The northern 'barbarians' took over much of north China, and in the south former military governors set up their own states. There was a great deal of fighting and rebellion, the ill effects of which were compounded by regional droughts and floods.

During the Tang the very considerable influence of Buddhism on Chinese affairs was forcibly controlled. Early in the dynasty its founder, the Gaozu emperor, issued edicts asserting Confucianism and Daoism as the religions favoured by the state, castigating Buddhism as a foreign religion. Taizong, the second emperor, further regulated the Buddhist establishment, restricting its influences in secular matters. Then in the ninth century the Buddhist establishment, tax-exempt and considered far too wealthy, was systematically dismantled. Thousands of Buddhist monasteries and temples were destroyed, and their enormous assets seized by the state. Millions of acres of land were confiscated and hundreds of thousands of monks and nuns forced to return to the lay community.

Meanwhile, the influence of this large, sophisticated neighbour on Japan had been irresistible. As Chinese culture flourished, the embassies from the *yamato* people became more frequent, in spite of the perils of the journey in the crude punt-like Japanese ships of the time. Many of those who did return brought books, ranging from the Confucian classics to treatises on medicine and history. These were the main avenues through which Chinese culture was transferred to Japan. An additional major influence came from the regular stream of Chinese and Korean migrants to Japan. They were educated and cultured far beyond the Japanese, and were welcomed as associates and advisers to *yamato* chiefs. They were able to teach Japanese leaders how to read and write Chinese, in spite of its difficulty and basic incompatibility with the Japanese language.

Early in the seventh century the governing regent for the empress, Prince Shotoku, encouraged a major Buddhist missionary effort in Japan, and probably asserted the divine origins of the imperial family for the first time. In the year 646, not long after his death, reforms known as the *taika*, or great change, were instituted, on the initiative of an admirer of Tang China, Fujiwara Kamatari. The Fujiwara family were to be of major importance in Japan into modern times. The *taika* reforms were intended to strengthen the imperial government at the expense of the regional clans, through a complex bureaucracy. These reforms closely followed similar changes in China, in which all land was vested in the emperor, reallocated among the peasants, and taxed. These modifications in Japan were carried out and policed by a public service modelled on the mandarinate. The custom of making compulsory military service part of the peasants' tax burden was copied. Since the Japanese army had no external enemy to fight, the conscripts were used as labourers on public works.

Such a project was a capital city, Nara, modelled on Changan. The Empress Gemmyo began this work in 694, copying Changan's layout of straight intersecting streets, its styles of architecture and landscape gardening. Tang music was also imported, and while it has disappeared in China, it has been preserved through the centuries in the Japanese Court. Nara was the first big city in Japan even though its ambitious early plans were never completed, and has given its name to the succeeding era of sinification of Japanese society.

The Emperor Shomu devoted his life and much of the energies of his people to good works inspired by Buddhism. Much of his work was to the benefit of the community – almshouses, hospitals, wayside halts for travellers, improved roads and bridges. Of less practical value was the building of a 53-foot high, 560-ton statue of the Buddha, the largest bronze statue in the world and still a major tourist attraction in Nara, although it is said to be much altered from the original due to an earthquake, many fires and general neglect during its 1500-year history. A plague of smallpox came to Japan from China that was so severe it inspired the emperor to build the statue in the hope that this would ward off the disease. This work became Shomu's greatest preoccupation, at enormous economic cost to Japan.

At least seven big monasteries grew up in and around Nara. These quickly became centres of considerable influence and wealth. Abbots armed their monks as a means of protecting the monasteries against bandits, but later used these small armies aggressively, even demanding concessions from the emperor. It was probably Buddhist pressure that induced the Emperor Kwammu to move to a new capital in 794. At first it was called Heian, meaning peace and prosperity, but was later simply known as the capital – *kyoto* – the name it bears to this day.

The Heian period saw something of an exhaustion of the impetus given to Japanese civilization by China. Regular contacts dwindled with the decline of the Tang Dynasty, and ceased altogether in 894. The spirit of the *taika* reforms had, in fact, vanished much earlier. The bureaucracy suffered from being a slavish copy of the forms of the mandarinate while lacking its traditions. Japan drifted back into feudalism. One by one the provincial governors and other high officials obtained land tax exemptions and used these to assert greater independence and power which eventually resulted in a pattern of almost autonomous fiefdoms.

The imperial family now came increasingly under the control of the Fujiwara clan. Fujiwara tactics, henceforward, were to marry regularly into the imperial family then force abdications in favour of heirs of tender years. This resulted in long periods of Fujiwara regency and the family became the effective rulers of Japan. This control of the nation by one of a number of powerful, competing cliques became characteristic of Japan, and is still manifest in the *ha* – factions – in modern Japan which make up so much of its political establishment.

Although Kyoto continued to be the capital until 1869, from this time on the emperors, with rare exceptions, were little more than prisoners – abstract symbols of inherited *kami*, too holy either to act on their own initiative or to be approached by ordinary men. The aristocracy grouped around the emperor drifted out of touch with the people, and, like the French Court before the revolution, devoted its time and resources almost exclusively to the pursuit of art and manners.

This society is described in clear and penetrating style in a remarkable novel called the *Tale of Genji*, written by the Lady Murasaki Shikibu, who was a resident of the Japanese Court, probably in the early eleventh century. Her diaries add to its portrayal of a shallow, amoral and luxury-loving society, at times capable of considerable artistic expression, but in the main occupied with, or bored by, trifles. The courtiers feared and disliked the crude ways of the rest of the country, and for an official to be sent from the Court to the provinces was regarded as a disgrace and banishment to a way of life virtually insupportable.

The truth was that the real power now resided in the regions away from Kyoto. New areas of settlement and cultivation were opening up and the great feudal families grew more powerful. Among them were two dominating clans, both offshoots of the imperial line, who involved Japan in her equivalent of the Wars of the Roses. These two families, the Taira and the Minamoto, engaged in a struggle to replace the waning power of the Fujiwara, who had been weakened by internal dissension. At first the Taira had some success but finally their enemy, under the command of Minamoto Yoritomo, was victorious. He established, in 1185, a military dictatorship which called itself the *bakufu*, which means camp government. This regime was based far from Kyoto in the town of Kamakura, not far from the present Tokyo. So Japan was set on a path of feudal militarism that extended through to the twentieth century.

The great military clans had been strengthened because of what was regarded as the disgraceful defeat of Japanese armies during a particularly stubborn revolt of the Ainu minority in the eighth century. This defeat, in the year 790, was the last to be imposed on the Japanese army until the tide turned in the Pacific phase of the Second World War more than 1100 years later. Widespread conscription was introduced to subdue the Ainu, who would never again be a threat to the Japanese. By the middle of the tenth century this military tradition had developed a code in many ways comparable with knighthood during the so-called age of chivalry in Europe. In Japan it was based on an hereditary caste of soldiers, the *samurai*, which was to dominate Japanese society into modern times.

Although the Kamakura period was one of military rule, it had distinguished artistic achievements, especially landscape painting and sculpture, with the first signs of an emerging style significantly different from the Chinese. Typical is a vivid statue of the *kami* of thunder, Rai-Jin, which still stands in Kyoto. It surges with a crude and even a cruel vitality: mouth open in a snarl showing savagely-bared teeth; right hand raised ready to strike; staring eyes and bulbous nose – all these bear eloquent witness to the artistic force of the Kamakura era.

It was at this stage that the military tradition merged with Buddhism, especially the Zen school with its stress on action and insistence on simplicity. It demands from its adherents a rigid discipline, hardship and great courage. It eschews logic – most of its few statements of belief are paradoxes – 'What is the sound of one hand?' It is therefore not possible to describe Zen accurately in words. The discipline, hardship, courage and long periods of calm meditation required of its adherents are designed eventually to create in them an inner experience which is beyond verbal description and which is the spiritual essence of Zen. This inner enlightenment is called *satori*. Nicheren Buddhism also significantly reinforced the militarist tradition, and, like the other popular form of Japanese Buddhism, the True Pure Land, obliged its adherents to little more than perfunctory observances – in the case of the former, granting salvation simply by reciting a set text, the Lotus Sutra.

Japanese architecture developed the simple, sparsely ornamented style that remains typical today. In other arts, notably flower arranging, the formal tea ceremony and garden design, equal restraint came to be practised. One classic garden consists of nothing more than 15 carefully placed stones on an area of raked, white sand.

In time, the spirit of the era seems to have inspired even the imperial family. The Kamakura government was ended in 1333 by the Emperor Go-Daigo. After some misadventures his forces were able to attack and defeat the *bakufu*. After taking, with much ceremony, the traditional small cups of Japanese rice wine, *sake*, the leaders and 1000 followers of the *bakufu* committed ceremonial suicide by the slow and painful process of disembowelling.

Go-Daigo did not, however, rule for long. His own general, Ashikaga Takauji, who had largely been responsible for the campaign against the *bakufu*, usurped power in 1338. A phase of almost constant war followed. The Ashikaga *shoguns*, or regents, were considerable patrons of the arts, but woefully inept at administration. Under their rule, Japanese society dissolved into civil war and banditry. In the fifteenth century Kyoto was sacked and burned. As almost all its buildings were of wood, much of the capital was destroyed.

During the confusion members of the imperial family had, at times, to beg and sell their calligraphy to stay alive. Two branches competed for the succession. Again there was something of a parallel with Chinese history, as society drifted off into anarchy. It was to wait a century for the strong men who would bring it back to order.

7 The Awakening of Europe and the Challenge of Islam

Europe still consisted largely of small villages and somewhat larger castle towns, scattered through the forests. To this comparative handful of uneducated people Asia was little more than a legend. While a few scholars were dimly aware that great civilizations flourished there, their concepts were largely of a region of queer, supernatural events, acted out by personalities either grotesque or larger than life.

Such a figure was Presbyter – or more commonly, Prester – John, a Christian monarch believed to govern, somewhere in Asia, an empire of fabulous wealth and power, administered by 72 subject kings. He was supposed to possess magical powers and devices, one of which was a mirror in which he could see events happening anywhere in his realm. It is symptomatic of the state of civilization in Europe that such stories were accepted with apparent credulity, not only by peasants but even by scholars and kings.

Through the first millennium a tenuous link with Asia had been maintained. The Venetian empire, dominating the Adriatic, became the European terminus of three trade routes: a caravan track east from the Black Sea, an overland and sea route from Damascus, and another route through the Red Sea. Trade with the East was essentially small in bulk, because of the small size and slowness of ships, and because the land routes followed a scattered chain of oases, crossing formidable deserts and regions of predatory tribes. Only expensive luxuries like silk, fine porcelain and spices were worth carrying in these conditions, but there was a steady and lively demand for them that kept the trade alive in spite of all difficulties. Spices, especially pepper, were in high demand in a Europe which had no reliable way of preserving meat, to eliminate traces of tainting during the long winters. Other spices were highly regarded as medicines.

The efficiency of the overland routes depended a great deal on political conditions. They were quickly affected by the advent, early in the seventh century, of a new and militant religion based on one god, Allah. This Islamic faith took a swift hold in the Middle East. It was still regional at the time of its founder Muhammad but grew rapidly under the control of his lifelong friend and supporter Abu Bekr, who became Muhammad's first *caliph*, or successor.

Islam drove eastward through the wandering nomad tribes, gaining adherents rapidly through its uncompromising choice of conversion to the faith or death. It absorbed and adapted the sophisticated Persian empire and penetrated to the borders of China. To the west it occupied Spain, Portugal and half of France, presenting a ringing challenge and a brilliant civilization that helped to lift Europe from its apathy and ignorance. Trade languished on the land routes; a flourishing sea trade to southern China developed, largely in Arab and Persian ships.

Nevertheless, the new Arab religion was not spread as far as south-east Asia in its original form. It had been adapted and liberalized considerably in Persia (now Iran), before it was spread to northern India and then on to Malaysia and Indonesia by merchants operating through the entrepôt port of Cambay. This is why there are major differences in the modern world among Islamic nations, especially in regard to women. As far east as Pakistan they are discouraged, if not forbidden, to become educated, are generally restricted to their homes, and are forced to wear the *chador*, the ugly and cumbersome all-over robe, if they venture out in public. In Muslim Indonesia and Malaysia women endure no such restrictions. Indeed, the Minangkabauer people of Sumatra are matrilineal, with women substantially controlling families and responsible for their finances and property.

Muslim culture was at its height around the end of the first millennium. It was Islam's capture of Jerusalem in 1076 that drew the European states into the great, if disastrous adventure of the Crusades. However, ultimately it was Mongol hordes who eventually captured the brilliant Muslim metropolis of Baghdad in 1258. Nevertheless, the Muslim Dynasty of the Ottoman Turks continued to present an effective block to European sea trade with the east by dominating the eastern Mediterranean and the Red Sea from the fifteenth century onward. Indirect access to India and the Spice Islands was still to be had across the land routes, but this was slow and expensive. A sea route, especially one that could be travelled wholly by European ships, was much to be preferred.

In 1453 the Ottoman Turks captured and used for their capital Constantinople (now Istanbul), until that date the seat of the later, truncated Roman empire. For 50 years afterwards the Turks made concessions to one Italian state, Venice, which allowed her a monopoly of the Asian trade. The merchants of Venice waxed rich, so giving the other states of Europe an even greater incentive to break this monopoly. This anti-Venetian, anti-Muslim drive, combined with a half-religious, half-commercial ambition to make contact with the empire of Prester John, induced a lifelong effort in a Portuguese prince, Henry the Navigator, to seek a sea route east via the west coast of Africa.

Henry encouraged marine studies at Sagres, in the south-west corner of Portugal, where the half-forgotten maps, sailing directions and methods of navigation of the past were carefully re-examined. Portuguese shipmasters pored over the Guide to Geography prepared by the Alexandrian Ptolemy in the second century. Henry was assisted by the Genoese, anxious to supplant Venice.

The wooden ships, often as small as 40 tons and tragically unwieldy and top-heavy, edged their way down the stormy leeshore of Africa. Many were lost, but the hard experience bought with the lives of ships and men led to important advances in naval architecture. A lighter, faster vessel named the caravel, and bigger designs – the armed carrack and later the galleon – were evolved and, in spite of their clumsiness, were able to survive the Atlantic storms. These larger ships also made trade in bulk commodities, rather than lightweight luxuries, feasible for the first time.

In 1487 Bartholemew Diaz reached and rounded the southern extremity of Africa – the Cape of Storms. With much rejoicing, it was renamed the Cape of Good Hope. In 1498 Vasco da Gama reached India, and the eagerly sought sea route to the east lay open. Portugal lost no time in exploiting it, despatching six expeditions between 1501 and 1505. The largest of these consisted of 20 ships manned by 2500 men, led by the first Viceroy of the East, Francisco d'Almeida. Efforts were made to drive away the interlopers, but the Portuguese won a major naval battle off the north-west Indian port of Diu in 1509. The following year the Portuguese established their base at Goa, and armed it as a fortress.

European infiltration of Asia had begun, and with it a new era. Profits on the early expeditions were so great that the share of the lowliest crew member could amount to a small fortune. A small consignment of pepper brought home by Vasco da Gama in 1499 paid for the entire cost of the expedition several times over.

Other nations of Europe were also resolved to seek adventure and fortune in the East. The dawn of the year 1520 saw the three small top-heavy ships commanded by Ferdinand Magellan four months and thousands of miles out from their home port of Seville. Sailing west, he made landfalls in the Philippines in March, and more than two years later one ship, *Vittoria*, reached home to become the first to sail around the world. By

Figure 5   Detail from a Dutch fortress gate in Malaysia

the end of the century a Spanish colony based on Manila in the Philippines was firmly established.

The Tudor monarchs of England built on the maritime tradition created by centuries of fishing in the stormy North Sea. Henry VIII brought in Italians to advise on the design of ocean-going ships, and offered a cash bounty to subsidize the building of new merchantmen. When Francis Drake returned in 1580 from his voyage around the world he brought a package of cloves acquired at Ternate in the Malukus, then known as the Spice Islands. On the last day of 1600 the East India Company was founded, with a Royal Charter giving it the monopoly of trade with the East. Holland was next in the field. In 1602 she formed her own East India Company, with the then immense capital of more than half a million sterling pounds. In 1619 the Dutch established a base at a fortified village in Java called Jakarta. They called it Batavia.

The geographic advantage of the Atlantic nations over those of the Mediterranean, especially Venice, was to set the pattern for the colonial era. One of the great 'might have beens' of history was the failure to bring to fruition the 1504 consideration by the Venetian Council of Ten for a Suez Canal. If the canal could have been built then, instead of 300 years later, Asia's major relationship with Europe would have been much earlier, and perhaps on more equal terms.

This period of exploration and trade expansion also brought the first crude enquiry into, and speculation about, economic forces. The earliest theorists, who maintained a persistent although diminishing influence for several centuries, were called the bullionists. They believed the prosperity of a nation was related to the amount of gold and silver bullion it was able to hoard. A further step was taken by the mercantilists, who held that this desirable accretion of bullion could best be achieved by having a favourable balance of trade with as many outside areas as possible – in other words, to take out more than was put in. One of the more profitable areas of commerce was the slave trade – around eight million forcibly seized and sent to America alone, plus perhaps two million more who died during transportation in the appalling conditions in the slave ships. Exploitation of other races soon found philosophic rationalization, notably from the eighteenth-century Swedish botanist Carolus Linnaeus. Linnaeus, who was highly regarded in Europe, firmly asserted the biological superiority of the white races, and this was at times used to justify the atrocities to come.

It is important to understand this mercantilist theory, since it was the justification for a policy followed into modern times, which assumed colonies to be chiefly valuable as places perpetually milked of their wealth to the benefit of the conquering country. Autocratic political control, backed by armed force, was used to make sure the system was maintained. This, among other things, led to the Boston Tea Party and the loss of Britain's American colonies. Its effects in Asia were, ultimately, to be no less profound.

8 Flood Tide in China: the Song, Mongol and Ming Dynasties

In 1206 a central Asian people, the Mongols, gathered in conference and elected a new leader, Genghis Khan. The choice was a wise one, for this man already had a high reputation as a military strategist among a people notorious for their ability and ruthlessness in war. Under the leadership of Genghis Khan and his successors the Mongols built up the largest empire the world had yet seen, occupying the greater part of the Eurasian land mass. The Chinese section of this vast empire was ruled directly by the Great Khans, Genghis himself, and his successors. Regions farther west were virtually autonomous, but their rulers owed a token allegiance to the Great Khan.

The most detailed account of the Mongol Empire comes from the Venetian adventurer Marco Polo, who claimed to be in the service of the Great Khan, at that time Kublai. Marco Polo's view of the Great Khan and his empire is always favourable and often sycophantic. This is not surprising, since he was Kublai's employee. He often exaggerates, his sense of geography is vague, and most deceptive of all, he attributes to Kublai a huge and sophisticated civilization which was really the creation of the previous Chinese government.

The Mongol subjugation of China, then ruled by the cultured, refined and broad-minded Song emperors, must be recognized as one of the major events of history. Although at the time of the conquest Song China occupied only the southern half of the country, the population under its rule had already passed the hundred million mark, making it the largest nation in the world.

The simple fact of the conquest in 1279, 44 years after the initial invasion and after three years of bitter fighting was, then, a resounding event in world terms, yet it was even more so in its implications for China's future. From this time onwards China was to diverge increasingly from the ideal culture it so much admired and which the Song so closely approached. There was to be only one more native dynasty, the Ming, but powerful

77

though it was, it became bigoted, inward-looking and conservative. In the Mongol conquest then, was the seed of the great Chinese disasters of the nineteenth and twentieth centuries.

A brief period of warlordism in north China followed the demise of the Tang early in the tenth century. There was a great deal of warfare and destruction, but the learning and traditions of China were preserved in the more peaceful south, especially in the Southern Tang and the Southern Han, states founded by Tang provincial governors who took control as the central authority declined. This considerable autonomy of provincial governments is something of a constant in Chinese history, still in evidence today.

In 960 yet another general was acclaimed emperor, but this time the founder, Zhao Kuangyin, was so able a negotiator that he persuaded the regional military governors to become part of a united China. The Song state he founded was not only more lasting than its predecessors, but also went on to an extraordinary brilliance for the world of its time. Chinese manufacture, especially the fine porcelain that came to be known as *china*, was in demand throughout the world and commanded an immense export trade by the standards of the time. Guangzhou became one of the world's biggest ports.

Book printing had become commonplace and many private citizens had libraries, centuries before the production of the Gutenberg Bible, Europe's first-known printed book, in 1456. Chinese printing used engraved woodblocks – by the eleventh century works employing more than 100,000 of these were printed. Seventeenth-century Western observers noted that the Chinese artisans doing this work could complete a page as quickly as a European typographer could handset it with moveable type. The woodblock system also had the advantage that illustrations could be fashioned into the same page. This was done to very good effect and eventually printing in four or five colours was developed.

This ability to reproduce both words and pictures quickly and relatively cheaply gave a tremendous impetus to the arts, especially painting and letters. The works of more than 1000 Song poets are known. Printing was used extensively for pamphlets on all sorts of subjects, and to produce paper money. Iron and bronze moveable type, invented by Pi Cheng in the eleventh century, was used in China to some extent in the fourteenth century, but were recognized as impracticable because of the large number of Chinese characters.

The world's appreciation of its debt to Song China is still increasing. There is, for instance, no known European record of the supernova explosion of

1054 that resulted in the Crab Nebula, even though the star grew so bright it could easily be seen in daylight. Yet, according to the British astronomer Fred Hoyle, modern science is much indebted to the careful records the astronomers of Song China made of this event. Sunspots, studied by Europeans for the first time in 1610, had been observed and recorded in the Chinese annals 59 times during the previous 1500 years. This has made it possible for modern astronomers to calculate the solar activity cycle during that time.

Song China pioneered many features of modern economies, using paper money, cheques, promissory notes and credit banking to facilitate inter-city trade. It developed inoculation against smallpox, maintained street lighting, street cleaning, sanitary and fire protection services in the cities; provided hospitals, almshouses, orphanages and homes for the aged which were financed by trusts to ensure inalienable income; and encompassed a remarkable number of inventions ranging from hand grenades and repeating crossbows to hydraulic machinery in the world's biggest ironworks.

Major textbooks covered almost all areas of science – architecture, mathematics, geography, medicine, horticulture. There was a specialist book on growing citrus fruit and in 1242 the world's first known book on forensic medicine was published. The so-called 'arabic' system of ten-digit numbering was used in China at about the same time as it appeared among the Arabs, prompting speculation that it originated somewhere in Indo-China. There was an enthusiastic science of archaeology researching earlier Chinese coins, ceramics and bronzes. The huge library at the Imperial palace housed four celebrated works – a literary anthology going back four centuries, a thousand-chapter encyclopaedia, a vast collection of strange stories and fables, and a massive anthology of political texts and essays.

The system of recruiting the mandarinate by public examinations became fully developed, so attempting an aristocracy of intelligence rather than of family and wealth. The fact that the ability of aspiring officials to paint and write poetry was tested has often been misunderstood. The examinations were primarily for administrative ability, but the mandarins were expected to be 'complete men' – accomplished in every way.

The lightly ornamented and simply styled porcelain, such as its green celadon, the delicate painting and understated poetry of the Song have in the past been dismissed as 'primitive' by earlier Western critics, bred to the florid Victorian taste. It is only the modern West that has recognized in Song art a sophistication it has itself approached.

One of the more eminent scholar-magistrates of the period, Su Dongpo, embittered by a series of reverses in his career, wrote this upon the birth of a son:

> Families, having a child, ask that it be intelligent.
> But I, through intelligence have destroyed my whole life.
> So I only hope the baby will turn out ignorant and stupid,
> then end a peaceful life as a Cabinet Minister.

The powerhouses of Song society were its intensive and highly organized agriculture and manufacture, producing silk, ceramics, huge quantities of iron, tea, alcohol, printed books, paper and lacquer goods among many other things. Rice yields were greatly increased by the technique of planting out seedlings and the selective breeding of higher-yield varieties. These basics created the great cities, some of more than a million people, along the rivers, canals and seacoast, and the world's largest merchant navy. Chinese ships had up to five masts, drop-keels, balanced stern rudders and watertight compartments, and could carry up to 1000 people. The Chinese 'fore and aft' junk rig and the stern-hung rudder made these ships not only much easier to sail but also more weatherly – able to sail reasonably well into the wind. Experiments in other forms of boats, especially for inland waters, were various, and included crank-operated paddle wheels. Some had up to 25 such cranks, linked by metal connecting-rods. Accurate maps and charts listed depth soundings.

The cities provided every form of pleasure and indulgence, with playhouses, shadow theatres, acrobatic and performing monkey shows, wineshops, gaming houses, brothels open until dawn. Viewing the first plum blossoms, by the light of a spring moon, over snow fields, was a popular cult – indeed Song poets and painters were virtually obsessed by the purity and simplicity of these flowers.

Zhang Zhi, a rich dilettante of the time, set out a list of what did and did not accord with plum blossoms. Strong wind, continuous rain, hot sun, bad poetry, gossip about current events, discussing financial matters and erecting purple screens opposite the flowers, were no-nos. The list of things that accorded with plum blossoms included gentle shade, fine mist, early-morning sun, making tea, playing chess on a stone board (according to Maggie Bickford in an article in *Orientations*).

The decline of Buddhism was followed by a renewed interest in Confucianism. This neo-Confucianism, which placed great stress on order in society, set rigid patterns that persisted through to the twentieth century. Although it was designed to assert Confucianism as an ethic supplanting Buddhism and Daoism, in many respects it turned out to be a synthesis of all three. The new system was certainly far removed from the thought of its nominal founder. Indeed Confucius himself was virtually deified. To him, as well as to the sun and the moon, the second-grade or 'middle' sacrifices were made.

However, Confucianism remained based on ancestor worship and the cult of the family. While having religious aspects, its main effects were ethical and conservative. This respect for established rites and definitions of conduct led eventually to the narrowness of the official mind and disinclination for change so much responsible for the Chinese disasters of the nineteenth century. All this applied more to the official class than the ordinary people – Buddhist influences persisted among them into Song times and undoubtedly contributed much towards the liberality and broadmindedness of the dynasty.

The Song state had a great deal of trouble with its army, in spite of spending vast sums on it. Soldiering was not highly regarded as a profession – 'Good iron is not made into nails nor good men into soldiers'. During the period between the collapse of the Tang and the rise of the Song China had suffered greatly from the depredations of warlords and the mandarins were concerned to keep the military in its place. The army had become more used to plundering than to battle. It lacked cavalry, and did not have the fine edge, good organization and utter disregard for human life of the Mongols.

Mongol methods were total war to a degree seldom equalled before or since. When they conquered the northern state of Jin, which had already forced the Song to retreat to the south, they virtually depopulated it. Its capital, Beijing, was almost wiped out, then burned. The Mongol troops were under orders to exterminate the population of cities that offered the slightest resistance and the fate of some of China's north-west cities was a terrifying example. Some of these have never again been populated, remaining desolate to this day. It is not surprising that the southern Song capital, Hangzhou, surrendered in 1276.

The populous and wealthy world of China presented an extreme contrast to the Mongols. They were largely illiterate and poor, and numbered perhaps three million. The victory brought into the conquerors' service some shrewd and able public servants, who were able to convince the Mongols they would be better off to maintain Chinese society as it was, and profit from taxing it. Not only was Chinese culture largely preserved, but it was able to exert an influence on the Mongols that refined and educated at least some of them. The great Mongol leader so admired by Marco Polo, Kublai Khan, was sinified in this way and developed a liberality and interest in Chinese art and culture that would have amazed his forebears.

The Mongols, who assumed the dynastic title of the Yuan, built a new, Chinese-style capital in inner Mongolia called Shangdu – the city which became known to the West as Xanadu. Thus the conquerors, although they strove to retain their own identity, were largely absorbed by the conquered. Chinese ways spread outside China itself and became fashionable in other parts of the Mongol empire. The military discipline initially imposed by the conquerors even allowed China to grow physically. What is now Yunnan Province was a separate kingdom called Nanzhao until 1253, when its Thai people were driven south into the valleys of Laos and other parts of south-east Asia.

As the Mongol empire drove deep into eastern Europe, it seems likely that knowledge of Chinese technology carried west in this way influenced the European renaissance. Certainly Chinese technicians and soldiers accompanied the Mongol armies – the army that besieged Baghdad in 1258 was commanded by a Chinese general. Such things as the stern-hung rudder, the wheelbarrow, the marine compass and gunpowder first appeared in Europe late in the thirteenth century, and the first paper was made then in Italy.

Kublai was unable to invade Japan in spite of two great expeditions he sent against those islands in 1274 and 1281. Seasonal typhoons scattered his fleet, with heavy losses. This great wind, or *kamikaze*, was regarded by the Japanese as divine intervention. In 1945, as Allied ships closed in on the Japanese islands, the same name was used for suicide aircraft that were deliberately crashed on the decks of warships.

By the early fourteenth century Mongol rule had already begun to weaken, its parasitic nature increasingly obvious after the death of Kublai in 1294. Mongol leaders had a curious and enthusiastic preoccupation with the mystic and at times obscene aspects of Tibetan Buddhism. Tibetan lamas became influential at the Chinese court, and were able to obtain huge endowments which contributed greatly to the size and wealth of their monasteries. The Tibetans had escaped mass destruction and murder by willingly accepting Mongol suzerainty – this is regarded as supporting the current view in Beijing that Tibet is a part of China. Chinese control of Tibet was reasserted by the Manchus in 1706, and continued until the fall of the dynasty in 1912.

In 1333 a series of unusually severe famines began and persisted for a decade. The reserve granaries were soon exhausted. Then in 1351 the Yellow River burst its levees, bearing thousands of acres of productive farmland down to the sea and destroying hundreds of villages. By 1356 paper money had become valueless and the printing of it was discontinued. The population fell, to perhaps 80 million.

The Mongol Dynasty had by then become decadent, with frequent disputes over the imperial succession, and a warlord phase began in which district governors asserted their independence. Pressure on the peasantry became extreme, and prompted widespread rioting and rebellion. These became almost general under the leadership of a secret society called the Red Turbans from about 1350 onwards, and led to the eventual overthrow of the Mongols and their expulsion from China. These mass movements were strongly influenced by *theravada* Buddhism and in many cases sought a renewed Song Dynasty.

From early times the peasant revolt had been China's natural answer to tyrannical or inefficient government and also, grimly enough, to pressures of population. Overpopulation, combined with the failure of the central government, resulted in famine. This in turn led to insurrection. As society became further disorganized, the population was hugely reduced by starvation, massacre and sickness. When stability was resumed under a new regime the cycle recommenced.

Perhaps because of this a certain lack of regard for individual human life became a part of the Chinese tradition. Modern China, for instance, finds it difficult to understand the criticism it attracts for continued capital punishment. The Great Leap Forward, the attempt to force China into an industrial breakthrough between 1959 and 1962, is estimated by Jonathan Spence (*The Search for Modern China*, p. 503) to have caused at least 20 million deaths from famine caused by the ruthless seizure and export of grain to pay for imported machinery.

When the Chinese peasants were pressed hard enough to revolt, they organized within mutual assistance societies, which remained dormant for many decades or even centuries, only to become active when circumstances demanded. These societies were so firmly based that even the mandarins hesitated to tamper with them. The oldest and most famous of the secret societies organizing the peasants was the White Lotus. It also appears to have played a consolidating role in the peasant revolts that ousted the Mongols.

The main impetus of revolt came from the south. Here Zhu Yuanzhang, who would soon drive the Mongols out of China, began his career. He was an orphan of humble origins, later to become a Buddhist monk, who rose to command a rebel group through sheer force of personality, ability in the art of intrigue, and the support of the Red Turbans. He concentrated on consolidating a significant area of power around the strategic Yangzi River city of Nanjing, which he occupied in 1356. Twelve years later, when he dominated south China, he sent a huge army north to Beijing. The Mongols fled before it without a fight. They had controlled China for barely 70 years; their successors would endure for almost three centuries.

The humble peasant-adventurer now became emperor, giving himself the reign name of Hongwu, which means 'vast military achievement'. The

dynasty he commenced in 1368 he called the Ming, which could be translated as 'brilliance'. As might have been expected from the nature of his
origins and career, Hongwu's authority was direct, brutal and decisive. He
is said to have had a highly suspicious nature and a furious temper, imposing the death penalty more or less on whim. Although an able administrator, Hongwu refused to have a prime minister, and when fair-minded
mandarins with a sense of duty ventured to remonstrate with him he had
them beaten with bamboo clubs, often to death. This set a pattern of
authoritarian government for the future, in contrast with the consensus
politics of the Song.

Strong parallels can be drawn between the first decades of the Ming and
those of the present Communist government in China. Both faced the need
to restore a complex agricultural system almost in ruins, both used a ruthless authority to get the necessary work done, both required the people to
plant vast numbers of trees, estimated at around a billion by some authorities. With an eye to restoring the maritime tradition of the Song, Hongwu
ordered the planting of at least 50 million of these trees for timber to build
ships.

Hongwu remained faithful to Nanjing, which now became the capital.
After his death the throne was inherited by his 16-year-old grandson, who
was immediately challenged by his uncle, the Prince of Yan, a warlord based
in Beijing and responsible for guarding the northern borders. He took
Nanjing in 1402, becoming emperor under the reign name of Yongle.
Nineteen years later he built a new capital at Beijing – the Forbidden City –
which, then on the edge of China, had a vulnerability that would ultimately
prove dangerous and, finally, fatal to the dynasty. The new structure was an
enormous cost simply in terms of building materials and labour. Beyond
that, situating the capital at Beijing not only placed it close to marauding
tribesmen on the other side of the Great Wall, but also involved a huge cost
in maintaining roads and canals to the south, including major repairs and
extensions to the Grand Canal. Finally, it tended to encourage the persistent
southern tendency towards autonomy.

In his 2002 book 1421 – The Year China Discovered the World, Gavin Menzies
describes the sumptuous banquet for the inauguration of the new capital as
indicative of 'China's position at the summit of the civilized world. In
comparison Europe was backward, crude and barbaric. Henry V's marriage
to Catherine of Valois took place in London just three weeks after the inauguration of the Forbidden City. Twenty-six thousand guests were enter-
tained at Beijing, where they ate a ten-course banquet served on dishes of
finest porcelain; a mere six hundred guests attended Henry's nuptials, and
they were served stockfish (salted cod) on rounds of stale bread that acted

as plates. . . . China's army numbered one million men, armed with guns; Henry V could put five thousand men in the field, armed only with long-bows, swords and pikes.'

Yongle had indeed inherited vast power – the empire was now larger and more populous than the whole of Europe, and its wealth and resources far greater. Even though she had diverged from her ideal of government China was now at the pinnacle of her material power. In no way is this more forcibly indicated than by the great sea expeditions sent out during the Yongle reign, and commanded by Admiral Zheng He. These vast ships, largely modelled on the Song fleet, were as much as 500 feet long and over 150 feet wide, and equipped to stay at sea for many months. The Chinese already knew about the dangers of scurvy, and carried large quantities of citrus fruits in the ships to protect the crews. Otters specially trained to herd fish into nets were carried and used regularly to provide fresh food supplies; desalination units were installed to distil seawater.

Chinese ships ranged throughout Asia – indeed as far afield as East Africa – and by the end of the first quarter of the fifteenth century had brought home token fealty and tribute from scores of Asian principalities. According to Chinese records a live giraffe from Africa was brought to Beijing, and presented to the emperor. There is well-researched evidence that these may have been the first mariners to sail around the world, and to establish mining colonies on the Australian coast.

A significant comparison can be made between Chinese sea power and the Portuguese fleet that took d'Almeida to India in 1505. With its 20 ships and 2500 men it was the largest yet to sail to Asia from Europe. Exactly a century before, in 1405, the Ming Empire sent its first fleet to India. It consisted of 62 ships and nearly 30,000 men, and was only the first of seven such expeditions. The total Ming fleet consisted of close on 4000 ships, at least 400 of them larger warships. The next most powerful fleet in the world then, according to Menzies, was that of Venice, which could muster 300 lightly-built galleys propelled by rowers and quite unsuitable for other than coastal voyaging.

It is interesting to speculate on the possible shape of events had the ships of Europe, coming to Asia a century later, found it already controlled by a Chinese navy, policing a Chinese maritime empire. Looked at in this way, the cessation of China's great sea expeditions in 1433 becomes a fact of major importance in European as well as Asian history. Yongle had all the means at his disposal to dominate the world and lay the foundations of an immense empire except the will to do so. He used his great fleets casually, almost as toys. He looked, always with anxiety, to the north. The thought of permanent dominion in south and south-east Asia seems never to have crossed his mind.

The Chinese felt that in their world they had achieved perfection and came to regard all other nations with a casual arrogance and suspicion as 'barbarians'. The term *Zhongguo* – 'Middle Kingdom' – for so long used by the Chinese as the name of their country, took on new overtones as they increasingly saw it as the centre of the world, with tributary nations arrayed around it. After 1430 Chinese were forbidden to leave the country without special licences. In the sixteenth century the harbingers of future trouble came with a revival of Mongol unity under a strong leader, Altan Khan, who mounted devastating raids into the Beijing region in 1550. A peace treaty was agreed with China in 1570, but the northern threat remained.

In 1514 the first Portuguese ships arrived in China. Early encounters were often unfortunate, since the Portuguese almost always mixed trade with piracy, confirming Chinese suspicion of Europeans generally. When a trading post was set up at Macao in 1557 it was carefully policed by the Chinese, and Europeans were restricted to their remote base on an isolated southern peninsula. Nevertheless there were exceptions, notably Jesuit intellectuals like Matteo Ricci, who lived in China for long periods, and whose writings provided the first significant cultural and technical interchange with Europe. The development on the windswept Dutch beaches in the seventeenth century of land yachts – then the fastest transport vehicles in the world by far – is said to have been inspired by the Chinese custom of attaching sails to wheelbarrows.

Land contact with Europe came from the north-west, as the Muscovite Ivan IV drove east from the Volga marshes, then the border of Russia. Within one more century Russian expansionism had given China a new and troublesome neighbour and border disputes that would persist into modern times.

Whatever the shortcomings of the Ming, they presided over a vast, intensely productive state. Its major catastrophe was what is considered the world's worst earthquake in 1556, which killed an estimated 830,000 people. Much of the antiquities the tourist to China sees today are of Ming provenance, including the dynasty's subterranean tombs on the outskirts of Beijing and most of the present fabric of the Great Wall.

The Ming Dynasty did not show serious signs of weakness until the reigns of the last four emperors, entering its phase of most rapid deterioration between 1620 and 1627, when the Tianqi emperor reigned. He was only 15 when he came to the throne and was dominated by a predatory official, Wei Zhongxian, who used his power to enrich himself and strike down any honest or courageous official who sought to oppose him. The architects of the Ming demise were a formidable army of eunuchs, probably as many as 70,000 of them towards the dynasty's end. Presiding over the elaborate and ritualized life of the court, they used their position to accumulate wealth and power at any cost, including mass murder of their opponents, intimidation and at times covert assassination of emperors.

When the last Ming, the Chongzhen emperor, came to the throne in 1628 he made a final desperate effort to reorganize the government, but matters had gone too far for reform. The competent and honest men had already been destroyed and the pervading selfish and cynical factionalism had eroded the dynasty of support. The Little Ice Age, which caused recession and starvation throughout the world, also had severe effects in China, and is regarded by some scholars as a factor in the Ming decline. Very cold weather and severe droughts during the first half of the seventeenth century caused such severe hardship the population may actually have declined.

Away from the intrigues of Beijing, the people suffered from a breakdown in administration, an increase in taxes, and tyranny from officials that set an ugly pattern for the future. Already the peasants were in revolt. When one of their popular leaders seized the capital in 1644 the emperor, in despair, could see no possible course except death. He hanged himself, from a branch of a tree, outside a graceful triple-tiered pavilion that still stands on Beijing's Coal Hill.

9 China: Ebb Tide

Power to replace the Ming was already waiting – to the north, as Yongle had feared. In 1583 a gifted leader called Nurhacu had persuaded a group of nomad tribes to unite in a largely military union, the Manchu confederacy. When in 1644 Beijing fell to Chinese warlord Li Zicheng, one of many who exploited and exacerbated the prevailing social disorder and poverty, the Manchus took advantage of a last desperate struggle between Li and the Ming loyalists to invade China unopposed. When they entered Beijing with the support of the Ming generals they at first insisted they were only there to support the lawful authority, but when a Ming prince was proclaimed in Nanjing they made war on him and proclaimed their own child emperor ruler of China. Seventeen years later the Ming prince was forced into exile in Burma but the Manchu agents, fully aware of the dangers of a living Ming pretender, pursued him even there and killed him by strangling with a bow-string.

Manchu rule was not easily imposed in the south, and never really accepted there. For many years, indeed, through the two and a half centuries of Manchu rule, there continued to be a persistent but small minority that affected to champion the Ming cause. Even today the slogan 'restore the Ming, supplant the Qing' (Manchu) remains in the rituals of Chinese secret societies in Singapore. It is said that one of the first actions of Dr Sun Yatsen, after the foundation of the Chinese republic at the end of Manchu rule in 1911, was to pray at the Ming imperial tombs.

The Manchus never allowed the Chinese to forget they were a conquered people. They required all men to shave the forepart of their heads and wear their hair in a queue – perhaps better known as a pigtail – as a sign of subjection. Manchus were not allowed to work except as civil servants and soldiers and the Chinese people had to feed this large, non-productive group, located in all cities and large towns. They were forbidden to inter-marry with Chinese and the original Manchu capital at Mukden was maintained.

In spite of these precautions Manchu had by the nineteenth century become little more than a court language and the invaders essentially sinified.

The Chinese had again demonstrated their remarkable ability to assimilate a conqueror. This cultural merging was very evident at the end of the reign of the second emperor, Kangxi, in 1722. A poet and a scholar with a deep interest in all aspects of knowledge, Kangxi encouraged Christian Jesuit missionaries to live in China. Many of them stayed for years, even taking Chinese names, protected by the respect the emperor had for their knowledge and his gratitude, for the Jesuits had cured him of malaria by using cinchona bark (quinine) their order had supplied from South America. Nevertheless, when the Jesuits took exception to established Chinese rites, the emperor discouraged Christian missionary activity, which had virtually ceased by the early nineteenth century.

In many respects the Manchu centuries can be regarded socially and culturally as an extension of the Ming. Nevertheless China expanded to its largest territorial extent in the eighteenth century, with the conquest of much of Xinjiang Province and renewed suzerainty over Korea and much of Vietnam – 13 million square kilometres, compared with the 10 million of today's China. The Kangxi emperor's interest in European art and science was reciprocated in Europe, where many cultural and artistic forms went through a phase of *chinoiserie*, an interest in and copying of things Chinese.

Chinese concern about civil war in Tibet led to an invasion in 1720, the inception of a Chinese nominee as Dalai Lama and the establishment of garrisons and a residency. By that time Tibet had ceased to be the ruthless military state which in the seventh century had controlled an empire extending at times through much of central Asia into northern Burma and northern India. Its martial tendencies were to some extent tempered by the advent of Buddhism which, with the much older animist *Bon*, remains the basis of Tibetan religion. Nevertheless for almost a thousand years, with brief interludes of unity, Tibet was torn by internal dissension. A particularly bitter phase of civil conflict early in the eighteenth century prompted the Kangxi emperor to intervene.

Although in some respects a reformer, Kangxi maintained the civil service examinations, now becoming increasingly formalized, and fully supported the Confucian ethic. To all outward appearances prosperity and order continued to be maintained during the rule of his grandson, who took the reign name of Qianlong. During his 60-year reign China showed little sign of the collapse so close ahead. The dynasty was now, for all practical purposes, Chinese. Qianlong took pride in his support for the Chinese arts, especially poetry, painting and calligraphy. He has left no fewer than 40,000 short poems of his own composition, and was a skilled horseman and archer.

Big improvements in agriculture and huge exports of ceramics, tea, textiles and lacquer ware made Chinese society stable and prosperous – even affluent – during the eighteenth century. Only in its last decades did the processes of decay become apparent. China was undergoing tremendous changes. The most significant was the huge growth rate of the population, which had reached 320 million by 1800 – almost twice that of Europe. Populations were growing all over the world but in the West the challenge was met by a ferment of experiment and the rapid development of new skills and technology. The Chinese government, however, was chained by an arid conservatism. Faced with the great swirl of forces for change, only dimly recognized and undoubtedly feared, it looked steadfastly to the past and resisted any attempts at innovation.

A most serious consequence was the failure to further improve agricultural methods. Overcrowding led to intensive cultivation of land until it became exhausted and would no longer bear crops. New land was often destroyed by erosion almost as soon as it was cleared. The Chinese were banned from the underpopulated grasslands of Manchuria because these had to be preserved as the Manchu homeland.

The mandarinate also deteriorated, and was now far from its ideal of broad-minded, educated men administering wisely and with moderation. Instead, arrayed in their robes of office the mandarins travelled their domains in golden palanquins, escorted by men with whips who lashed out at any who obstructed the way or who failed promptly to grovel in obeisance. Unusual and cruel punishments became common, and were administered for trifling reasons. Death was not enough. Men were whipped on the soles of their feet until gangrene set in, or their heads confined in the cangue, a heavy wooden square which made it impossible for them to feed or care for themselves, then left to die slowly and painfully.

Manchu suspicion of the south led the government to forbid foreign trade except from Guangdong, which was badly located in relation to the sources of the main export products, tea and silk. The administration became increasingly lazy and effete. Pirates ravaged the coast, but little was done to control them. When Qianlong died in 1799 his favourite, Heshen, was impeached on charges of amassing a huge fortune looted from the administration, and forced to commit suicide.

Yet all these abuses, all the clamouring social and economic problems, did not lead to reform and correction, but rather to an even more repressive conservatism. Poverty grew year by year as the population grew, and famines of alarming proportions arose from quite mild seasonal variations. Rural poverty gradually developed towards its full horrors – the exposure of newborn girl babies in the fields at night to die, the selling of children into slavery, the growing rapacity of officials and landlords, themselves struggling on the edge of the abyss. In 1795 poverty was so acute in Shanxi, Hubei and Sichuan Provinces that the White Lotus Society raised a major peasant revolt that was not to be controlled for nine years. Two desperate attempts were made on the life of the emperor, in 1812 and again in 1814, which led to harsh reprisals.

China was not to be at peace for a century and a half. Bandits and Manchu armies under the control of warlords marched through the unhappy countryside, raiding and destroying crops, burning villages, pressing conscripts into their service. So the largest country in the world, the society that had prided itself on its superiority and civilization, plunged into the trough. There had been such troughs before, but never with the same implications, for this one coincided with the reaching of the despised European 'barbarians' for the crest of the wave.

> Therefore, O king, as regards your request to send someone to remain at the capital, while it is not in harmony with the regulations of the Celestial Empire, we also feel very much that it is of no advantage to your country. Hence . . . we have commanded your tribute envoys to return safely home. You, O king, should simply act in conformity with our wishes, by strengthening your loyalty and swearing perpetual obedience. . . .

In these words Qianlong addressed the choleric George III of England when, in 1793, the British government sent its first official mission to China to establish a resident at the Manchu court. The fiction that all foreign representatives came as bearers of tribute and fealty was maintained throughout this period of early contact with the West. Moreover, China could speak from the complacency of self-sufficiency. There was nothing she wanted from the outside world. A decision was taken to cease trade with foreigners altogether.

Britain, however, was anxious to trade more extensively, especially to sell opium in China, and pressures grew rapidly after abolition of the East India Company's monopoly in 1833 brought spirited competition between a dozen companies for the lucrative return trade in tea. This inevitably brought the two nations on a collision course. The Chinese government had become concerned at the swift growth of the opium habit, especially when it began to drain silver – the effective Chinese currency at this time – out of the country. The trade had been declared illegal in 1729 and imports forbidden in 1800, but it continued to flourish nevertheless. In 1838 Beijing had sent a mandarin, Lin Zexu, as special commissioner to end the import of opium through Guangzhou, which was still the only port foreigners were allowed to use. In that year opium imports had reached the massive total of more than 2000 tons a year, and the number of habitual users has been estimated as high as ten million. The fact that many of these were soldiers and officials increased the unease of the Chinese government.

Specially built, fast ships, clippers like *Thermopylae*, *Nightingale* and *Cutty Sark*, raced from China to London at speeds as high as 18 knots. Since these ships were built for speed rather than large cargo capacity, they required a commodity they could carry economically on the outward- as well as the homeward-bound passages. Opium, with its high value for its weight and ready demand in China, suited this specification and was specially grown in India for the Chinese trade.

Commissioner Lin attempted negotiation to control the trade. He even wrote to Queen Victoria, saying, 'if there were people from another country who carried opium for sale to England and seduced your people into buying and smoking it, certainly you would deeply hate it and be bitterly aroused'. There being no response, Lin demanded the surrender of all opium stocks held in Guangzhou. In June 1840, a British naval squadron silenced the Chinese batteries protecting the mouth of the Yangzi. Next, the two large ports of Xiamen (Amoy) and Ningbo were occupied. In alarm the regional authorities agreed provisionally to restore trade, but Beijing repudiated this and in January 1841, the war was resumed.

Britain's bombastic Foreign Secretary, Lord Palmerston, had sought authorization from Parliament for a punitive expedition to compel the Chinese to resume trading. 'The Chinese,' he said, 'must learn and be convinced that if they attack our people and factories they will be shot.' William Gladstone, then an Opposition member, thought differently, saying: 'a war more unjust in its origin, a war more calculated in its progress to cover this country with permanent disgrace, I do not know, and I have not read of . . . Our flag . . . is become a pirate flag to protect an infamous traffic'. Parliament carried the motion for a punitive expedition by only nine votes.

The British warships were able to proceed up the Yangzi to the point, near Nanjing, where the Grand Canal joins the river. With the southern capital defenceless under the guns of the foreign fleet and the batteries guarding the entrance to the Grand Canal silenced, the gravity of the situation could no longer be concealed from the Court. Among the British fleet was something new and deadly – the steam-driven ironclad *Nemesis*, whose shallow draught and manoeuvrability permitted her to do enormous damage.

China was forced to sue for peace and, as a result of the consequent Treaty of Nanjing, agreed reluctantly to the resumption of trade. Britain had already seized Hong Kong (Xianggang) as a base, and it was now ceded to her. Not only Guangzhou but also four other 'treaty ports' were to be opened to British shipping. The opium trade flourished, imports doubling between 1830 and 1850. American merchants brought opium in from Turkey, and poppy plantations in China itself proliferated rapidly. These events, and the fundamental injustice of forcing narcotic drugs on the Chinese, are a very important element of history taught to Chinese school-children, and will continue to be in the future. They also featured prominently in the celebrations and media coverage in China to mark the return of Hong Kong to China in 1997. Westerners dealing with China in any way would find themselves at a disadvantage if they betrayed ignorance, or lack of a proper appreciation, of the Opium Wars and their consequences.

The Treaty of Nanjing proved unsatisfactory. The Chinese considered it to have been imposed on them by force, so they saw no reason why they should not evade its provisions if they could. The enforcement of similar treaties to the benefit of several European countries and the United States increased their anger.

This apparent Chinese intransigence resulted in a further war in 1856, designed to force her to comply. China was again defeated easily, and had to accept even more humiliating terms under the resulting Treaty of Tianjin. Now, the importing of opium was legalized, foreigners were allowed to travel anywhere in China, and Christian missionaries were given freedom to operate wherever they chose. All these provisions were accepted by the Chinese, but with a bitter underlying hatred, especially for the final one, allowing the 'pale ghosts' to preach a militant Christian ethic to compete with Confucianism. Even though there were many converts and the missionaries did a great deal of good (founding hospitals, schools and orphanages for the thousands of girl babies left out to die slowly from exposure), a solid core of opposition to them persisted, and was covertly encouraged by the mandarins.

Resistance to the treaties brought war again in 1860. A joint Anglo-French mission – 38 men in all – had gone to Beijing under a safe conduct agreement to discuss the deadlock over the treaty terms. They were arrested on the orders of the Court, and 20 of them died in agony. They were tightly bound in new rope, then water was thrown on them, causing their bonds to shrink slowly. A combined Anglo-French expedition marched on Beijing. Manchu cavalry, attacking at the charge, was blown to pieces from a safe distance by French artillery. Beijing capitulated and the emperor and his mother, the Dowager Empress Cixi, fled. The beautiful Summer Palace near the capital was looted and destroyed in revenge for the death of the prisoners. One of the force that carried out this work was an English officer named Charles Gordon, later to become famous for his defence of Khartoum in the Sudan, and his tragic death there. Gordon

wrote to his mother: 'You can scarcely imagine the beauty and magnifi-
cence of the palaces we burned. It made one's heart sore to burn them. In
fact these palaces were so large and we were so pressed for time that we
could not plunder them carefully. Quantities of gold ornaments were
burned, considered as brass.'

This was the last attempt by the Manchus to resist foreign domination
overtly, and the Western powers now began to carve up China into 'spheres
of influence'. Only jealousy between the powers, carefully cultivated by the
Chinese, prevented the complete partition of the country. Nominally, it was
allowed to remain independent. However, Manchu rule was now on the
foreigners' terms. These included foreign control of Chinese trade and
revenues – the mainstays of government. An Englishman, Sir Robert Hart,
was inspector-general of the maritime customs for more than 40 years
from 1863.

Having secured the compliance of the Manchu Dynasty, the powers now
supported it against rival contenders, in particular the Taiping rebels. They
were led by a visionary schoolteacher named Hong Xiuquan, who, in 1851,
named himself emperor of a rival dynasty. The new regime, which attracted
enormous support throughout the anti-Manchu south, was based substantially on ideas its founder had acquired from Christian tracts. The Taiping
revolt was, in fact, a major civil war, similar to those which had led to the
foundation of the Han and Ming dynasties. Some observers see in it the first
large-scale manifestation of growing unrest and the desire for reform; a
forerunner of the Communist revolution to come a century later.

Although it did advocate ideas of freedom, including the equality of the
sexes and redistribution of land to the peasants, it is best not to regard the
Taiping in too idealistic a light. For instance, recruits to its army had to
memorize the Lord's Prayer and the Ten Commandments within three
weeks on pain of execution; and the wives and children of the Manchu
garrison in Nanjing were burned alive after the fall of the city.

The Taiping achieved vast initial support. Its armies swept north to the
Yangzi River and may well have overthrown the Manchu but for the
support the dynasty got from European gunboats, artillery and the 'Ever-
Victorious Army', led by British officers. It is worth noting, however, that
the Taiping were not well supported in north China, and lost much of their
initiative after their capture of Nanjing. Hong from that time onwards
retreated into an ever more bewildering maze of religious mysticism and
religious oppression. The Taiping aroused wide opposition in the countryside because of their habit of destroying Buddhist and Daoist temples. A
notable victim was the nine-storey, 250-feet-high Porcelain Pagoda at
Nanjing, sheathed in white and gold tiles.

The cost of the revolt and others – there had been an independent Muslim state in Yunnan for 15 years – to China was appallingly high; it has been estimated that between 20 and 40 million people were killed over the 23 years of this huge convulsion – this represents probably the largest death toll from conflict in human history. Many cities were destroyed and conditions rapidly became worse in the ravaged countryside. China, which had been a substantial industrial economy, now reverted to a largely agrarian one – and an inefficient one at that – because of huge damage to complex infrastructures.

So inefficient were the Manchu armies that efforts were made at improvement – modern weapons were bought and German instructors recruited. But it was too little too late; these measures could not prevent China's defeat by Japan in 1895 in a war over the control of Korea, which had long been a Chinese tributary state. The resulting Treaty of Shimonoseki obliged China to surrender Formosa (Taiwan), the Pescadore Islands and the strategic Liaodong Peninsula of Manchuria. Japan now had a foothold on the Chinese mainland itself.

The decisive nature of Japan's victory led many Chinese intellectuals to believe China's only chance of survival as an independent nation was an urgent process of modernization like that Japan was undergoing. One of these, Kang Youwei, was able to persuade the young Chinese emperor to issue in 1898 a series of commands that would have started such a process of reform. Instead, the dowager empress, supported by the mandarins, acted before the new measures could operate. The emperor was imprisoned until his death ten years later. Kang Youwei escaped from China in the nick of time, but six of his associates were executed. Kang was something of a socialist utopian – his writings foresee a human condition in which nation-states give way to world government; private property and the family are abolished; marriages last only a single year; children are brought up in communal nurseries.

In 1900 came the last wave of violent reaction from the old regime – the attack on foreigners and, in particular, Christians, by the so-called Boxers. The Boxers, members of a society of peasant origins called the Righteous Harmony Fists, were encouraged by the dowager empress and some of her supporters in a final effort to 'destroy the foreigners'. In fact, those to suffer most were the 'devil's disciples', the Chinese Christian converts, of whom 16,000 were killed. Armed Boxer bands attacked European missionaries in many parts of China, then converged on Beijing. They destroyed the German legation and killed the minister. All Europeans withdrew into the embassy quarter, which withstood a siege for nearly two months. In August China was invaded by an international force, including Japanese, which captured Beijing, relieved the embassies and effectively ended the uprising. The Chinese court fled to Xian, in the north-west. Huge reparations demanded by the Western powers completed the ruin of the Chinese economy.

It was impossible that the old order should survive such events for long. It seemed to be maintained only by the iron willpower of the dowager empress. However, even she could see the inevitability of change. In 1901 she ordered reforms in important directions, notably in methods of education. In 1904 the old civil service examinations, based on Confucian studies and the stilted, highly formalized 'eight-legged essay', were abandoned. Western-style schools were introduced and accepted eagerly by the Chinese. By 1910 there were 35,000 such schools, teaching more than a million pupils the rudiments of a modern education. Many other Chinese studied abroad, especially in Japan.

The younger men and women educated in this new tradition became deeply concerned for the future of their country. The material of change was now in place, an explosive mixture awaiting the lighting of the fuse. Nor was this long in coming. Late in 1908 the captive emperor died under mysterious circumstances, probably poisoned by the Court mandarins, when it became obvious that the aged dowager empress was near her end. She died the following day, having nominated the infant Puyi the tenth Manchu emperor. Only three years later, still in early childhood, the last of the Manchus was deposed.

The contrast between China and Japan at this stage is very significant. Like Japan, China might have been transformed into a modern economy and her agonies over the next half century might have been avoided. But it was not to be. The shortsightedness and conservatism of those who ruled China, and the exactions of her Western predators, condemned her to the decades of chaos and poverty which were now to ensue.

10 The Three Makers of Japan and the Tokugawa Period

Japan as a unified nation was the creation of three opportunistic and treacherous men, artful enough to outwit and confuse the multitude of regional lords who in the sixteenth century controlled the country, and strong enough to set an imprint that would endure for many centuries.

The Ashikaga *shoguns*, acting as regents for the Imperial family, brought political chaos to Japan but also – perhaps the one advantage of weak government – rapid advances in overall culture because of the freedom weak government gives to strong individuals and families. Although poor administrators, the Ashikaga were great patrons of the arts, which flourished, surprisingly, in conditions of almost constant war. This culminated in a bitter and largely pointless internecine conflict, the Onin wars, which commenced in 1467 a pattern of civil strife that would continue for nearly a century.

Many of the ancient families were destroyed and power became concentrated in the hands of around 150 powerful lords. Towns grew up around the fortified castles they built – the origins of many of the regional cities in today's Japan. These power figures, called *daimyo*, were to be an important factor in Japanese life from now on. Fortunes rose and fell rapidly and in this fluid environment the old feudal stratification of the community became blurred. In some cases bandit leaders rose from obscurity by sheer force of personality and came to command great influence. The relaxation of central authority made it possible for the peasants to break free of their masters for a time and revolts were frequent. Some of these led to the creation of new regions of power. However, it was the peasantry generally who bore the brunt of deteriorating economic conditions, exacerbated by locust plagues, flood and drought. Tens of thousands starved to death during the fifteenth century.

It was this world of distinct, almost autonomous states controlled by the *daimyo* that the Portuguese found when they reached Japan in the middle of the sixteenth century, in search of Japanese silver. Generally speaking, the

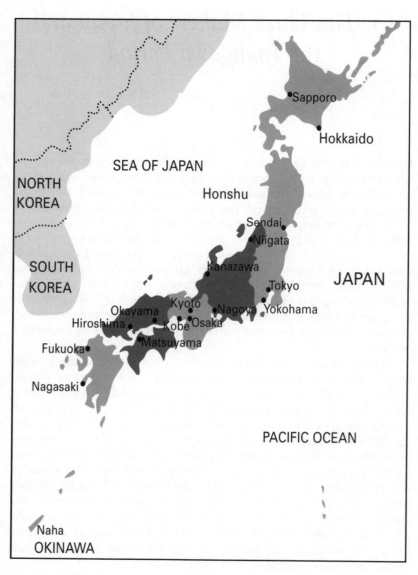

Map 3 Japan

daimyo were willing to trade. They were intrigued by the matchlock musket and quickly saw the significance it could have in the struggle for power. Almost at once the Japanese learned how to copy these weapons and make them for themselves. Japan's tradition of regarding weapon making as an art is manifest in both the long and short muskets, delicately chased in silver, made at this time.

The heir to a small principality in the Nagoya region was one of the first to ponder the significance of firearms. This man, Oda Nobunaga, equipped an army with muskets almost as soon as he inherited his small estate. He used a skilful blend of force, intrigue, treachery and marriage alliances to extend his influence until in 1568 he was able to seize Kyoto. He consolidated his position by building a great castle high on the slopes of a mountain – an almost impregnable stronghold of a kind not seen in Japan before. From this secure base he launched an attack on the centuries-old Buddhist monastery complex on Mount Hiei which, by this time, amounted to several thousand buildings – almost a city. Nobunaga destroyed it completely, and massacred 2000 monks and their dependents on a single day in 1571 without a shadow of pity, so bringing a time-honoured pressure group to an end. There is no evidence that Nobunaga was a particularly religious man. His dislike of Buddhism and his interest in Christianity sprang alike from political motives.

Roman Catholic monks of the Jesuit order had arrived in Japan hard on the heels of the Portuguese traders. Christianity flourished with amazing speed, and the number of converts soon ran into hundreds of thousands, representing all classes from the *daimyo* down. Nobunaga's support undoubtedly helped. Another great persuader was the association of missionary work with trade – often the monks actually controlled trading operations.

Oda Nobunaga was at the height of his power in 1582 and in his fiftieth year when he was treacherously killed by one of his generals. He was avenged by another general, a vigorous, arrogant man named Hideyoshi. At first Hideyoshi ruled as regent for Nobunaga's infant grandson but within a year he had usurped the leadership. It was nevertheless his role to build on the foundation Nobunaga had laid down – he commanded an army of a quarter of a million men towards the end of the decade. In thus supporting the *samurai* he reduced the peasantry to an almost serf-like condition, forbidding them to leave their land and forcing them to hand in all their weapons.

Both Nobunaga and Hideyoshi were loyal to the Imperial line, and at no time tried to usurp the functions of the emperors. In fact, both men did much to restore the pomp of the throne and freely conceded they ruled in its name, probably because they understood the emperor system would reinforce the rigid social structure. The *daimyo* in power at this time remained in their positions and the *samurai* – about one in ten of the population – were confirmed as a specialized military class which the unfortunate peasantry was compelled to support and obey without question. Enormous skill and effort were exerted to make the fine steel blades of the *samurai* swords, which, as the most significant possessions of the warrior class, acquired major symbolic importance and are still regarded as important works of art. Pieces of iron and pure pine charcoal were patiently hammered and folded together until after hundreds of repetitions a high-carbon steel was produced that could be sharpened to a razor edge.

Like his predecessor, Hideyoshi had been favourably disposed towards the Christians, but towards the end of the century his attitude changed. The new faith was perhaps growing too fast for his liking and he suspected the Jesuits of political ambitions. In 1567 he issued an edict ordering all foreign missionaries to leave the country within 20 days. For ten years he enforced this new law only sporadically, but the problem of Christianity emerged again when the Japanese looted the wreck of a Spanish galleon blown off her course from Manila to Mexico. The Spanish captain objected vigorously, telling the Japanese about the mighty empire Spain had gained through the use of the Bible and the sword. When Hideyoshi was told of this he concluded that the missionaries might spearhead a bid for foreign political control of Japan. The following year, 1597, he crucified six Spanish Franciscan monks, three Portuguese Jesuits and 17 Japanese Christians after first torturing and mutilating them.

Hideyoshi was a swashbuckler of low birth, an adventurer, something of a *bon viveur* and an exhibitionist. He gave huge parties in the great castle he built at Osaka, delighting in showing off its utensils – even its doorhandles – of pure gold. He seems to have felt the need for constant action to maintain his position. This was perhaps the reason for the expedition he launched against China in 1592, without any clear idea of the vast power of the Ming empire. The advance was made through Korea, which resisted the Japanese strenuously. China took a somewhat leisurely decision to send an army. It crossed the border at the Yalu River early the next year and forced the Japanese to withdraw. However, they were back again a few years later. Hostilities continued on and off until Hideyoshi's death in 1598 ended the pointless conflict. The Koreans, who were almost completely Chinese in their culture and outlook, bitterly resented this apparently wanton attack from the people they called the *wa* (dwarves), which caused immense distress and hundreds of thousands of deaths.

Like his predecessor, Hideyoshi had left an heir, his son Hideyori, who was in the charge of two regents. These men, however, engaged in a struggle for power which ended in a great battle at Sekigahara in 1600, when the victor was a Tokugawa named Ieyasu. The Tokugawa clan was now to control Japan for two and a half centuries, into modern times.

Hideyori, who had been betrayed in this way by the man into whose charge his father had given him, retreated with his supporters into the great castle in Osaka. Its eight-storied, many-gabled central keep was defended by a series of moats and walls – the outer one two miles long – and was virtually impregnable. Ieyasu besieged it for years, and finally took it by trickery in 1615. He had promised Hideyori and his family favourable truce conditions and so persuaded them to weaken their defences. At the end of a treacherous surprise attack only one of Hideyori's family remained alive – his eight-year-old son Kunimatsu. Pitiless to the end, Ieyasu killed even this child, the last of the family of his former master.

So began the period known as the Tokugawa, during which the ruling elite imposed an iron conservatism and the rule of repression and fear throughout Japan. Of a population of 20 million about one in ten were *samurai*. The peasants, the vast majority and the mainstay of the almost totally agrarian economy, were not allowed to be educated. They were told what to grow and how, were taxed as high as 70 per cent of yield, and ordered to be frugal, diligent and submissive. In contrast to the matrilineal society in early Japan, women were now compelled to an almost slave-like state. Their property rights were removed and their husbands, who were free to be as promiscuous as they chose, could kill their wives if they were unfaithful, or even if they were considered lazy in their domestic duties. Even to look up and meet the eyes of a man other than her husband was forbidden. A husband could divorce his wife at any time, but she could not divorce him.

Thus measures were taken which froze Japanese culture along these lines so that, 250 years later, it presented a scene apparently medieval to the amazed eyes of nineteenth-century Europe. Even today, the Tokugawa centuries influence modern Japan.

While in Kyoto Ieyasu lived within the moated, massive-walled Nijo Castle in a small wooden house distinguished by its beautifully decorated and painted colour panels and 'nightingale floors' – boards laid in such a way that they squeaked when trodden on, giving warning of the approach of a possible assassin. However, the later Tokugawa avoided Kyoto and instead based themselves on the little fishing village of Edo. The city which grew up there is now Tokyo, where the *shogun*'s castle walls still encircle the Imperial palace. During the Tokugawa period it became one of the biggest cities in the world, with more than a million people.

Urban life flourished under curious circumstances. The new *bakufu* – camp government – understood that its continued existence very much depended on the subjection of the great *daimyo*, especially the 'outside lords' who had opposed Ieyasu at Sekigahara. Ieyasu required them to sign regulations limiting their power and permitting a close supervision even over their personal affairs. They were forced to leave their wives and families in Edo while they were themselves absent, and were required personally to spend a certain amount of the year in the capital. Along the great high roads, such as the famed Tokaido between Kyoto and Edo, guards working at special roadblocks checked constantly on the traffic, looking for 'women coming out and weapons going into' Edo.

An elaborate spy system was introduced to check on the great families. The slightest suspicion of disloyalty could lead to part, if not all, of the estates of the *daimyo* being confiscated. They were not allowed to enter into marriage alliances, build new castles or even repair old ones, without the permission of the central government. The obligation to spend regular periods in Edo led not only to the city's mushroom growth, but also helped to keep the *daimyo* too poor to cause trouble. Every great family had to maintain an establishment there. In fact, as the centuries passed, Japan was impoverished to pay for the infrastructure and amusements of the city.

The flood of money into Edo from the heavily taxed peasantry created a wealthy merchant class and a varied entertainment industry – both new departures in Japan. A family originally occupied in brewing *sake*, the Japanese rice wine, branched out into rice distribution, the general retail trade, and then banking. A *samurai* named Iwasaki Yataro set up a shipping line which rapidly expanded after Japan again became open to the world. These were the origins of Mitsui and Mitsubishi, two industrial giants of today's Japan.

An entertainment complex called the *ukiyo*, 'the floating world' – teahouses, taverns, puppet shows, brothels, theatres, public baths and circuses – accumulated in Edo to serve the wealthy and leisured. There are restaurants in Tokyo that serve the same dishes – unchanged – now, as then. More specialized entertainment was also available – *sumo* wrestling and popular playhouses, the *kabuki* theatre. Because its productions were so often ribald and erotic the *bakufu* forbade the employment of actresses in *kabuki*, so female roles had to be taken by men. Brightly coloured costumes, lively music and dancing were all part of *kabuki* productions, which became enormously appealing to the ordinary people.

Then there were the bath girls and the *geisha*, a specialized female pleasure class. Particularly pretty small girls were sold to the *geisha* houses, and carefully trained in the social arts – flower arranging, the lengthy and

Figure 6   The Golden Pavilion, near Kyoto, is one of Japan's national treasures

formal Japanese tea ceremony, singing, dancing. Their occupation was then as paid companions for wealthy men.

The Tokugawa quite early considered any foreign contacts dangerous, and sealed Japan off from the outside world. A first step in this direction was to stamp out the major foreign influence – Christianity. Trade and missionary activity had earlier been closely associated. It was a time of intense commercial and religious rivalry between the Protestant and Catholic nations of Europe and Ieyasu could not fail to be influenced by this. Both factions tried to make him suspicious of the other. Finally, he seems to have been impressed by the fact that the English and Dutch brought with them no organized religious activity like the Jesuits. The fact that many of those defending Osaka castle had been Christians increased his suspicions. In 1614 he ordered all foreign missionaries to leave Japan permanently.

However, it was the second Tokugawa, Hidetada, who began a major campaign of torturing and killing Christians extending over two decades. Many priests, and some of the congregations, accepted their cruel fate as martyrs and at least 3000 people died, in the most agonizing ways. They were immersed in caustic water, thrown on to red-hot gratings, dropped into pits of poisonous snakes, or most commonly, crucified upside down. People suspected of being Christians were called on to trample on a picture of Christ or the Virgin Mary, and were tortured until they agreed to renounce their faith or died.

The city of Nagasaki had become a focus for Japanese Christianity, nearly all the people in the city and its surroundings having been converted. It was here that the persecution reached its terrible climax. Bad local government and ruinous taxation led the people of this region to revolt in 1637, and the uprising inevitably became associated with the Christian faith. The local *daimyo*, Matsukara, was a man of unusual cruelty and rapacity even for those times, notorious for his habit of boiling people alive in the hot springs of the region. The peasants were compared with sesame seed – the more they were squeezed, the more they would give. Almost everything was taxed – doors, shelves, candles among other things, and the appalling torture of the Mino dance was applied to those who could not pay. They were dressed in a bulky straw coat, their hands tied behind their backs, and set alight.

Desperate from the religious persecution and the ruinous levels of taxation, 37,000 Christians and their families gathered in an old fortress called Hara on the Shimabara Peninsula, and fought to the end a force of 100,000 Tokugawa *samurai* who besieged the castle for three months. The end came in April 1638. Of those still alive in the fortress only one, a traitor imprisoned in the dungeons, was allowed to live. At Hidetada's request a Dutch ship had used her guns to breach the fortress walls. Fifteen thousand of the government's force were killed.

This terrible civil conflict, which is still well remembered in popular arts in today's Japan, had two major effects. The first was to convince the *bakufu* that the only way to preserve Japanese society was to cut adrift as completely as possible from contacts with Europeans. Japanese were forbidden to leave the country. Those who did leave faced the death penalty if they returned. Shipbuilders were forbidden to construct anything bigger than coastal craft. After the Shimabara revolt the Portuguese traders in Japan were told to leave and warned they would be killed if they made any further attempt to make contact. At the time the traders were expelled, the Japanese still owed them considerable sums. A ship sent from Macao (on the south Chinese coast) in 1640 to try to collect the money was burned and 61 of her company beheaded. Thirteen who were spared were sent back to Macao with instructions 'to think of us no more, just as if we were no longer in the world'.

Spanish ships had already been warned away and England had abandoned its trading post in 1623 as unprofitable. Only the Dutch were permitted to remain and they were confined to a tiny, artificial island called Deshima in Nagasaki Harbour. Once a year they were allowed to leave this island to present gifts to the *shogun* in Edo. Normally they were treated with respect but sometimes they were forced to dance, jump and roll about as if drunk – these indignities apparently being designed to demonstrate the crudities of Europeans. Nowadays, thousands of Japanese a year visit a multi-million dollar 'Dutch' theme park in Nagasaki.

The *bakufu* had made distinctions between European and Asian traders, Ieyasu encouraging trade with south-east Asia, where Japan's silver was much in demand. In the first three decades of the seventeenth century some 400 trading passages were made by Japanese ships, which voyaged as far afield as the Thai capital of Ayudhya. That city had its own Japanese quarter, housing more than a thousand residents.

The second major effect of the extermination of the people in Hara Castle was to cow the populace to the extent that most would accept any privation, any indignity from sheer fear. No force for reform or change was likely to persist. Japanese society, now substantially removed from any outside influence, proceeded along the lines dictated by the *shoguns*. If restrictive, this at least enforced a kind of peace, although the heavily taxed and much abused peasants revolted from time to time. Crop diversification and more intensive agriculture resulted in a modestly expanding economy, although there were severe famines causing thousands of deaths in the eighteenth and nineteenth centuries. The autocratic nature of the government encouraged extremes of authoritarianism which are almost incredible, the most celebrated example being the measures introduced by Tsunayoshi, the so-called 'dog' *shogun*. He was worried by the fact that he had no heir and was told by a soothsayer that his childlessness would continue until a campaign of kindness was introduced to all animals, in particular dogs, because the *shogun* had been born in the Year of the Dog. Over the next 20 years a set of regulations forbade killing or ill-treatment of animals. Canine shelters were built outside Edo to house 50,000 dogs and all Japanese, when talking to a dog, had to address it as 'Honourable Dog'.

In spite of the constraints of Tokugawa rule and their tradition of restrained and formal public behaviour, the Japanese people managed a certain wry and ribald vigour – an ambivalence still apparent today. By the late eighteenth century a deep respect for learning and letters had resulted in a relatively high rate of literacy. Towards the end of the Tokugawa, close on half the boys and perhaps 10 per cent of the girls were said to be attending schools, although this seems unlikely to have been the case among the peasants, only the wealthiest of whom could afford to send their children to temple schools. Book publishing was a flourishing trade, but because the modest incomes of most people made ownership of personal libraries prohibitive, lending libraries, often carried around on the back of their proprietors, were popular. There was a rigorous book censorship of any criticism of the regime. When author Santo Kyoden published three popular satires, he was sentenced to 50 days in handcuffs and his publisher was heavily fined. Such happenings inclined most writers away from the controversial towards the fanciful, the ribald and the exotic. Erotic fiction was very popular.

The Tokugawa used the *samurai* to enforce their orders – they even had the right 'to kill and go away', not to be brought to account by the law for murder. There has been a regrettable tendency to romanticize the *samurai* and *bushido*, their so-called cult of honour, in television programmes for children, among other things, so a few balancing facts might not be out of place.

The appalling torture meted out, often to quite innocent people, indicates a sadistic desire to kill in the most painful and prolonged way possible. For instance, pirates captured in the Straits of Korea were boiled alive in copper kettles. The terrible deaths devised for Christians were carried out by *samurai*. *Daimyo* travelling between Edo and Kyoto would be accompanied by scores, even hundreds of *samurai* hangers-on. Any commoner who did not prostrate himself abjectly enough in the dust beside the road was liable to be literally cut to pieces by the *samurai*. Hideously masked and dressed in leather and steel armour, the *samurai* were a specialized coercive force preying on their own people.

However, by the early nineteenth century their formidable image was much diminished. The class had not actually done any fighting since the Shimabara revolt of 1637, and had become a caricature of its former self. While they affected to despise the growing merchant and banking class, increasingly the real power was moving to this mercantile sector. The great *daimyo* and many of the increasingly corrupt and idle *samurai* came to be deeply in the debt of the merchants. So the coming of the nineteenth century saw strains and tensions inside Japan which augured change in the not-too-distant future.

A small minority of scholars, who, from 1716, were licensed to import Dutch books through the Deshima post, acquired a purely theoretical knowledge of the advances Europe was making. It was noted that more ships seemed to be appearing off the coast. In 1805 a Russian ship lay for months off Nagasaki, seeking permission to land an official envoy, but finally had to sail away without achieving success. In 1824, the crew of a British whaler landed, killed cattle, and generally seem to have behaved in a lawless way. This led to a renewal, in 1825, of the decree providing that any foreigner landing should be killed. In 1837 a United States ship was fired on.

The Japanese were not altogether ignorant of the outside world. They were aware of and alarmed by news of the Opium Wars and the unequal treaties that had been forced on China, and they understood that the *samurai*, with their antique weaponry and total lack of experience of war, could not defend Japan against the feared Westerners. The resulting public dissatisfaction with the regime was to be exacerbated by four years of disastrous weather and resultant famines from 1833. Even at this time there was considerable criticism of the neo-Confucian ethic of the *bakufu* as foreign and 'un-Japanese' and a resurgence among scholars of the idea that the emperors really were, as the ancient myths had it, descended from the sun goddess and virtually divine.

However much the Japanese wished the outside world would go away, it was not to be denied. The isolated isles with their Rip van Winkle atmosphere had become a source of intense curiosity. In 1846 an American mission, led by Commodore Biddle, was forced to leave without negotiating the trade treaty it sought. So the next time the Americans came they made sure it was with a suitable display of force. On 8 July 1853, Commodore Perry entered Edo's Uraga Harbour with a squadron of two steam and two sailing sloops, the largest of 2400 tons and carrying 16 guns. Under the guns of these ships Perry was able to deliver a letter from the President of the United States requesting that some Japanese ports be opened for trade. On 16 July the 'black ships' departed, leaving Japan in a confused ferment. Commodore Perry had undertaken to return the next year for the *bakufu*'s reply. This was affirmative, although cautious, and led to the opening of two small ports remote from Edo; a token gesture only. But America followed up by sending as its first official representative Townsend Harris, a shrewd, forceful but tactful man who, after much patient negotiation, succeeded in gaining audience in 1857 with the *shogun*, Iesada. This was followed by a comprehensive treaty, not only with the United States, but with other nations.

These treaties were signed without the approval of the emperor and those who advised him in Kyoto or the majority of the *daimyo*, and because of this they occasioned widespread opposition, further eroding support for the *bakufu*, and firmly establishing two words – *sonno-joi* – 'revere the emperor, repel the barbarians' – as popular national sentiments.

Nevertheless, the centuries of isolation had ended, and with them all pretence that Japan's society was itself static – an illusion the *bakufu* was striving to maintain. Not surprisingly, a major victim of change was the *shogunate* itself, supplanted by a restoration of the Japanese Emperor to a position of symbolic national primacy. This reversion to the past was engineered not by the wealthy merchants but by disgruntled *samurai*, leading Japan into half a century of unbridled militarism and aggression.

PART II
The 'White Man's Burden'

11 *The Dominators and the Dominated*

The nineteenth and early twentieth centuries saw the development of imperialism on a scale never known before. The long and traumatic Napoleonic wars were over, Europe was industrializing, and there were radical advances in the means of transport, notably shipping and railways, and naval power. A crucial factor in the conquest of empires was the development of deadlier light weapons. American farm machinery technician Richard Gordon Gatling developed a machine gun in 1862 that would fire 350 rounds a minute, a new device for mass killing which was quickly adopted by all the colonial powers. For the first time, natives inclined to fight back could be – and were – mown down in hundreds.

By this and other means it became technologically possible for a single nation to dominate much of the world. At its maximum material extent during the 1920s the British Empire occupied nearly a quarter of the land surface of the planet inhabited by about 500 million people, then almost a quarter of world population. Wherever the eye fell on the map of the world, there were the daubs of red, marking the empire on which the sun never set.

This empire, like those of other major European powers, was substantially in Asia. The British colonies there consisted of what are now seven countries: India, Pakistan, Bangladesh, Sri Lanka, Burma, Malaysia and Singapore. There were other smaller outposts, like Hong Kong, and also spheres of influence in countries nominally independent, but prepared to accept British advice.

The imperial dissection of Asia followed a definite geographic pattern. The British Empire was westernmost, extending east from India through Burma to small, lately acquired possessions in Malaysia. Beyond Thailand, kept independent as a buffer state and twice lopped of some of its territory, was French Indo-China, now Vietnam, Cambodia and Laos. Holland controlled the western half of archipelago south-east Asia – what is now Indonesia. The 400 islands farther east became the Philippines, the colony first of Spain and later of the United States.

China was too big a fish for any single European state to swallow whole or, indeed, to be permitted by its rivals to do so. Instead she became divided into 'spheres of influence'. The imperialist powers exacted important concessions in major ports like Shanghai along the Chinese coast. These grew into big cities, in which a seemingly inexhaustible resource of cheap labour drove both a massive industry and a massive accumulation of human suffering, poverty and disease.

Japan maintained her independence only because she had 'westernized' her economy and industry with remarkable speed and energy and gained the respect of the dominators by becoming a colonial power herself, annexing Korea, Taiwan and Manchuria. Thailand, under the shrewd control of her Chakri kings, escaped colonial status by bending to the wind – surrendering territory where this seemed expedient and accepting European – especially British – advice.

This geographic organization of Asia to suit the dominators, informed largely by an incessant, uneasy rivalry between them, had some strange and at times disastrous consequences. Everywhere one now looks in Asia anomalies remain – peoples divided between two or more nations, minorities cut off from the majority of their race, frontiers that defy the facts of geography. The tensions caused by these things are important, active influences in the Asia of today and will have unpredictable future effects. But for colonialism it is likely that Indonesia would have been more than one country. Sumatra might have been associated with the Malay Peninsula which it neighbours and which its terrain and people so closely resemble. Java and Madura, with their dense populations and distinctive cultures, might have made up a second. The eastern islands and the Philippines could have comprised a third.

There are hill-tribe people in north-east India who are ethnically identical with others now Burmese. The border between Afghanistan and Pakistan divides the Pushtuns. There is a substantial Malay minority in southern Thailand. The people of north-east Thailand are Laotian by language and tradition. India is showing indications of division into three regions of different interest, and throughout her history as an independent power regional influences have gained ground on those that seek to unify. Nearly all these anomalies resulted from the organization of colonial empires, which successor states have insisted on as a basis for their own boundaries.

The dominators' manipulation of the economy of the colonies to their own ends was facilitated by the association of soldier and merchant so typical of the colonial era (the British East India Company maintained distinct civil and military divisions), and by a policy of actively discouraging political development in the colonial peoples. The use and enforcement of monopolies was a typical economic practice. Those formed to sell opium are notorious examples. For instance, in 1867 the contribution made by the East Indies to the Netherlands government was almost exactly the amount raised by government monopolies in opium and salt and the management of pawnshops. While Laos was a colony, even as late as 1945, its major export was opium, and during the Japanese occupation of Korea production of the drug was legal. Throughout Indo-China opium, alcohol and salt were government monopolies so profitable they doubled colonial revenues in the first decade after their inception. Opium exports from India did not cease until 1909. It is interesting that while the dominators made money out of opium its production was seldom criticized and it was freely used in patent medicines. It is only since those revenues have ceased that campaigning against it as an illegal drug has become so strident.

It has been estimated that the drain of money from south-east Asia alone in the form of profits from the colonies was $3007 million in 1930. In 1925, 51 per cent of all imports into India came from Britain, although Indian exports to Britain were only 22 per cent of her total. Imports from France represented 52 per cent of all into Indo-China. The economies of the colonies were manipulated so they could be a cheap, fruitful source of raw materials, while industrial development was retarded to discourage competition with the industries of the dominators. India, before the colonial era the world's major supplier of cotton fabrics, lost this position in the nineteenth century to the massive textiles industry that developed in the English Midlands. Effectively, Asia's share of world GDP fell from almost 60 per cent in 1800 to less than 20 per cent by 1940. This enormous decline was no accident. While the industry and economies of the dominators boomed, those of the colonies were deliberately restrained.

These economic policies contributed towards major social changes in the colonies. The most significant were a massive turnover of land to export crops, rapid population growth and underdevelopment – a lack of adequate material resources and only a tiny and limited pool of educated people. These continue today to be common problems in most of the former colonies, and are the root causes of millions of avoidable deaths, especially of children, and of disease and poverty. Unbalanced economies and a rising demand for cheap labour to work the expanding plantations drove populations into rapid growth. Java and Madura, with five million people in 1815, had twice that number a generation later, ten times as many at the time of independence, more than 20 times as many now. There were similar increases in all the 'plantation' regions of Asia.

Development of the human resource – education – varied from place to place but in none did it even begin to approach that in the dominators' home countries. At the end of the colonial era, when virtually the whole world outside the colonies was literate, the vast majority of the dominated peoples remained illiterate.

Much the same situation existed with material infrastructure. Some roads, railways, port facilities and cities were developed but these, paid for out of colonial revenues, were designed to suit the needs and interests of the dominator. Development was generally much below that achieved outside the colonies. In 1950, which could be considered the end of the colonial era, the three largest Asian nations, China, India and Indonesia, had a total of 38,000 miles of rail track, compared with 217,000 in the United States and 237,000 in Europe. Statistics on roads, factories, power-generating stations and the other resources of modern states indicate equal or more serious underdevelopment.

The fact that the colonies were regarded as the property of the master country is, then, central. The first objective of the colonial system was to make money. The colonies were businesses, run by businessmen, through most of their history, regardless of the Kiplingesque ballyhoo to the contrary. As late as 1913, J. Dautremer, the author of a standard book, *Burma Under British Rule*, wrote: 'The colonies are countries which have been conquered. They are the property of the country that administers them, governs them, and develops their riches for its own profit. Since the colony is the property of the nation, it has no right to be put on the same footing as the governing country.' These statements are broadly typical of publicly expressed attitudes at that time.

The colonial governments triggered a grotesquely large disparity of wealth and privilege within the Asian peoples, a situation which persists in the modern nations. Before colonialism the basic social structure was the small village community, with long-standing traditions of mutual help and consensus decision-making tempering the authority of leading families. Generally land was available to anyone who wanted to work it. But the new rulers brought with them the concepts of the European state, and a require- ment for private ownership of land so it could be taxed efficiently. One man in the village became chief, who levied taxation on behalf of the central authority. That authority backed him with military force. This new system created massive financial disparity, considerable absentee ownership of land, and a bottom layer of poor, landless families. When times were bad, as during the great depression of the 1930s, this alienation of land acceler- ated, typically to the stage where in many places more than half the villagers lacked enough land to support them and their families. Their only recourse was to work as labourers for the wealthy.

It could be asserted that Britain made the greatest contributions of value to her colonies, especially in the twentieth century. It is reasonably clear that Dutch rule in Indonesia contributed the least. They left the huge archipelago only 3000 miles of railways, compared with 16,000 in India. The Dutch refused to recognize, even at a late stage, the possibility of the East Indies becoming independent, considering only a state within the Netherlands commonwealth to be governed by the 250,000 Dutch living there.

There can be little doubt that the relatively orderly history of India and Malaysia since independence, for instance, has been due to efforts made during the later colonial era to educate some local people in business and administration, and to provide a reasonable administrative framework. That these were primarily to the benefit of the colonial business machine is beside the point. On the other hand, the chaotic problems of Indonesia during her first decades of independence were due largely to a lack of such efforts to educate. This factor is difficult to overestimate and one that those seeking to understand Indonesia should keep in mind. At the outbreak of the Second World War in 1939, the literacy rate was only seven per cent. Such educated men as there were had in most cases been sent to schools overseas by their families. But even when these returned to Indonesia they could find only subordinate positions.

It is fair to add, however, that in Indonesia, as elsewhere, the nationalist movement came from among the tiny educated class. Also, research scholars of the colonial powers were largely responsible for bringing to the attention of these nationalists the glories of the past. French archaeologists patiently unravelled the history of the vast buildings of Angkor and began the work of restoring the ruins of the great Khmer city. Dutch scholars did as much for Indonesia. The traditions of Shrivijaya and Majapahit, which came to mean so much to the nationalists, might never have been recovered, even to the present extent, but for the work of these Dutch enthusiasts. Later pre-colonial Indonesian society, for instance, had no inkling of the meaning of the great monument of Borobadur, simply shunning it as 'a place of ghosts'.

The nationalist movements were, then, organized and perpetuated substantially by a small minority educated in Western ideas of politics. For decades the language of the Indian Congress was English. Its leader, Jawaharlal Nehru, was English-educated and the Indian constitution was drafted on Western precedents. Ho Chi Minh was educated in Communism in France. Indonesia's Sukarno was literate in several European languages and widely read in European political theory. But the future may well lie elsewhere, as some Asian statesmen recognize. I can recall many years ago hearing a speech by the architect of modern Singapore, Lee Kuan Yew, in which he predicted the arrival of new, as yet unknown, political forces and the eclipse of Western-educated leaders such as himself. The beginnings of this process are now apparent.

A second contribution of colonialism was the rule of law. Europe obtained its basic concept of an impartial codified legal system, binding equally on all citizens, from the Romans. Attitudes towards law in Asia, with few exceptions, were quite different, the law being almost invariably customary rather than codified. In south-east Asian principalities law was generally such a savage, unfair instrument that people hesitated to use it. In China there was one law for the privileged, another much harsher code for the mass of the people, and, if the popular literature, classics like the *Jin Ping Mei*, can be believed, readily and regularly influenced by bribery. In Japan one class, the *samurai*, became virtually immune from the law.

During the colonial period most of the European powers imposed their own systems of law on the subject territories for long enough to train a significant body of local people in those legal methods. Places like Japan and Thailand, even though they were not colonies, found it expedient to accept Westernized legal systems because if they had not done so, the much-hated principle called extraterritoriality, under which foreigners were immune from local law, would have continued.

12 South-east Asia: the European and Chinese Incursions and the Later History of the Mainland Peoples

Many chapters could be devoted, without much profit, to the dynastic successions, transitory empires, and constant wars which, over the centuries, make up the chronicles of south-east Asia. However, since the source material deals almost exclusively with the affairs of ruling families, and frequently shows scant regard for credibility, much less truth – for instance, we are told that a Vietnamese king, Phat Ma, straightened a sagging pillar in a ruined temple simply by looking at it – it is largely unreliable.

The real history of this region is the ebb and flow of village life; the succession of scores of generations of ordinary people, humble, unlettered but tenacious, without great possessions, patiently growing rice according to methods and rituals already so old their beginnings have been forgotten, and just as patiently devoted to traditions and art forms of considerable significance. In the 1930s Europe became fascinated with these qualities in the Indonesian island of Bali – a way of life involving personal accomplishment in one or more of the arts, a minimum of personal possessions, a disregard for any more money than is necessary, a proper regard for personal tranquillity and social harmony. There is, of course, also a downside – conservatism, strong pressure on individuals to conform, an almost complete lack of personal privacy, and, beneath an outer appearance of tranquillity, a potential for cruelty and savage mob violence.

These things are in many ways typical of village south-east Asia in most of its diverse settings. To these, the real people, the struggles and ambitions of their warring masters meant trouble from time to time, but very little more. The figures of kings appeared almost Olympian: gods, whose actions, often tyrannical and usually unpredictable, were in some vague, magic way linked to the overall prosperity of the realm and the productivity of the soil. Where great affairs of state were concerned, the people were

Map 4 South-east Asia

largely powerless – and usually ignored. Little has changed. Contemporary chronicles – the modern media – when they concern themselves with Asia at all, almost invariably report on the activities of the elite classes living in capital cities that might make up, at most, five per cent of the Asian population.

Nevertheless, in the seventeenth century parts of south-east Asia passed through a considerable though restless phase of urbanization, with several cities exceeding populations of 100,000. Malacca was one of these prior to its occupation by the Portuguese in 1511. These merchant entrepôts, which included Aceh, Makassar (Ujung Pandang) and Ayudhya, were comparable with major European cities of that time. London had fewer than 200,000 people then. Significant location on the trade routes and highly productive hinterlands were the major economic reasons for this urban growth. Another was the diversion of much of the rural wealth and national manpower to the purposes of the rulers. In Thailand, for instance, the corvée could amount to as much as half the labour time of the peasants, to support a large bureaucracy and army and to carry out the physical construction of cities like Ayudhya.

Much of the population of the trading ports were transients, obliged to stay over for months at a time until the monsoons changed. They needed, and paid for, food, accommodation and other services during that time. They also provided the rulers of the city-states with a reliable source of income, with imports and exports taxed at between five and ten per cent. This urban growth proved to be fragile. It depended tenuously on the authority of kings or emperors, which was frequently disputed, especially at times of succession. Bitter and protracted civil conflict at these times, and destructive wars between neighbouring realms, greatly reduced these mushroom cities, or even, as in the case of Ayudhya, led to their abandonment. Many of their population were slaves captured in war, or peasants forced into corvée labour or military service. Weakening or collapse of regimes inevitably and rapidly affected the entire urban structure. During its phase of occupation by the Portuguese, Malacca's population fell by two-thirds, and other cities later to be used as bases by the colonizers were similarly affected.

The evolution of nation-states in Europe did not then, have its counterpart in south-east Asia until recent times, although Burma and Thailand did achieve a kind of unity. This circumstance did much to assist colonialism. At first sight it seems strange that relatively small numbers of Europeans were able to gain a foothold in countries which were basically strong and wealthy, and had a considerable and sophisticated cultural and economic past. The reason was that everywhere local petty lords were at each other's throats. They were only too ready to make concessions to European adventurers to use their guns and ships against a neighbouring rival. Often enough these concessions involved the critical but mundane bread-and-butter tasks of administration, such as tax collecting. Provided some money came to the sultan or rajah, it was a matter of little concern that vastly more was extorted from the unhappy peasantry by tax 'farmers'.

Parallel with the arrival of Europeans on the scene was another virtual invasion of foreigners, the overseas Chinese, in much greater numbers and almost certainly more significant in the long term. Their descendants in south-east Asia now exceed 20 million people. It is probable that if the Chinese government had supported its people in south-east Asia to the extent that European governments supported theirs, the evolution of European colonial empires in Asia might have been greatly limited. But the Chinese government did not. The Manchus did nothing to help or support Chinese leaving for what became called the *nanyang* – the southern ocean – nor did it prevent them. Poverty, lawlessness and injustice were powerful incentives to seek a new life overseas and during the centuries of growing European influence the Chinese did so in millions. Everywhere they went they took with them their tradition of hard work and singleness of purpose, building ships, opening gold and tin mines, lending money to rulers, cornering rice markets, involving themselves in virtually every area of trade and commerce.

More than 600 junks arrived in Manila in the 30 years following its establishment as the Spanish colonial capital of the Philippines. There were 10,000 Chinese there by 1586, compared with well under a thousand Spaniards. The flood of Chinese was resented and resisted by the local people, with half a dozen massacres during the seventeenth century. Nevertheless the Chinese population of Manila had risen to 40,000 by 1750.

The large Chinese quarter in Ayudhya was perhaps the most solid and prosperous part of the city. The government used the Chinese as tax collectors and managers of state enterprises. Most of Thailand's trade at that time was with China, and the Dutch, French and English were unable to gain an early foothold. This was an important element in Thailand's continued, although qualified, independence during the colonial era.

In Batavia (now Jakarta) Chinese control of commerce and manufacture became almost pervasive, and with the encouragement of the Dutch a large Chinese minority spread throughout Indonesia. By 1740 more than half the inhabitants of Batavia were Chinese. Many became wealthy through a system of taxation which granted the tax farmer the right to levy a range of taxes after he had offered the largest cash bid for the concession.

Figure 7 This group of woodcarvers on the Indonesian island of Java are maintaining traditional crafts

Everything else he could wring from the populace was his – including taxes on ports, salt, opium, gambling, even duties on travel within the colony.

Opium was an important area of trade. Its use was uncommon in south-east Asia until the late eighteenth century, when the British growers of the poppy in Bengal and the Dutch adopted a deliberate policy of encouraging it. The Dutch administration bought the opium in Bengal to serve its monopoly in Indonesia. They farmed out the distribution of the drug to Chinese dealers. It was enormously profitable, Anthony Reid (*Cambridge History of Southeast Asia*, p. 500) estimating that profits were 3000 per cent over the Bengal cost price.

There were several important consequences of the Chinese migration to south-east Asia. The most obvious was the transplanting into the region of a large, widely dispersed and permanent Chinese population. Singapore, for instance, a major independent city-state, is mostly Chinese. One-third of the population of Malaysia is Chinese, and there are minorities in all the south-east Asian nations, often running into the millions. A second fundamental was the virtual domination of trade and commerce in south-east Asia by the overseas Chinese. While this has been resisted strenuously by the independent nations, it remains a major factor, with considerable portents for the future in the light of China's emergence as one of the world's largest economies. A third effect, deriving from the first two, has been a deep-rooted and violent resentment of the Chinese by the indigenous peoples. In thousands of south-east Asian villages the shopkeepers, moneylenders, and substantial landowners are Chinese, and are objects of suspicion, envy, and barely suppressed hatred.

The destruction of the south China kingdom of Nanzhao by Kublai Khan drove increasing numbers of the Thai people from that area southward. This migration established several important and related groups, who are now split up among several countries. These groups are the Shan tribes of north-east Burma, the Thais, the Laotians, and the people of Yunnan Province of China. National boundaries inherited from the colonizing powers can be most deceptive. The Mekong River, for instance, on the map appears to be a logical border between Thailand and Laos; yet because the river is the main means of transport in areas with few roads and no rail links and because people who are ethnically the same and speak the same language live on both banks, it is a factor that tends to unite rather than divide them. As late as 1964 Thai government officials in Nongkai Province of Thailand near the Mekong found villages in which the inhabitants were firmly convinced they were Laotian and had pictures of the King of Laos on their walls as the object of their loyalties.

Thailand, then called Siam, became independent when a subject city of the Khmer Empire called Sukhothai broke free in 1238 CE. So preoccupied was Angkor with wars on its other frontiers, it was forced to accept the situation. A century later Sukhothai's people moved south, far into the fertile delta plain of the Chao Phraya River, where they built a larger city. This was Ayudhya, named for Rama's capital in the *Ramayana*.

Off to the west, the Burmese gradually welded together the northern section of their old empire, called Pagan, around a city named Ava, not far from the present Mandalay. This empire used Thai mercenaries, who ultimately set up their own kingdoms in the north under hereditary lords called *sawbwas*. These kingdoms are the Shan states, which are still fighting to become independent from Burma.

Burma achieved significant territorial cohesion under the rule of her final line of kings, founded by a strenuous and ambitious soldier named Alaungpaya, who had been a village headman. He established an entrepôt port in the southern town of Dagon, and renamed it Yangon, which means 'the abode of peace'. Rangoon is a European rendition of this name. Next Alaungpaya turned his armies east. In 1760, while directing an attack against the Thais, he was killed when a cannon burst near him. However, his army kept up the assault. It took the northern Thai city of Chiengmai in

1763, and four years later sacked and burned Ayudhya after a 14-month siege.

Burma was so strong militarily that it was able to withstand attack even from China when the Qianlong emperor sent an army across the border from Yunnan State in 1766. Although the Chinese columns advanced several times from the hill passes on to the Irrawaddy River plain, each time they were driven back. In 1770 the Manchus were obliged to agree to peace terms. The Burmese were aware of British expansion in India and both knew a collision of interests must come in time. This was the more obvious following Burmese conquest of the Kingdom of Arakan on the Bay of Bengal towards the end of the eighteenth century. Early in the next century Burma occupied the big hill state of Assam, so gaining a foothold on India itself. Matters became worse when the assertive General Bandula prepared to attack Bengal.

Before he could act Britain struck the first blow. In 1824, a British fleet made a surprise attack on Yangon and captured it easily. So began the first Burmese war. Bandula fought well, but he had no idea of the scale of the resources behind his enemy. Like other British campaigns of the time, the execution of this one was criminally inefficient. Constantly plagued by disease, the death rate was appalling; 15,000 British troops died, all but a few hundred from disease and infected wounds. In the end the Burmese sued for peace. They paid an indemnity of £1 million, although the war cost Britain £13 million. Burma also lost – and Britain gained – a significant section of the Burmese coastline and it was agreed a British resident should be located at Ava, mainly to foster trade.

The Burmese were by no means anxious for closer relations, and the peace did not last long. It was reported back to India from time to time that British subjects in Yangon were being treated with indignity, and feelings mounted on both sides. Matters came to a head when two British sea captains were arrested on trumped-up murder charges. The British Viceroy in India, Lord Dalhousie, sent a squadron to Yangon under the command of a peppery naval officer, Commodore Lambert. In the river Lambert's ship, HMS *Fox*, was attacked rather ineffectually by a shore battery, which made some holes in her sails. Lambert, acting with an energy and lack of discretion quite beyond his instructions, used the guns of *Fox* until he had sunk everything in sight that might conceivably have been a Burmese ship of war. So the opportunity for negotiation passed at once and war became inevitable.

Lambert's attitude – epitomizing as it does the jingoist era of British colonialism – is evident in his letter to the government of India: 'It is with deep regret that I have had to commence hostilities with the Burmese nation, but I am confident that the government of India and Lord Dalhousie will see it was unavoidable and necessary to vindicate the honour of the British flag.' In fact, the government of India and Lord Dalhousie were not at all pleased, but had to accept the second Burmese war as an accomplished fact. Constantly under fire from the British press, the dismal war dragged on, leading finally to the capture of Ava and the addition of several more Burmese provinces to the British Empire.

The resulting demoralization did nothing to improve the ethics and standing of the ruling dynasty. The court at Mandalay became notorious for its violence, injustice and squalid immorality under King Thebaw, the last of his line, who succeeded to the Lion Throne after Mindon's death in 1878. Mindon had not nominated a successor and the resulting intrigue for power led to a horrifying slaughter of princes and princesses of the royal house, both adults and children. As in other parts of mainland south-east Asia, it was forbidden to touch the person of any of the royal line, and sacrilege to spill their blood. Thus the executions ordered by Thebaw were in the macabre tradition of the past. The victims were first sewn inside red velvet sacks and then despatched by breaking their necks with blows from sandalwood clubs.

This atrocity deeply alarmed British residents in Burma, caused an outcry around the world, and brought the British government under strong pressure to put an end to Thebaw's misrule. Almost at once Thebaw began to intrigue with the French in Indo-China, with the idea of playing them off against the British. The British government now waited only for a suitable pretext for war, which Thebaw provided soon enough. A money dispute arose between the Court and a big teak monopoly company, the Bombay–Burma Trading Corporation. The British government intervened. An expeditionary force occupied Mandalay in 1885 and the following year the monarchy was deposed. The conquest of Burma was complete. Conversion of the royal palace into a British club became an ironic symbol of Burma's new status as a mere province of British India.

The burning of the Siamese capital, Ayudhya, had destroyed one of south-east Asia's most beautiful and populous cities – a source of marvel to the European traders who visited it. However, a small Thai army had been able to fight its way out of the ruins and, in spite of four more Burmese raids, regained control of the Chao Phraya River delta, the region's rice-bowl. An army officer, General Chakri, became king under the title of Rama I. So began the dynasty that still reigns, as constitutional monarchs, in Thailand today.

The destruction of their capital had taught the Thais a bitter lesson, and Rama I was guided mainly by strategic considerations in choosing a site for a new one. He decided to place the broad stream of the Chao Phraya River between him and his enemies, and found the site he needed at a village named Bangkok. Foreigners still use this name, but the Thais call their capital Krungthep, which means 'the city of angels'. Old people who had known Ayudhya in its glory were called in to advise the architects of the new city, for it was intended that it should resemble its predecessor as closely as possible. Ayudhya had been situated on low land almost completely enclosed by a great bend of the river, criss-crossed with hundreds of canals, which are called *klongs*. This was how Bangkok acquired the *klongs* which were such a distinctive feature, although most have now been filled in to provide wider roads for the city's hectic motor traffic.

The early Chakri monarchs continued to rule in the traditional barbaric and despotic fashion. The king was regarded as a god. People had to enter his presence on all fours, and as much as to touch his person meant death. His title was 'lord of life' and he held summary powers over all his subjects. When he travelled outside his palace, which gleamed with gold leaf and multi-coloured tiles, the ordinary people shut themselves away inside their houses, to avoid the risk of being seen with their heads higher than the king's, for this, even if inadvertent, was a capital offence.

In 1848 a young official, using the services of a marriage go-between, sought the release of a young woman from the king's vast harem so he could marry her. The mere intention was construed as treason. Not only were the young man and woman executed, but also eight other people, since they had known what was going on and had not informed the Court. Apart from protecting the interests of the king and aristocracy, the government took only the most casual interest in law and order. In civil cases especially, the law was so partial and illogical that few people had the temerity to resort to it.

Fortunately, the country was not then poor or overcrowded. Most people lived in little villages along the many waterways, vacant land was available to anyone who wanted to take it up, and the only serious burden imposed by the government was taxation. Under Rama III this burden became greater because the government let out the right to collect taxes – the so-called 'tax farming' system. These agents, who were mainly Chinese immigrants, bid for the right to collect taxes and were allowed to keep whatever they could realize above their bid. The tax system resulted in a large slave class, perhaps as much as a third of the population. Most were persons who had voluntarily gone into slavery for non-payment of debts. They were free to transfer themselves from one owner to another and could redeem their freedom simply by repaying the debt. Few chose to do so because slaves were exempt from taxation.

Rama III agreed reluctantly to a trade agreement with Britain in 1826. The Thais did their best to ignore or circumvent it, because they had no wish to follow the Indians and Burmese into the imperial maw. It was apparent to Rama III that every skill he could muster would be needed to escape colonial domination – this became the policy of the dynasty. It was served best by Rama IV, better known to the rest of the world as King Mongkut because the reminiscences of his children's English governess, Anna Leonowens, use this personal name. It is a pity that the Western image of this shrewd and intelligent ruler should have so much been formed by the film and musical comedy freely adapted from what were, even in their original form, rather inaccurate observations. Anna's main interest to history comes from the simple fact of her appointment. This sprang from Mongkut's awareness that his descendants might the more easily ward off the colonizing powers if they spoke English. His judgement in this matter and many others more important were major reasons for Thailand remaining at least nominally independent through the colonial era.

Mongkut was a Buddhist monk for 27 years before he became king in 1851 at the age of 47. Largely due to his reform of the Buddhist organization in Thailand it has become one of the best-organized religious orders in the world. Mongkut's own character was formed by these years of monastic discipline, devotion to education and self-denial for, like other monks, he was enjoined to celibacy and could own no property other than his yellow robe, sandals and a few other necessities. He was polygamous as king because that was the custom, inspired more by the political advantage of binding many families to the throne than by the personal desires of the monarch. He permitted members of his harem to marry others in certain cases and it has been recorded that a man who abducted one of them was let off with a fine amounting to about $5.*

Thailand was set on the path for major reform under his rule, largely on his own initiative, for he was no reactionary forced into reforms by a nationalist movement. Indeed, he had to cajole and encourage his people into accepting liberality and change. His energies seemed to flow in every direction. He set up printing presses, encouraged Christian missionaries, promoted education, issued a modern system of currency and democratized the monarchy by making himself far more accessible to the people.

He welcomed advice and help from the West and accepted advisers from many countries to assist in the reform of Thai law and institutions. There was a limit to what he could do in a 17-year reign, but in that time he gave

* Throughout the book all figures given in dollars are US dollars.

his country a decisive push from the medieval into the modern world. Mongkut was a man of considerable energy and intellectual curiosity, and even the circumstances of his death are typical. He died in 1868 as the result of a fever he caught when returning from a scientific expedition he had organized to view an eclipse of the sun. His epitaph might well have been the words of an English missionary who knew him in Thailand and who described his rule as 'the mildest and best heathen government on the face of the globe'.

The situation in Thailand's neighbours to the east, the Indo-Chinese states which are now Vietnam, Laos and Cambodia, was quite different. A group of French Jesuit missionaries had an early and major influence. They persevered in spite of considerable persecution and the Christian community, almost entirely Roman Catholic, numbered several hundred thousand by the end of the seventeenth century.

In the final quarter of the eighteenth century a major revolt broke out in the Tayson district in the mountains of northern Vietnam and then spread to the plains. It was an expression of mass discontent with levels of taxation and the rule of the mandarins, and was the beginning of the end for the two rival dynasties in the north and the south, the Trinh and the Nguyen. The Nguyen were driven out of Hue, their vulnerable and unstrategic capital sited according to the predictions of astrologers, and went into hiding in the far south, which was then largely unpopulated jungle.

They lived as outlaws on the islands of the Gulf of Thailand until, finally, their cause was taken up by the French Apostolic Vicar, Pignane de Behaine, who negotiated an agreement with the French government to restore the Nguyen to the throne in return for a trade monopoly and the cession of certain territories to France. At first de Behaine had difficulty persuading the French authorities in Asia to implement this agreement, but they eventually mustered a small French mercenary army which, using modern weapons, was highly effective. Not only was the southern kingdom recaptured but Hanoi was also taken in 1802. The conquest of the north was relatively easy, since the Trinh leaders had already been displaced by the Tayson popular movement. Unity of Vietnam under single rule was, then, largely the result of French exploitation of rival factions. A treaty was signed in 1862 ceding three southern provinces to France and permitting missionaries to work anywhere in the country. Six years later the French occupied three more provinces. They also established a protectorate over Cambodia in 1864, and, 19 years later, over north Vietnam.

These colonies became known as French Indo-China.

13 The Malay World: Majapahit and Malacca

The Javanese empire of Majapahit was one of the last of the major Hinduized states of island south-east Asia, and probably the best remembered. In this lies possibly its greatest importance, for the Majapahit tradition has been adopted as part of its national heritage by modern Indonesia. Some Indonesians have seen in Majapahit a pan-Malay empire which might again be realized in the future.

There is a good deal of disagreement about how large Majapahit actually was. Tradition claims it extended beyond Java and Sumatra to most of Malaya, the Celebes (Sulawesi) and even parts of what are now the Philippines, possibly also to New Guinea and parts of northern Australia. Such contentions are based substantially on what is a suspect source – an account of the empire given by Majapahit's court historian, Prapanca, in a long panegyric poem.

Indonesia's independence leader and first President, Sukarno, referred to Prapanca's account of Majapahit during discussions, in the final years of the Japanese occupation of Indonesia during the Second World War, about the form a future independent republic might take. At these discussions the Malayan peninsula, Borneo and New Guinea were mentioned as once having been part of the Majapahit realms. While it would be extreme to regard this as evidence of Indonesian expansionist ambitions to all of these territories, the vision of a 'new Majapahit' seems to have remained in the minds of some Indonesian leaders.

Apart from its contributions to the nationalist ambition, Majapahit has had important and lasting social consequences in East Java, which is still extensively Hinduized. This is especially true of the aristocratic, or *priyayi* class. This region has only a thin layer of Islam over much earlier animist and later Hindu influences, and Bali, which can properly be associated with it in this context, remains almost entirely Hindu. It is not without interest that President Sukarno's father was from the *priyayi* class and that his mother was Balinese. The next president, Suharto, also came from the Javanese heartland.

Majapahit became in the fourteenth century the major co-ordinator of the spice trade to Europe, based on the port city, Surabaya, and Majapahit itself some distance up the Brantas River, on a rich, rice-growing plain. It seems to have been a loose confederation of convenience between autonomous spice-producing states owing only token allegiance. Hence, far from being an empire derived by conquest, Majapahit appears more to have been a kingdom controlling East Java, Madura and Bali, with widespread reciprocal commercial contacts with the spice-growing Indonesian islands on one level; on another, trading relations with China and with Europe, via the Mameluke Empire of Egypt, which passed commodities on to Venice.

Majapahit appears to have been at its zenith during the prime ministership of Gaja Mada in the latter part of the fourteenth century. Whatever the facts about this, Gaja Mada is regarded as a national hero. One of Indonesia's largest universities, established in Jogjakarta during the struggle for independence from the Dutch, is one of many national institutions named after him. Majapahit declined in importance after Gaja Mada died in 1364. We are told it was found necessary to appoint four ministers to do his work but in spite of their efforts the kingdom drifted into a phase of less competent government from which it never recovered. As always, a stronger enemy was ready to take advantage of weakness. It was probably a league of Muslim princes, based on the port of Demak, that conquered Majapahit about 1520.

The Muslims who spread the faith of Allah to south-east Asia were mostly Indian. When Islam reached Indonesia and Malaysia it was substantially modified from the stern ascetic faith of the desert, and because of this was more readily acceptable. The mystic Sufist school of Islam has elements of magic, and a certain flexibility which allowed the incorporation of ancient animist beliefs when it reached south-east Asia. And since Islam did not have professional priests, the missionaries were usually traders; adoption of Islam gave a definite commercial advantage to ambitious local rajas.

These elements have important present-day implications, making necessary a large distinction between Islam in Indonesia and Malaysia and that in the Middle East, especially the fundamentalist branches. In the Middle East, Pakistan and Afghanistan, Muslim orthodoxy is conservative and restrictive, whereas in Indonesia the religion is much more pliable. Women have a high degree of personal freedom and independence, play an important part in government and business, and are not limited in their movements and freedom to gain an education.

The last of the larger Malay maritime empires was the first to be located on the Malayan peninsula itself. This was Malacca, a port on the straits which bear its name. According to a sixteenth-century Portuguese observer, Tome Pires, in his Suma Oriental Parameswara, the founder of Malacca may have been of Shailendra descent, of the same blood as the dynasty that had ruled Shrivijaya. Certainly development of the two empires was similar, and they both had the same commercial motive – domination of the Malacca Straits trade. Singapore is their modern equivalent.

Nowadays Malacca's river has silted up and is useful only as a haven for a few fishing boats. The sleepy town looks out over a shallow, muddy stretch of sea over which the monsoon drives an endless succession of short, steep waves. But 600 years ago both the river and the sea approaches were readily navigable, providing a convenient port for sailing ships. The weather is seldom stormy and the two monsoons, the trade winds of this region, blow with remarkable regularity.

Because of this, Malacca was a useful stopping place for the Ming armadas. Peace, and its location on the main sea route through south-east Asia, permitted Malacca to grow rapidly. Indeed, China issued an order to Malacca's main potential enemy, Siam, not to attack the city. In the two decades from 1411, five Malaccan rulers journeyed to the Chinese court. The Gujerati Muslims from India played a major part in its brisk trade. They came to Malacca in hundreds, using all the efficiency in trade and commerce that distinguishes their descendants in India today; indeed, Indian cotton cloth and spices were the major commodities traded. Malacca's revenues came from a six per cent duty levied on the value of all cargoes brought in.

The first Portuguese ships to arrive in Malacca, in 1509, found the city at the height of its influence. The arrival of the Europeans caused much uneasiness among the Gujerati Muslims, who, from their experiences off the west Indian coast, knew something of Portuguese methods. They anticipated a commercial challenge in south-east Asia, and persuaded the rulers of Malacca to agree to a sudden attack on the European squadron. The Portuguese were forced to withdraw, leaving behind two burning ships, many men killed, and 19 members of a shore party held as prisoners. Revenge was not long delayed. Two years later the second Viceroy, d'Albuquerque, arrived off Malacca personally with a fleet of 18 ships, demanding, at gunpoint, the return of the Portuguese prisoners and compensation for the ships that had been destroyed.

Malacca decided to resist, and the Portuguese then took the city by storm, after several days' hard fighting. The European force was small – European forces in Asia usually were – but its discipline, superior arms and the supporting firepower of the ships allowed it to win the day. Also, resistance was far from general. Many of the merchants living in the town had no real loyalty to its rulers – they were mainly interested in ending the fighting quickly so trade could be resumed. Following their usual custom, the Portuguese consolidated their victory by building a strong, stone fortress near the river mouth. Its gateway can still be seen in Malacca, surrounded by green lawns in a park that looks over the sea.

The Portuguese had not been long in Malacca before its prosperity began to decline. Like most colonial powers, their primary objective was to make money, but the Portuguese set standards of rapacity never equalled afterwards, and so doomed their empire in Asia. Eventually they became so well hated for their treachery, cruelty and greed that shipping began to avoid the port. Most of the Gujerati traders now went to ports in north Sumatra. Another European power, Holland, was to be the Portuguese nemesis. Dutch ships bombarded Malacca in 1606, and from then on blockaded the port more or less continuously. Malacca's trade became almost non-existent, and eventually the town even ran short of food, for it was dependent on rice imports from Java. The Dutch, in an alliance with Malacca's former Malay rulers, attacked it in force in 1640 and six months later the fortress capitulated.

Malacca never recovered, because the Dutch did not allow it to do so. While they held Malacca nobody else could reinstate its trading potential and so commerce was diverted to the East Indies (now Indonesia) in which the Dutch were more interested. Dutch military government in Malacca was harsh, and much misery resulted from the hostility between the Protestant Hollanders and the Catholic Malay and Eurasian converts. Thus, the early promise of Malacca came to nothing. It became one of the first victims of the age of imperialism.

However, it was not the only one. For 200 years from 1400 south-east Asia was engaged in a busy trade with much of the world, carried in Chinese, Indian and Arab ships. This was to change as the European colonizers took over the region, usually at gunpoint. Additionally, climate change, the Little Ice Age that was to cause poverty, even starvation, in many parts of the world, resulted in a global trade recession.

Although the kingdom of Johore, at the extreme south of the Malay peninsula, achieved a certain continuity of rule it, too, was riven with dissension and strife. The rest of the peninsula reverted to small, primitive river kingdoms, passing through restless alliances and perpetual, if sporadic, warfare between neighbours. The northern states became vassals of Thailand. For a time, dominance over much of the rest of Malaya was exercised by a race of sea pirates, the Bugis of Sulawesi.

British merchants began to trade in a limited way with this small, under-populated Malaya during the eighteenth century. One of them was a sea captain named Francis Light who, after much argument, persuaded the British East India Company to establish a port on Penang, the small mountainous island off the north-western coast. This settlement, Georgetown, founded in 1786, was the first British foothold on Malayan soil. As usual, trade was the main consideration. The East Indiamen, as the company's ships were called, needed a base to break the long journey to and from China for tea. This trade was fast expanding. Ship design improved and tea, unknown in England before the middle of the seventeenth century, was fast displacing coffee, and stronger beverages, in popularity, its appeal to the rapidly developing British morality succinctly described in the poet William Cowper's description of 'the cups that cheer, but not inebriate'.

Thomas Stamford Raffles, who had been governor of Java during the Napoleonic wars, landed in 1819 on a small, swampy island off the Johore coast, separated from it only by a narrow, shallow channel. This island of Singapore, inhabited only by a few fishermen, seemed worthless to the Sultan of Johore, who agreed to lease it in perpetuity. The new settlement quickly proved its value. As early as 1824, the date of the first official census, more than 10,000 people had settled there. In 1824 Dutch and British spheres of influence were regularized by treaty. Holland withdrew her objections to Singapore and exchanged Malacca for the only British post in the East Indies, Bencoolen, on Sumatra. Two years later Singapore was united with Georgetown on Penang and Malacca as a separate colonial territory, the Straits Settlements.

14 Indonesia: the Last Independent Kingdoms and the Extension of Dutch Rule

The merchant adventurers of Holland began that country's three and a half centuries of association with the fertile islands they called the East Indies under a haze of cannon smoke. They were treacherous, cruel and rapacious, and from first acquaintance excited fear and hatred among the native people.

In these respects they differed little from their fellow European traders in this region. Journeys to and from the Indies were so hazardous that generally only criminals and others of desperate character and uncertain morality would take the risks. For many years an average loss of a quarter of the crews of ships trading to the Indies was regarded as normal. The first Dutch fleet of four ships to reach the islands in 1596 lost 145 of its complement of 249 during a voyage of 14 months. Many of these deaths were from scurvy.

Dutch exploitation might never have gone further than the casual mixture of piracy and trading typical of this earliest penetration of European influence had it not been for the ambitious vision of Jan Coen, who was appointed the first Governor-General in 1618. He foresaw a vast Dutch commercial empire in the East, with ramifications far beyond the Indies. Coen achieved control of the trading port of Jakarta in West Java and built there a strong fortress and a miniature Dutch town. Its rows of small white houses huddled close together along the banks of muddy canals, with their brown-tiled roofs, lead-light windows and heavy shutters, were inspired by a keen homesickness for the Netherlands. In 1619 this town was given Holland's ancient name, Batavia. The small Dutch outpost did not, and could not, initially challenge the still-powerful rulers of Java. It successfully withstood some probing assaults from them, then signed agreements which technically accepted their overlordship.

Because of the remoteness of these islands from Europe, their spices had always commanded very high prices. At that time the Malukus (Moluccas)

Map 5 Indonesia

were the only place where cloves grew, and the nutmeg tree was found exclusively on Banda and Ambon. Jan Coen used a mixture of persuasion and force to secure a monopoly on this lucrative trade. He then consolidated his position by driving trade competitors, especially the English, from Indonesian waters. There were many obscure but violent incidents, of which the best remembered is the killing of a few English traders and their Chinese assistants at Ambon in 1623. In spite of an ensuing battle of words between the Dutch and English governments, the British East India Company was not interested enough to finance a lengthy war. The English disappeared from the Indies, except for a single post at Bencoolen in Sumatra.

The Dutch applied rigid controls on the economy of the islands, for they were determined not to allow the price of cloves and nutmeg to fall because of over-supply. They forced the local people to cut down and burn their trees, until spice production had fallen to a quarter of the former crop. Villagers who resisted were ruthlessly hunted down and shot, and their homes burned. Coen's expedition against Banda to secure the nutmeg monopoly is one of the horrifying incidents of colonial history. The islanders fought back bravely, but were overwhelmed by the superior weapons of the Dutch. Fifteen thousand were killed, and the survivors were forced to grow the spices for the Dutch under conditions little better than slavery. The company determined the price it would pay, and forced the growers to accept trade goods from Batavia in payment.

This barter system was very much to the disadvantage of the Indonesians. The prosperity of the islands diminished, and over the next century the population of Ambon declined by a third. So deep was the bitterness aroused by these policies that when world demand for spices increased in the eighteenth century even extreme measures could not induce these people to increase production of cloves and nutmeg. Finally the trees were successfully grown in India and the Dutch monopoly ended.

Meanwhile, the toehold on Java was precariously maintained. The last major Indonesian state prior to the colonial period was based on an inland capital, Mataram, in Central Java. It became large and powerful during the lifetime of an outstanding leader, Sultan Agung, who came to the throne in 1623. According to the Court records of the time, he regarded himself as the successor to the great rulers of Majapahit, even though he was a Muslim. By 1625 he ruled all of Java except for small areas at the eastern and western tips of the island, which were controlled by Bali and the state of Bantam. Bantam was a vigorous state based on the west Javanese pepper trade. The society on Bali, led by Hindu-Javanese families who had fled from Majapahit, maintained a well-organized opposition to both Mataram and

Figure 8 Balinese temple dancing represents part of complicated religious dramas, usually from the ancient Indian epics

the Dutch, keeping their own island and the small enclave on Java independent.

Between 1627 and 1630 Agung made determined efforts, both by treachery and direct assault, to destroy Batavia. The armies of Mataram placed a dam across the river that provided the fortress's water supply, and, when all else failed, instituted a siege involving thousands of soldiers. However, this massive army soon ran short of food. Dutch naval power was vastly superior – the Dutch ships destroyed a fleet of 200 boats carrying rice – and within weeks the starving army of Mataram was forced to retreat. A treaty followed guaranteeing Batavia's continued existence.

In many ways Mataram followed the traditions of Majapahit and was probably representative of even earlier Javanese kingdoms. It is consequently of some interest because there are many written descriptions of it by European observers. Social changes are slow in Asia. Mataram resembled in a number of ways the Indian kingdoms of more than a thousand years before its time – the first of which we have independent accounts. The observations of the Greek Megasthenes about the Mauryan empire in north India in the fourth century and those of Dutchmen who visited the *kraton* – the palace complex – of Mataram, bear witness to this continuity of tradition.

One similarity was the king's guard, composed of women armed with spears and lances, who were the only people allowed near the ruler when he appeared in public. Far more basic was the sacral role of the king, his place as an intermediary between the people and the feared and worshipped forces of nature, which are impressive enough in Java, with its active volcanoes and sudden, violent thunderstorms, in some places occurring on more than 300 days a year. Only the king, supported by the spirits of his ancestors, could negotiate with these forces, on which the common prosperity and safety so much depended. There are links with east Asia in the *pusakas*, or sacred objects, on which the welfare of the kingdom was believed to depend, hidden away in a secret place deep within the *kraton*.

The Sultan of Mataram's life, and that of all Javanese princes of his tradition, was surrounded by magic and mystery. He was believed to possess sacred weapons, such as swords, that could make him invulnerable; he would spend nights near the graves of his ancestors, gathering magical influence, and was believed to obtain dynamic power from the soil itself, from thunder and lightning, and other manifestations of nature. In spite of being Western-educated and well read in European political theory Indonesia's independence leader, President Sukarno, consciously followed this tradition.

The sultan was above and beyond the law. If he behaved in a peremptory, brutal, even, at times, hideously criminal fashion, this was seen by the ordinary people as a manifestation of divinity in him. The ruler was expected to live in a more extravagant, dynamic and flamboyant way than ordinary men – to be a great user of women, among other things. Because of this belief in his superhuman qualities, the rulers had absolute powers of life and death over even the highest-born, and these seem never to have been questioned.

Some Indonesian people, although apparently very gentle, have hidden capacities for violence and can be suddenly taken with a killing frenzy, described by the word *amuk* – mad. The violent murder of as many as a million people after the fall of Sukarno in 1965 is indicative. European observers were shocked when Agung's commander ordered the summary execution of 800 of his soldiers because they had failed in the attempt to take Batavia. The aristocracy, made up of princes of the royal house and of associated states, had to live in the *kraton* with the king and could be (and sometimes were), killed at a word from him at the slightest suspicion of disloyalty. Royal wrath was visited on high and low alike without mercy. The peasants suffered, as peasants did in every feudal state, and in much the same ways. They were taxed and sweated to support the *kraton* and regularly conscripted to fight the king's wars. As elsewhere in south-east Asia, such armies could number 100,000 or more, and casualties among them were often high. The relatively small population of the region before 1800 has been ascribed to this.

Nevertheless, Mataram did have a considerable prosperity and a definite system of law. Dutch observers say the region around the *kraton* was intensely cultivated, with hill after hill built up into a complex of terraced, irrigated ricefields. Several million people lived under Mataram's rule, in perhaps 3000 villages of 100 families or more, each surrounded by their fields. It was an organization of rural life still typical of much of Asia today. Although Agung was a Muslim, he did not base the law of Mataram solely on that of Islam. The religious courts existed, but the law was a mixture of the Islamic and the traditional Javanese customary code, called *adat*, which retains considerable force today.

The *kraton* itself was a rambling collection of red-brick, stone and timber buildings, gardens, pavilions and courtyards. Certain parts of it were semi-public. Much of the rest housed the king's retainers and the nobles who were kept constantly under his eye so they might have no opportunity to plot rebellion. Other parts of the *kraton* were never open to visitors or any but the highest officials. Building work for the ruler was a constant occupation for much of the community because new *kratons* were required constantly. There is an interesting echo of Angkor in the fact that every new ruler was expected to build a new *kraton*. Sometimes the residence was shifted after the passing of a certain number of years, or if the old *kraton* were defiled for ritual reasons.

Those who reflect on the difficulties of Indonesian democracy, the privileges assumed as of right by its rulers and their families, the vast economic advantages they have over the ordinary people, the ruthless decimation of whole communities, as in Aceh, Irian Jaya and Timor Leste (East Timor), might also consider the extent to which these things are simply part of a long-standing tradition, likely to persist into Indonesia's future.

The rulers of Mataram did not regard the Dutch as superiors, or even as equals. Initially they were welcomed because competition between them and the Portuguese drove up spice prices. However, the sultan treated the Dutch with contempt, because they were merchants, and forced them to wait for hours in the hot sun. On the other hand, the officials of the company treated the rulers with deference, regularly offering gifts imported from Europe.

Nevertheless, during Agung's reign the Dutch had been able to consolidate. The third Governor-General, Anthony Van Diemen, took Malacca from the Portuguese. This, with the eviction of the British, left Holland as the major trading power in the Indies. Van Diemen and Agung died in the

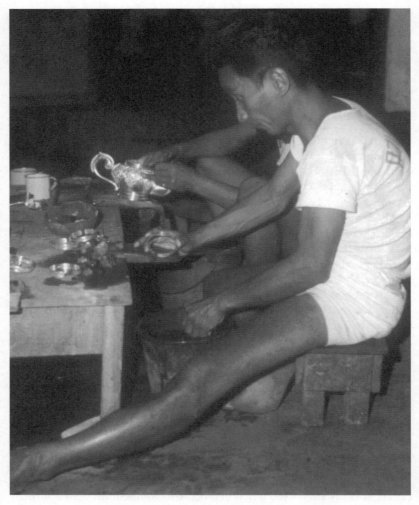

Figure 9   Silver has always been an important source of wealth and art in Asia, and is still handcrafted in most parts of the region

same year, 1645, and the relationship between the company and the state of Mataram began to change. Agung's successor, Amangkurat, was a less formidable man than his father. In 1646 he concluded a new treaty which made him dependent on the company for much of his personal income. He reined in the power of the religious courts and is said to have killed 6000

Muslim 'priests' in a single massacre after calling them together in confer-ence. This reaction against Islam, and his desire for absolute control of the empire, caused dangerous trouble in the outlying vassal states. The ruler of one of these led a revolt that dethroned Amangkurat. His *kraton* at Mataram was burned, his treasures looted.

Amangkurat died shortly after he escaped from the ruins, but before he did so he advised his son to seek a closer alliance with the Dutch. Amangkurat II, who was said to be of weak character, was restored to power by a Dutch army. The price was control of the Mataram empire by the company, which now had troops stationed permanently at the new *kraton*. With Mataram subject, Bantam's years of independence were numbered. The Dutch took advantage of a royal quarrel there to manipu-late the succession and control the state.

So the eighteenth century began with the Dutch empire greatly extended. Although the old kingdoms had lost their power, the Dutch did not disturb their traditions and essential social organization. The rulers and the aristocracy remained in their traditional positions, but were not permit-ted to make war on one another. The Dutch, in fact, used them as agents. The nobles became 'regents', responsible for exacting a certain amount of tax from the peasants, which they had to pass on to the company. The worst features of the independent states remained – but added to them was the burden of tribute going to the Dutch. Thus the old social relationship was maintained into modern times, the privileged position of the *priyayi* still remaining an essential feature of Javanese society.

Batavia itself was afflicted for a hundred years with a contagious fever – probably malaria – which caused a high death rate among the Dutch settlers. The large numbers of Chinese who had settled in Indonesia now became increasingly influential. The 'regents' appointed by the Dutch were usually lazy and inefficient, and had a contempt for the details of commerce. Chinese immigrants were ready to act as intermediaries, provided they saw a good profit in it for themselves. Internal highway tolls, another burden on the ordinary people, were often 'farmed out', like other forms of taxation, to the Chinese. Because of this direct relationship with the people in what came to be an extortionist role, the Chinese came to be despised and hated. This attitude is still strong today, and lies behind regu-lar episodes of anti-Chinese violence since independence.

Like all institutions that exist for a long time without change, the Dutch East India Company gradually deteriorated. The Chinese made money but, increasingly, the company did not. It was dissolved in 1799 because of its heavy losses and overheads and a bad record of corruption among its officials. Direct rule by the Dutch government did not mend matters significantly. Holland became embroiled in the Java War, which dragged on for five years from 1825. It was caused by Dutch interference in the succession in Jogjakarta. A prince named Diponegoro, the eldest of his family, was passed over by the Dutch, who installed a younger brother as sultan. Diponegoro led a revolt that combined many different hostilities, including those of the aristocracy against the Dutch and the ordinary people against the Chinese who were their immediate oppressors. Vague and mixed though its motives were, the war was intense and destructive. It resulted in the loss of 15,000 Dutch soldiers and the death of perhaps a quarter of a million Chinese and Indonesians – mostly civilians not actually concerned with the fighting.

From 1830 Holland was involved in war at home – a nine-year revolt of her Belgian provinces that completed the exhaustion of the Netherlands Treasury, already depleted by the Napoleonic Wars. To restore her finances Holland imposed on the Indies the cultivation system, requiring the planting of one-fifth of all agricultural land in a crop dictated by the colonial power. This crop became the property of the government. Added to existing burdens, this resulted in such a severe 'squeeze' of the peasants that there were major famines in Java. This cultivation system introduced new crops to the island – sugar, coffee and indigo, and later tea, produced entirely for export.

The vast sums pouring out of Batavia made up close to one-third of the entire Netherlands budget over a period of 50 years. Yet barely half this revenue came from the cultivation system. A further large sum came from land taxes, customs duties, and monopolies in salt, opium and pawnshop operation. Little was provided in return. No attempt was made to develop a basic education system of any consequence, nor to train Indonesians in the professions. Introduction of universal basic schooling was considered once or twice, late in the colonial period, but dismissed as being too expensive.

15 India under Two Masters: the Grand Moguls and the East India Company

After the decline of the Gupta empire no other unifying force comparable with it emerged for nine centuries, leaving north India at the mercy of any marauding band that chose to ride down through the passes. Revealed instead are cruel and extortionate north Indian kingdoms, like those of the Muslim sultans of Delhi, and the petty empires of scores of warlike princelings, each the predator of a tract of country dominated by a central fortress. Although incessantly preoccupied with war, these rulers, the Rajputs, contributed to their country's defencelessness by their quarrelling, lack of a common purpose, and retention of old-fashioned if romantic military methods against enemies who had cannon and had advanced the use of cavalry to an exact science. Reckless, indeed suicidal, bravery was no effective answer to these things. It was a tradition of the Rajputs, when one of their fortresses was doomed to fall, to burn all their women and children alive on a funeral pyre while the men sallied out to meet death at the hands of their enemies.

Many of the invaders who drove down from central Asia were simple destroyers, like the Huns, who were execrated in India just as they were in Europe and China. Later 'barbarians' were more cultivated although just as cruel. They were Muslims, practising a form of Islam derived through and influenced by the civilized and artistic Persian (Iranian) culture. To these people the ornamented architecture of the Hindu temples, their many statues of gods and goddesses, elaborate rituals and use of music for worship, were evidence of an idolatry the removal of which, by fire and sword, was a religious duty. It was one that associated itself conveniently with looting. In his book *India* (2000), John Keay compares these pre-Mogul invaders with the subsequent European ones: 'Like the white *sahibs* of European colonialism, the true believers of the (Delhi) sultanate saw India simply as a source of wealth, a scene of adventure, and a subject for moral indignation spiked

Map 6 South Asia

with prurient fantasy. They too, indeed, were colonialists. Compromise with the natives was as unthinkable as it was preposterous' (p. 308).

Buddhism in India was hastened into decline by the Muslim invaders, who slew its peaceful monks in thousands and destroyed the great teaching monasteries. Nalanda, with more than 10,000 monks and students in the thirteenth century, was sacked, and thousands of its occupants killed. The survivors fled north to Nepal and Tibet. One of the last to go, Vikramashila, was demolished so completely that no trace of its considerable buildings remains.

This phase of conquest and brutality is balanced somewhat by a blending of indigenous and Islamic art, notably painting and architecture. The delicate building of this time, with its shady courts, fretted walls, water gardens, and tall graceful minarets, owed much to Persian influence and the dislike of the conquerors from the clean air of the hills for the hot mugginess of the Indian plain in the months before and during the monsoon rains. It is a style still very much alive, and one which spread far beyond India, as the railway station in Kuala Lumpur and the extravagant marble mosque in Brunei can testify.

It also seems likely that the spinning wheel was introduced to India from Persia about 1350, massively benefiting a cottage industry that would soon provide most of the world with its cotton fabrics.

Order and authority returned to north India with the advent of the Muslim Dynasty Europe called the Grand Moguls. They added glamour, pageantry and a strange collection of legend to the world's story but, more than that, brought a unity and established methods of government that, in many respects, foreshadowed the patterns of today. At its best, it was a remarkably able administration for its time.

In 1525, with a force of only 12,000, the King of Kabul, who was to become the first Mogul emperor, Babur, marched through the Khyber gorges to conquer India. He met a defending army of 100,000 on India's traditional field of decision, the plain of Panipat, 50 miles north of Delhi, and won decisively. Babur's victory was due substantially to good discipline, highly trained cavalry, and possession of an artillery train. Fifteen thousand of the Indian army died in that battle. Judging from his own diaries, Babur was that rare combination – a visionary and a man of action with almost the skills of generalship of a Napoleon. 'I put my foot in the stirrup of resolution, set my hand on the rein of trust in God, and move forward,' he says, but nevertheless he maintained a close interest in the casting and transport of his field cannon.

The people of north India were accustomed to these periodic raids from the north. When Babur pushed on from Delhi to Agra, the Indians sought to placate him with the gift of an enormous diamond, thought by some to be the great stone now called the Koh-i-noor. But unlike his forerunners, Babur did not return to the mountains of the north. In Agra he laid out a garden, and made other preparations for a permanent stay, in spite of complaints in his memoirs that India lacked interesting fruits, baths and graceful buildings, and that it was steamy, hot and unattractive. Although capable enough of harsh, even cruel, actions by the standards of today, Babur was moderate and cultured for his time. He was reflective and thoughtful, with considerable powers of personality, which were fully engaged persuading his homesick followers to stay in India.

According to a chronicle of the time, when Babur's eldest son Humayun became seriously ill Babur followed a custom of his people in offering his own dearest possession, his life, in exchange for his son's restoration to health. He is said to have walked three times around Humayun's sickbed and to have pledged his own life in exchange. Humayun recovered, but Babur died at the age of 47. Humayun, heavily addicted to opium, had little of his father's powers of leadership and came close to losing the empire. He spent practically the whole of his life on the move, intriguing against, fighting with, or running away from his enemies. An enthusiastic astronomer, in 1556 Humayun missed his footing and fell down the stairs to his death when leaving his rooftop observatory. His son Akbar was several times taken hostage before his father's death made him emperor at the age of 13.

Against all expectation, all the powers of his grandfather, and more, returned to the dynasty. Akbar brought a rare genius to the task of controlling his difficult heritage. During his reign of nearly 50 years, to 1605, the Mogul Dynasty was firmly established, and even integrated with the older elements of Indian society. Although he was a Muslim for most of his life, Akbar went out of his way to win the respect and assistance of the traditional Hindu leaders and, as the decades passed, even the intolerant and wild Rajput princes came to serve him loyally. Akbar was astute enough to see that pride and self-esteem were the mainsprings of their lives, and he won them over by allowing them status symbols – the right to sound their drums in the capital, which was a privilege of royalty, or to enter the royal audience chamber fully armed.

Akbar used them in his civil service, which was organized with fixed, graded salary scales so officials did not have to depend on bribery and extortion for their incomes. This, his regularization of taxation, standardization of weights and measures, and improved legal code, made India relatively peaceful and prosperous. Taxation of the peasants was limited to around a third of gross product, and the detested poll tax levied on non-Muslims remitted. Mogul India became one of the principal sources of wealth in the world, and its major port, Surat, one of the world's busiest, exporting huge quantities of cotton cloth – calico was soon to be found in almost every European and British home in large quantities. Gold and silver to pay for these cottons, silk, molasses, saltpetre and indigo – much in demand to dye military uniforms – and also huge food crop exports, flooded into India from all parts of the world. This wealth derived from the huge resource of manpower; at this time India's population was well over a hundred million – at least three times that of the whole of Western Europe.

Unfortunately, Akbar's lively mind turned to a restless mysticism as he grew older. He established a new religion, a court cult based on the assumption of his own divinity, which sought to blend Islam and Hinduism. He even went so far as to wear the caste marks and sacred thread of the Hindu twice-born. This alarmed the orthodox among his Muslim followers, and a period of reaction set in after his death.

It was an added misfortune that his heir, Jehengir, was cruel by temperament, and reverted to such forms of punishment as flaying alive and impaling. During Jehengir's reign, in 1615, Sir Thomas Roe led a British embassy to the Mogul court. The gifts it brought were scorned as trifles, and Sir Thomas was not able to achieve as much as he had hoped. However, Jehengir formed an admiration for the quietly courageous Englishman, who stubbornly refused to knock his head three times on the floor before the Mogul, the required form of homage. Roe was able to make some trading arrangements and consolidated the first British mercantile post, which had been established by Captain Will Hawkins in Surat in 1609.

The extravagant wealth of the dynasty was at its most lavish during the reign of Jehengir's son, Shah Jahan, who is remembered chiefly because his great and lasting passion for a woman inspired one of the world's most beautiful buildings. The emperor was wholly devoted to his wife, Mumtaz Mahal. When she died in childbirth at the age of 39 after bearing him 14 children, Shah Jahan set 20,000 men to work for 22 years to build her memorial, the Taj Mahal at Agra, the most famed and lovely of all Indian monuments.

The last of the Moguls to hold more than a shadow of power was a devout and bigoted Muslim, Aurangzeb, who damaged the empire through the narrow-minded religious zeal that marked his reign from 1659 to 1707. Aurangzeb failed to control the ever-present Muslim extremist faction, which sought to persecute the Hindus. They seized the opportunity to loot and burn Hindu homes and temples, and to force Hindu officials out of office. When Hindu protestors took to the streets in large numbers they were subdued by force – on at least one occasion by sending elephants among them to trample them to death. Aurangzeb quickly lost the support of the Rajput princes, on which the empire so much depended. His most persistent enemy was the Maratha confederacy from the mountains of west India, led by a warrior chief called Shivaji. His name is important because it was later used by Hindu extremists as a symbol of their opposition to Indian Islam. In spite of his wealth and pomp, his 800 war elephants and huge army, Aurangzeb steadily lost ground against the rebels.

In 1701, six years before his death, the emperor had granted the British East India Company the right to collect revenues from land near Kolkata (Calcutta), and their influence on the trade of Bengal increased steadily from then on. During the next 40 years eight Mogul emperors, increasingly out of control of the empire, sat on the throne. Over these decades the realm split into fragments as, one by one, local officials or governors set up virtually autonomous states. So began the princely states, which were to endure into the twentieth century. The largest of these states became as populous and wealthy as some of the world's leading powers of the day, the greatest of them the central Indian state of Hyderabad, whose hereditary rulers, the Nizams, became the richest men in the world.

The Moguls and their administrators were, of course, a superstructure above, and supported unwillingly by, the real India, which was very different. Eighteenth-century Europe spoke in glowing terms of the treasures of Ind, but in reality the flamboyant prosperity of the Moguls was based on the exploitation and poverty of the mass of the people. After Akbar's death, the villagers suffered acutely. Mogul taxation was increased to as much as half of all produce, and even this does not take into account additional amounts extorted, less formally, by tax gatherers and local lords. Virtually all the national income that came into the hands of the governing class was spent on high living, paying retainers and the creation of private buildings, tombs and monuments. Public works like irrigation canals, roads and bridges, which would have improved the lives of the villagers, were not seen as a state responsibility. Instead local officials exacted highway tolls at strategic points, such as river fords and crossroads, for their own benefit.

Villages, then as now, stood dirty and impoverished, an untidy network set on the dusty plains. Their people were poor, vulnerable to the vagaries of the seasons and the cupidity of their rulers alike, limited in their ambitions and almost all suffering from one or more debilitating diseases. Women, worn out by bearing large families when they had scarcely left childhood themselves, were lucky indeed to survive their twenties. Those who died young were perhaps the most fortunate, since widows were frequently burned alive on their husband's funeral pyre.

The caste system was by then fully developed. It divided Hindu society into a myriad of small groups, each of which sought to maintain its special position or privileges. In many respects the caste amounts to an exclusive society, with established rules and discipline imposed on all its members, and designed to serve their interests. Often membership of a caste group is associated with occupation, as guilds were in Europe, with work skills passing on from father to son. Closely associated is the influence and authority of the extended family, still very important in India today. The system seems to have evolved to its present form prior to and during the later Mogul period, and is consistent with the necessity for small social groups to maintain their identity.

India, in spite of its problems and staggering social disproportions, has evolved a remarkably diverse and vigorous culture, a reflection of a society full of subtleties and surprises. Its dance and music are distinctive, highly developed and formalized. They have also been pervasive, to the extent that the same arts throughout south-east Asia are plainly derivative. The elegant dances performed on the steps of Angkor Wat, and in Bali, have evolved from Indian forms. Indian art is a part of life, intimately linked with the everyday life of individuals, rather than a separate 'package' as in the West, where appreciation of the arts tends to be a spectator sport.

Perhaps because of this much Indian art is ephemeral – one gets the feeling that its great works have survived almost by accident, usually because their original intent was decorative. There is a strong sense that it is the act of creation that is important, rather than the finished work. Frequently, large amounts of time and effort are put into displays for processions, carnivals or religious occasions, using temporary materials, that are destroyed or disregarded soon after they are complete. It is very much art of the moment, using colour, form, sound, light and fire to create as vivid, often as bizarre, an effect as possible.

A further dimension of Indian culture is the mysterious, even the miraculous, based on meditation and prolonged mental training. This can manifest itself in apparently impossible physical events – people who can walk on fire without being burned, who have been buried alive for long periods, withstood what would be for most people terrible injuries amounting to torture, the stopping of the heartbeat and breathing for long periods. How much of this is genuine and how much trickery is difficult to determine, and is a constant area of controversy.

During the early Mogul period the first European trading posts continued to exist in a small way, more or less on sufferance. The merchants neither exercised political power nor sought it. Their motive was trade, their ambition to amass enough capital to retire at home in comfort as soon as possible. These *nouveau riche* 'nabobs' excited some resentment and curiosity when they retired to the English countryside, not the least for their habit of bathing regularly.

During the seventeenth century three major posts were established by the East India Company. These, in the order of their founding or acquisition, were: Fort St George, later to become Madras (Chennai), on the Coromandel, or south-east coast; Bombay (Mumbai) on the central-western coast; and Fort William on the Hughli River in the Ganges delta of Bengal. Fort William was later to become Calcutta (Kolkata), one of the world's biggest cities and the place from which Britain's empire in India was largely to develop.

The struggle to inherit Mogul power was intensified with the coming of the eighteenth century. At first circumstances seemed to favour the Hindu Maratha princes, but they were too self-seeking and disunited to take advantage of the situation. Some modern Indian historians look back on the Maratha campaigns at this time as a patriotic Hindu uprising against Islam, but the Marathas cannot really be viewed in this way after the death of their leader Shivaji in 1680. They became more interested in plunder than politics, and their power was broken in a battle with a coalition of Afghan raiders and the Muslim princes of Delhi. The Afghans emerged from this battle, at Panipat in 1761, as the strongest single force, but they had no pretensions for empire. Hence there was no Indian power left that was strong enough, and ambitious enough, to take over government of the country.

At this stage the British also had no desire to rule India; indeed, the East India Company's policy was to avoid involvement in local politics if possible. This was not necessarily the view of its officials on the spot, who understood the value of political power in promoting trade. Their influence had a far-reaching effect. One of them, Robert Clive, began the chain of events that led on to British India when he first eliminated a French foothold on the Coromandel coast, for reasons of commercial rivalry, then intervened in the succession in Bengal.

An inexperienced ruler of Bengal – he was only 19 – attacked the British settlement at Kolkata. He is said to have had more than a hundred people locked in a small room, 18 feet by 15 feet, through one tropical night. Most of them were said to have died in this 'black hole'. The apparent enormity of this event, prominently featured and coloured in almost all British histories of India written during the imperial period, depends on a single suspect source – the account of one of the survivors, one J. Z. Holwell. Now the 'facts' are disputed by several modern historians; the emotive term 'black hole' was in fact British army slang for a barracks prison; probably 64 people went into the prison, 21 survived.

Clive led a punitive expedition, regained Kolkata, and defeated a much larger Indian army at Plassey in 1757, substantially because of a secret pact with some of the Indian commanders, notably Mir Jafar, to defect. Clive, then aged 32, virtually installed Mir Jafar on the throne. The payoff was the disbursement of more than £1 million from the Bengal Treasury, of which Clive personally acquired the then huge fortune of almost £250,000. The East India Company was now in a position to control Bengal. It did so through local officials it appointed and kept in office, then consolidated its political power when in 1765 it exacted from the puppet emperor the right to collect the revenues of Bengal, Bihar and Orissa, worth as much as £3 million a year. Anarchic conditions through much of the country made further increases in British power almost inevitable. The three rapidly growing ports under British rule and British law were islands of relative peace and order amid chaos, and attracted business of all kinds.

One of the fatal weaknesses of the Mogul empire had been its inability to foster a flourishing mercantile class with rights and influence of its own, like the sturdy British middle class even then laying the foundations of empire. The Moguls and their provincial governors dominated manufacture and trade and forced artisans and craftsmen to work for them almost as slaves. Even though merchants acquired wealth, they had no standing and no privileges. These mercantile families, who wanted only to trade fairly and lawfully, flocked to the British enclaves in thousands.

British policy from this time on was designed to subdue the entire subcontinent. The next 50 years would be decades of regional wars to conquer Indian provinces – notably the Maratha region in the north and Mysore in the south. Two members of the Wellesley family, Lord Mornington and his brother Arthur – later to become the Duke of Wellington of Waterloo fame – were prominent in these military adventures.

Bengal, in 1769–70, suffered a famine of such intensity that, on Warren Hastings' estimate, one-third of its inhabitants died – probably as many as eight million people, generally in the most atrocious circumstances. Contemporary accounts speak of vultures, dogs and jackals eating those so weak they could no longer move, cannibalism, and the agonies of those trying to survive by eating bark and leaves. After this huge disaster a severe labour shortage disturbed the whole balance of landownership, and perhaps a third of the land of Bengal was left uncultivated for more than a decade. This was perhaps the blackest period of British exploitation of India, since the forcible extraction of huge sums in tax from the peasants was maintained in spite of the extent of the famine. Tax revenues were £1.38 million for 1769/70, while famine relief offered by the company was less than £10,000.

British rule and revenues were guaranteed by taxes on land and monopolies on salt and opium, both of which were taxed. Tax exaction could be as
high as 50 or even 80 per cent of a peasant's production. If the tax were not
paid promptly, land and chattels were subject to seizure. However, the
British enclaves prospered and grew rapidly. The Indian population of
Kolkata was over a quarter of a million in 1788, in spite of a huge fire in 1780
that destroyed 15,000 homes. Mumbai and Chennai were not far behind.

The East India Company remained a commercial undertaking, based on
trade and exploitation. High prices were paid for posts as company officials
at the courts of Indian rulers, and large fortunes were made through 'tax-
farming' the unfortunate people. The ostentation of these returning
'nabobs' continued to attract unfavourable comment at home. Clive, who
became the first governor of Bengal, and his successor Warren Hastings
drew widespread criticism because they had made large fortunes through
the exercise of their influence. Clive was forced to defend himself on the
floor of Parliament in 1772 and, after an all-night debate, was exonerated.
Two years later he committed suicide in London. A similar controversy
marred the reputation of Warren Hastings. Mainly as a result of these scandals the British government passed, in 1773, a regulating act which brought
the operations of the East India Company under the surveillance of the
Crown. While the company maintained its trading monopoly for another
40 years, political control was henceforward to be a matter for a council of
directors in London, and a governor-general in India, responsible to
Parliament.

The extension of British rule, while often initially resisted strenuously,
was eventually accepted largely without dissension because the British,
while still imposing land tax, usually kept it a little lower than had been
exacted from the peasants previously. They also dealt directly with the
landholders, rather than using middlemen. Collecting these revenues fairly
required administration by English trained staff – this era was the real
beginning of that devoted, honest, competent and unbelievably self-right-
eous band of Britons, the Indian Civil Service. From 1809 these young men,
mostly from the public schools, were trained at the company's college at
Haileybury, where they learned at least one Indian language, some Indian
history and a sense of their almost divine destiny to rule and educate the
'heathen and backward natives'. Of them Rudyard Kipling wrote:

> Take up the white man's burden
> Send forth the best ye breed
> Go bind your sons to exile
> To serve your captives' need.

Unshakably convinced of their mission to govern, they were at least constructively reformist. Widow-burning was outlawed in 1829, although it continued illegally long after that. The more responsible British thinkers and statesmen began to feel the wider implications and responsibilities of their vast dominion. In 1834 the celebrated historian and essayist Thomas Macaulay, who had taken a seat on the Supreme Council for India the previous year, argued successfully for a system of education, based on the English language and European traditions, to produce 'a class, Indian in blood and colour, but English in taste, in opinions, in morals and intellect'.

This education minute has been severely criticized, especially its assertion that 'a single shelf of a good European library is worth the whole native literature of India and Arabia'. Yet English as the official language and vehicle of education, from 1835 onward, gave India, for the first time, a single language that was understood throughout the country. To some extent Persian, the court language of the Moguls, had met this requirement but it was used only by a small restricted class. A very much wider range of people learned English and India's debt to it as a unifying agency is recognized by most thoughtful Indians.

The most bitter conflicts of the expansionist phase came with the two Sikh Wars, which by 1849 resulted in the addition of the 100,000 rich square miles of the Punjab to British India – although at the cost of more than 2000 British lives. But that year also brought the 'doctrine of lapse' – a legal device requiring any Indian state where there was not an heir of natural issue to lapse to British rule. Indian princes without sons routinely adopted an heir. When they no longer had this option, seven states came under British rule over the next six years, adding several million pounds a year to the imperial revenues.

Education in the historical traditions of Europe during a phase of liberal revolutions brought to the evolving Indian intelligentsia some new and disturbing concepts – nationalism, democracy, the freedom of the individual. Up to this time no one had seriously thought of India as an entity, a possible nation. But now the tightening of the imperial grip caused serious misgivings among both Hindu and Muslim traditionalists, who could now be in no doubt of British intentions to transform Indian society.

Some historians, in particular Indian historians, regard the Indian 'mutiny' that broke out in 1857 as a consequence of this disquiet, and as the beginning of Indian nationalism. *Sepoys*, Indian soldiers in the Bengal army, turned on their officers and their families. The uprising began in Meerut after native soldiers saw 85 of their number gaoled for refusing orders to bite the new Lee Enfield rifle cartridges, which had been smeared with pig and cow fat, an act forbidden to Muslims and Hindus respectively by their religions. A change of law in 1856 permitting widows to remarry – also something contrary to Hindu religious custom – may have been a contributing factor. Although the scale of the revolt was relatively small and its duration brief, the horror of it, especially that of the killing of English women and children in Cawnpore, made a tremendous impact in England. It should be recorded that British retaliation was equally brutal and a good deal more extensive, involving the destruction of whole villages, and the extermination of whole families, often completely innocent of any involvement in the rebellion.

Christopher Hibbert's *The Great Mutiny* (1978), largely derived from carefully documented contemporary accounts, presents army officers, especially the notorious Colonel James Neil, in a very unfavourable light. When Delhi was occupied by the British, it was virtually destroyed by indiscriminate burning and looting. Thousands of the people were hanged, shot or bayoneted. Another account describes how villages, many of them near Cawnpore, were surrounded by cavalry, the women and children brought out and all the men burned alive in their houses. If they tried to escape the flames they were 'cut up'. Flaying alive of mutineers was actively proposed, although there is no evidence it actually happened. In London Queen Victoria, deeply disturbed by the savagery of the reprisals, made a public appeal for moderation, and called for all Indians 'to enjoy the equal and impartial protection of the law'.

There was considerable fear that the revolt might spread throughout India, although in the event this did not happen, most *sepoy* regiments remaining 'steady'. The army at that time consisted of fewer than 50,000 British troops and more than 200,000 *sepoys* – a disproportion to be corrected after the 'mutiny'. The 'doctrine of lapse' was abolished in 1858 for fear it might prompt further revolt. More than 500 princely states would now be permitted to continue intact under British protection.

The 1857 uprising is a convenient point at which to observe the declining influence of many of the old Hindu and Muslim aristocrats. British land reforms, designed to make tax collection more efficient, disturbed the interdependent communal nature of rural communities and instead substituted definite landlord and peasant classes. In general the energetic, unscrupulous and businesslike became landlords, rather than the traditional ruling class, which was too proud to appear anxious for financial gain. When, in 1788, agricultural depression led to the forced sale of 14 per cent of Bengal lands to meet tax arrears, the buyers paid on average less than a single year's revenue. Common land, perhaps 10 per cent of all Indian land, became private property so it could be taxed, further depressing the condition of the poorest. A major survey of village India towards the end of the colonial era, in the 1930s, showed that only 39 per cent got enough to eat and that 20 per cent were virtually starving. Infant mortality was almost one in four births, life expectancy at birth about 30.

In many respects influence was going over to the mercantile middle class, the new class of British-educated, based mainly on the three big cities of British India, but especially on Kolkata. These were almost invariably from the highest castes, and were largely people who, through association with their colonial masters, had the best opportunities to improve their lot. One may perceive in them the direct ancestors of the wealthiest and middle classes of today's India.

During the final century of British rule, then, Indians on average became poorer, famines killed more people, an educated class dependent on their rulers prospered, and the colonial hold on the country tightened. In 1876 Queen Victoria was proclaimed Empress of India, leaving no doubt about how the Britons of that generation saw their imperial destiny. Back in public life after a long period of mourning for her consort Prince Albert, the queen became an enthusiastic supporter of Prime Minister Disraeli's campaign to strengthen the British empire by any means. Imperial power was now to be vigorously advanced, especially in India, which Victoria saw as the main jewel in her crown.

Autocratic though the methods were, much of this effort was of value. An impartial and codified system of law, well-adapted to and largely based on local traditions, did much to reduce oppression and injustice. Telegraph lines and a cheap, efficient postal service were developed after 1850. Even if the devout deplored railways because they jostled all castes together in shocking proximity, Indians did not hesitate to use them after the first passenger line was opened in 1853. Also the trains were able to move food quickly, and this helped to mitigate the intensity of famines. Nevertheless rural poverty continued to increase, and in 1877 India experienced its worst famine of the century, taking perhaps five million lives. In 1883 a code was developed that placed the responsibility squarely on the government to provide adequate famine relief. After the turn of the century this proved reasonably effective, with one massive and disastrous exception – the Bengal famine of 1943.

16 Gandhi's India: the Struggle for Liberty

Universities teaching the Western humanities were founded in the three main Indian colonial cities, Kolkata, Mumbai and Chennai, in 1857, the same year as the 'Indian mutiny'. Of the two events the first was arguably the more significant, since Indian nationalism developed largely among the graduates of those universities. During the next 30 years nearly 50,000 Indians passed the entrance examinations, which themselves required literacy in English, and 5000 achieved the Bachelor of Arts degree.

Christianity was an important influence on Rammohun Roy, the first Indian reformer of consequence. It was he who led a vigorous campaign that persuaded the British government to overcome its reluctance to interfere in religious customs and prohibit the custom of *suttee*, which obliged, and often forced, a widow to be burned alive on the funeral pyre of her husband. Roy had watched his own sister die this way. In 1828 Roy founded the Brahma Samaj, which sought to reform Hindu society by introducing into it the Western ideals he so much admired, and by abolishing the caste system. His ideas interested the increasingly large middle class of officials and professional men who owed their opportunities to the British.

There was also concern for the depressed and unhappy position of surviving widows. They were condemned almost to a living death, unable to remarry and forced to live out the rest of their lives in sterile seclusion. Their hardships were the greater because for a variety of religious and social reasons girls entered into arranged marriages very young. Normally their husbands were older, and in a society which then had a life expectancy of about 30 wives frequently became widows younger than the average Western girl becomes a bride – sometimes as young as eight or nine.

The issue was, of course, important in its own right. However, it also brought another consideration that was to cast a long shadow on India's future. This was the immediate conflict between the reformers and the forces of Hindu religious conservatism, and the revelation that the latter were easily the stronger. The educated reformers talked a great deal, but flinched from actual defiance of caste discipline. Even after remarriage became legal, religious and social pressures generally prevented it.

The second wave of reform was based on a political and social revival of Hinduism itself, as revealed in the ancient epics. This came with the founding of a number of regional religious organizations, one of which was the Arya Samaj, established in 1875 by Dayananda Saraswati, an Indian sage who spoke no English and had no Western education. He went back to the 'Aryan'classic text, the *Rigveda*, for his inspiration, and attempted to identify a 'pure' Hinduism free from the contamination of later influences. These religious movements were of lasting importance. They influenced many Indians to oppose social reforms introduced by Britain on the grounds that it was best for Indians first to achieve political influence and reform their society afterwards. Hence a revivalist Hinduism became a central theme of nationalism.

The dusty brick mounds of Harappa and Mohenjodaro were still unrecognized. Half a century would pass before these ruined cities would be acknowledged as the remains of the first important Indian civilization, and no hint of their significance was available to the Hindu revivalists. Accordingly, they looked back for a tradition to the epic writings of the later Aryan-speaking invaders of India, and so attributed to the beginnings of Indian society a pastoral simplicity quite unlike the sophistication and urbanity the Harappa ruins indicate. Even after the discovery of Harappa, these early ideas tended to be rationalized, and still persist in the modern Indian's sense of national identity – belief in a Golden Age long before India came under the domination of foreigners, in which happiness and simplicity were thought to have prevailed.

There were also material facts that gave impetus to nationalism. From 1837 on, a selected number of English planters were allowed to take up land and settle in India – there were almost 300 such plantations by 1870. Even though they were subject to certain conditions – for instance, planters must live on their holdings – the very fact that they were there at all was a source of uneasiness to Indians. There were many peasant revolts of one kind or another during the nineteenth century, but the Indigo Revolt of 1860 was among the most significant. When the European planters used at times violent and unjust methods to force peasants in Bengal to grow indigo for low financial rewards, there was a massive reaction that approached armed rebellion. Educated Indians and recently founded newspapers supported the peasants. Confronted with what became in effect a popular political movement, the colonial government finally limited the power of the planters and insisted that any further disputes must be decided in the courts.

Another influence for nationalism was the growing pressure of poverty and landlessness among the villagers. The British themselves did not usurp land to any major extent, but they did introduce a land tenure system open to abuse. In many cases tax assessments were unfairly high – at times approaching double those during Akbar's rule. This forced hundreds of thousands of peasants from their land, which passed into the ownership of moneylenders who foreclosed on mortgages. Famines persisted, in spite of relief measures introduced by the government. The steady and massive drain of India's wealth to the imperial coffers, combined with plague and drought-induced famine, caused a nightmare of poverty and mass death so serious that India's population declined during the decade to 1905.

A sense of competition between the two major communities, Hindu and Muslim, induced both towards political organization. An educated Muslim, Sir Seyed Ahmad Khan, warned his people as early as 1883 about the nature of the communal problem. 'If the British were to leave India,' he said, 'Who would then be the rulers? Is it possible that two nations, the Muslim and Hindu, could sit on the same throne and remain in power? To hope that both would remain equal is to desire the impossible and the inconceivable.' Sir Seyed was the leader of a movement to raise Indian Islam from the apathy and disunity into which it had fallen after the collapse of the Mogul Dynasty. Due to his efforts the Anglo-Oriental College was founded in 1875 at Aligarh, near Delhi, to provide a place at which 'Muslims may acquire an English education without prejudice to their religion'. Almost all the national leaders of what was to become Pakistan were educated at Aligarh.

The first organization with the declared objective of Indian self-government was the Indian National Congress. Its political offspring, the Congress Party, was to lead India to nationhood in 1947. However, the first Congress, in 1885, was far from being a political party in the modern sense. Of its 72 delegates only two were Muslims, and there was a solid commitment to establishing Anglo-Saxon political institutions in India. Congress members did not at this stage envisage India as a nation – rather, as ' a nation in the making'.

However, a militant anti-British nationalism was also developing. It emerged first in Mumbai and was founded not only on the Hindu revival, but more specifically on that of the Maratha people who, under their great leader Shivaji, had successfully defied the Moguls in the seventeenth century. The movement gained terrorist overtones. In 1896 bubonic plague spread from Mumbai south to Pune. Strong measures were needed to control it. A British official named Rand used soldiers to evacuate houses thought to be infected and to destroy property, if necessary at bayonet point. The following year an extremist murdered Rand and an associate.

The extremists found renewed opportunities during the autocratic term of office of Lord Curzon, the Viceroy from 1898. Curzon, a dedicated Conservative, was a man of restless energy and efficiency. Almost constantly in pain, for he had to wear a leather and iron harness because of a back complaint, he was overbearing and tactless to the point of rudeness. He had no patience with 'political Indians', and stated an objective of 'assisting the Congress to a peaceful demise'. Two unpopular measures towards the end of his term led educated Bengalis to oppose him. The first restricted their influence on university administration, the second partitioned the huge state of Bengal. The partition was ostensibly to provide better government for its predominantly Muslim eastern section, the present-day Bangladesh, but was seen by Indian intellectuals as a simple 'divide and rule' situation. The protest was substantial, resulting in riots and demonstrations. These having no effect on the government, a campaign called *swadeshi* was organized to boycott British goods, especially textiles, and remained a favourite tactic of the nationalists from this time onwards.

World war in 1914 became as much the end of an era in India as in Europe. More than a million Indians were recruited into the imperial forces – thousands were killed on the Western Front in France by the first German advance on Ypres. The influence on Indians returning from the war is perhaps most graphically illustrated by a work of fiction, John Masters' *The Ravi Lancers*, which describes the profound disillusionment with European ideas caused by the senseless carnage of the war. The war effort seriously weakened British administration in India, and the loss of a considerable trade with Germany and of other export markets caused severe recession. Bubonic plague swept the country in 1917 and the following year came an even greater scourge – the world epidemic of influenza. It killed 12.5 million Indians.

The consequent unrest and rioting were aggravated by the extension of wartime laws to control revolution and sedition. The Congress in 1916 negotiated a remarkable accord in which Muslims and Hindus pledged themselves to support the common cause of home rule for India. The Congress, until now the compliant and willing partner of the imperial government, was henceforward to be its antagonist. Against this tumultuous background a new player would enter the stage, a figure of enormous significance not only in India, but throughout the world.

Mohandas Gandhi, a Gujerati who went to England in 1888 for an education in law, was admitted to the Bar at the Inner Temple in London three years later. Subsequently he went to South Africa and acquired an international reputation as leader of a movement which resisted discrimination against the Indian expatriate minority there. World attention was attracted

Figure 10   Most people in village Asia still shop in traditional markets like this. The hanging roots of a giant banyan tree are in the background

not so much by the cause itself as by Gandhi's novel methods of mass passive resistance. Patient and non-violent acceptance of an adverse situation had long been a tradition of Hinduism, but Gandhi, who had read Tolstoy and was impressed by him, added to it the firmness of the Russian's concept of a more militant non-co-operation with the evil and destructive. He was 45 when he returned to India in 1914 to work for the Congress, becoming its unquestioned leader in 1920.

The extension of the wartime anti-sedition laws triggered serious opposition. Gandhi rallied support against these repressive Rowlatt Acts. His intention was for a day of fasting and prayer and a business strike, but that event on 18 March 1919 led to severe rioting in Amritsar, the holy city of the Sikhs, in which five Europeans were killed and a number of buildings burned. Three weeks later a British army officer, General Reginald Dyer, issued a proclamation warning that any public assemblies in Amritsar would be fired upon.

Two factors bore on the situation. One was Dyer's order that all Indians passing through a street in which a European had been attacked should crawl, and the second, noted in the report of the later investigating commission, was that in many parts of Amritsar Dyer's proclamation had not been read. Hence a large proportion of the population was unaware of the warning.

The following day a large crowd gathered in an enclosed square called the Jallianwalla Bagh, which could be entered and left only through a few narrow gateways. Although the crowd was unarmed, and listening peace-fully to a speaker, General Dyer ordered 50 Gurkha riflemen to start firing on them. They continued until they ran out of ammunition. The people inside were unable to escape the deadly, individual marksmanship, which was so effective that of 1650 rounds fired almost all found a mark, since 379 people were killed and more than a thousand injured. Many were women and children.

The brutal overkill of the Amritsar massacre and its consequences are of immense importance, for they destroyed any remaining feelings of good-will and faith in Britain so many educated Indians had had. The world-renowned Indian author, Sir Rabindranath Tagore, renounced his knighthood. Gandhi described British rule as 'Satanic'. These reactions were due not only to the massacre but also to the fact that so many influ-ential Englishmen approved of Dyer's actions, the House of Lords support-ing a public subscription by the *Morning Post* newspaper which raised £26,000 to Dyer's benefit, some of which was spent on a sword studded with jewels. Rudyard Kipling was a subscriber. The repercussions were still considerable as late as 1997 when Queen Elizabeth, making a visit to India, was told she would not be welcome in Amritsar.

By 1920 there was open unrest in India. The Congress issued an ultima-tum: complete self-rule within a year or massive civil disobedience. When this was ignored Gandhi called for civil disobedience throughout India. Outbreaks of mob violence, notably the burning alive of 22 police in 1922 inside their station at Chauri Chaura, shocked Gandhi so much he with-drew from the campaign, retiring to a religious retreat to meditate. The rest of the decade passed without major event. One ominous tendency was the steady deterioration of relations between Hindus and Muslims, with a growing number of deaths from communal violence.

During Gandhi's absence from active politics the nationalist cause was led by a successful lawyer, Motilal Nehru, who had given up a life of wealth and privilege to follow Gandhi. Motilal Nehru died in 1931. He was succeeded as leader of the Congress by his son Jawaharlal. Born in 1889 of blue-blood Kashmiri stock, Jawaharlal Nehru had all the advantages of a privileged birth and environment. A *brahmin* by caste, he was educated at Harrow and Cambridge and was admitted to the Bar in 1912. Like his father, he renounced his career and former way of life to work for the nationalist cause but, nevertheless, remained essentially a product of Western ways of thought and an English education. Throughout a long life of immense influence he was impatient of Indian traditionalism and caste barriers. Although he fought bitterly for Indian independence, his influence on its final form was almost entirely derived from Western political traditions.

The younger Nehru and Gandhi were close friends and associates, and with the advent of Jawaharlal to major influence, Gandhi left the spinning wheel and looms of his secluded *ashram* to return to the political battle. Within a year came a further call for independence and a civil disobedience campaign. Gandhi began this with an inspired gesture – one of protest against the much-hated government tax on salt. Making and selling salt was a government monopoly, and it was illegal for anyone else to do so. In March 1930 he began a 240-mile walk to the coast. Gandhi, then aged 61, led the procession, which grew steadily in volume during the 24 days before the Arabian Sea was reached. There he scooped illicit salt from the beach. He urged Indians to make their own salt, and thousands did so illegally.

The incident was typical of Gandhi's genius, which reached the hearts and inspired the enthusiasm of the vast mass of the Indian people. The peasantry, who had formerly not been involved in the nationalist struggle had, indeed, for centuries regarded themselves as too humble to be concerned with matters of power. Gandhi fought ferociously for the poor and downtrodden, and especially championed the cause of India's millions of untouchables. This deep concern for the underprivileged permitted Gandhi to act as a bridge between the people and the intelligentsia.

The defiance of the salt tax was vigorously repressed. By May 1930, 60,000 people were in prison, including Gandhi, Nehru and most of the other Congress leaders. Not long after Gandhi was imprisoned 2500 Indians marched on the government salt factory near Mumbai, where, according to a newspaper correspondent, Webb Miller, 'scores of native policemen rained blows on their heads with steel-shod *lathis*. Not one of the marchers even raised a hand to fend off the blows. They went down like ninepins. The waiting crowd of marchers groaned and sucked in their breath in sympathetic pain at every blow. Those struck down fell sprawling, unconscious or writhing with fractured skulls or broken shoulders. The survivors, without breaking ranks, silently and doggedly marched on until struck down.' Miller reported that two men died and 320 were injured.

Incidents like this attracted attention and sympathy throughout the world for the nationalist cause. From now on Britain was never allowed to forget it. Imports of cloth from Britain were halved, and revenues from other products, like cigarettes and liquor, considerably reduced. The Indian Communist Party, formed in 1920, grew steadily, and, due largely to Nehru's influence, socialism strongly influenced the Congress. The world depression of the 1930s affected India severely as export markets dried up. Millions of Indians abandoned their land and drifted into the cities, begging on the streets for the means of bare survival. Limited provincial self-government was introduced in 1937. It resulted in the training of a pool of experienced Indian administrators that would stand the new nation in good stead after independence.

There were also special provisions designed to encourage the princes controlling the large and small states outside British India – governing a quarter of the total population – to enter an Indian Union. Bickering, self-ishness and apparent lack of wider vision made it impossible for them to avail themselves of this last chance to unite and form a significant area of power. A few years later they passed out of history largely unlamented, shorn of political power but with some even now enormously wealthy and influential within their own territories.

PART III
The Modern Nations

17 The Second World War and the End of Empire

Granted peace rather than war in 1939, the colonial era could have dragged on longer in Asia. But as it was, the next six years of conflict saw the empires crumble. Their demise after the end of the war in 1945 became only a matter of time.

Hitler's rapid advance – the *blitzkrieg* – across Europe brought two of the major colonial powers – France and Holland – to their knees. These countries faced four years of often brutal German occupation during which their ability to maintain the colonial machine became virtually non-existent. Germany dictated the terms of interim government for Asian colonial regions, and these could be no more than perfunctory in the face of the continuing conflict in Europe. For the time being the colonies became a side issue.

Almost without exception they were at this time plantation economies, closely linked to those of their colonial masters. The hugely increased workforces resulting from rapid population growth depended on these plantations of export crops for their livelihood. The war in Europe caused disruption of trade and widespread unemployment, which in time led on to almost universal hardship, often extending to actual starvation. The self-sufficiency previously conferred by traditional agriculture had meanwhile been severely curtailed.

Then there was a moral effect. To a large extent, and particularly in British India, colonial rule depended more on a qualified but none the less real respect for the master country and its officials on the spot than on actual military compulsion. After Dunkirk Britain was at bay within her own islands, France and Holland occupied. The colonial masters no longer appeared all-powerful to their subject peoples, were no longer arrayed in a mystic superiority that gave them an apparent mandate to rule. It became plain that they could be defeated, they were no more than human.

Nor had the lesson of colonial affluence been lost on the Japanese, who for a decade before the Second World War had had ambitions to acquire an empire in Asia. By 1939 Japan had conquered Korea, Taiwan, Manchuria and much of the rest of China, but that was not enough. The power vacuum in southern French Indo-China, a prolific rice producer, and the Dutch East Indies, rich in oil, offered tempting opportunities. But Japan's initial attempts to expand into these areas came under strong opposition from another major Pacific power – the United States of America.

When in 1941 Japan occupied the southern part of what had been French Indo-China, the United States retaliated by cutting off oil supplies on which Japan was almost totally dependent, and demanded that Japan withdraw from China. The Japanese rejected this last demand. With only enough oil reserves to keep her navy active for 18 months, a rapid push as far south as the Dutch East Indies oilfields became central to Japanese war planning.

By November of 1941 both sides knew that war was virtually inevitable, but the Americans had no idea how it would start and what its eventual course might be. This became obvious at dawn on 7 December, when the Japanese launched an unsuccessful attack on the American naval base in Hawaii, Pearl Harbor, with five midget submarines. Four of these were sunk by American destroyers – effectively the first action in the Pacific war. Very damaging bombing raids by more than 300 Japanese aircraft followed. Within two hours 21 warships had been sunk or severely damaged, 350 aircraft had been destroyed, mostly on the ground, and more than 4000 Americans were dead or wounded. A warning of the Japanese approach was ignored, the radar signal being attributed to friendly aircraft. The day being Sunday, most of Pearl Harbor's defences were unmanned or otherwise unready.

The Second World War had spread to the Pacific. The Japanese moved through south-east Asia with terrifying speed. Within three months they had taken the Philippines, Malaya and the Dutch East Indies, and the Pacific islands north of New Guinea. Singapore, which the British regarded as impregnable, was captured with relative ease, due mainly to a confused and inept defensive effort which culminated in the surrender of 130,000 Allied troops to a Japanese force half that size. Bad administration and inefficiency at the command level, rather than lack of courage on the part of individual units, were responsible.

The Japanese had given priority to aircraft carriers, as opposed to the battleship mentality which still dictated British and, to a considerable extent, American naval planning. Her carrier-borne force of 500 aircraft was the largest in the world. This taught another early and severe lesson when the brand-new British battleship *Prince of Wales* and the battle cruiser *Repulse*, which had sailed from Singapore without air cover, were sunk in two hours by Japanese torpedo bombers.

By 1942 the Japanese had occupied Burma, reaching Yangon in March of that year, so threatening British India. Almost half of 30,000 Allied troops were left behind dead or missing during a 600-mile retreat to the Indian border. Only the onset of torrential monsoon rains averted an invasion of India. When the Japanese again attempted to invade India in 1944 they met sharp resistance, and after 80 days of bitter fighting, were forced to withdraw. To the south-east, the occupation of most of New Guinea placed Australia at risk. The Japanese were able to exploit the invaluable resources of oil, rubber, non-ferrous minerals and food from the Dutch East Indies, and, for the time being, safely export them to the service of the Japanese war industries.

The Japanese took thousands of European prisoners of war, who were treated with the utmost brutality in camps and as forced labour on projects like the Burma–Thailand railway. One of the worst such episodes came after the fall of Bataan, in the Philippines. The American garrison were already starving and weakened, but the Japanese forced them to march 65 miles north to a prison camp. Around 30,000 Americans and Filipinos died during the last hours of the defence of Bataan or during this march. Another 22,000 died in the camp within two months. While these prisoners attracted much sympathy from the indigenous people of their former colonies, the lesson was taught again that Europeans were not superior masters, but could be reduced, even destroyed, by terrible indignities and brutality.

Initially, the Japanese positioned themselves as liberators – there was to be a new pan-Asian movement led by Japan which would eventually lead to liberation of the colonies as free peoples. At this stage the tiny Burmese independence movement was encouraged by Japan, and in the East Indies Sukarno and the other nationalist leaders were led to believe that the end of the war would bring a new independent nation, Indonesia. The Japanese organized and trained a military force that would later be the core of the army that would fight the Dutch for Indonesian independence.

However, although the Japanese had gained the empire they wanted they were not to be allowed to keep it. The staggering six million square miles they occupied had to be policed by only 11 army divisions – 25 others were kept in China to maintain Japanese ascendancy there. This involved supply lines of impractical length and demands that Japan's limited industrial capacity could not meet. American submarines took a heavy toll on Japanese shipping. By 1943 ten times as many ships were being sunk than could be replaced by new construction.

Although Australia's northern city of Darwin was bombed, the country was never invaded, largely due to tenacious resistance by Australian soldiers that stopped the Japanese tide in the jungle-clad mountains of New Guinea, and a naval battle in the Coral Sea in which the Japanese were, for the first time in the war, defeated. Cut off from their supply lines, only 13,000 Japanese soldiers in New Guinea eventually survived of 140,000 who had been sent there. The huge productive capacity of the United States was now coming into play, and in August 1942 an American attack on Guadalcanal, in the Solomon Islands, raised the curtain on a series of ferocious and bloody maritime invasions that forced the Japanese north.

The Japanese fought back with almost maniacal tenacity – their soldiers had been indoctrinated with the conviction that to surrender and be taken prisoner was a disgrace and a betrayal of the emperor. Hence they almost always fought to the last man. On the insignificant eight square miles of the island of Iwo Jima, 22,000 Japanese and 7000 Americans died during a five-week battle. The Japanese took very high casualties almost everywhere – more than a million soldiers and almost half a million navy men died during the war. On Saipan a thousand survived of 32,000, on the atoll of Tarawa in the Gilberts every one of 4800 Japanese marines was killed.

In a desperate duel between carriers near the island of Midway in 1942 fortunes swayed from side to side, suggesting a Japanese victory until, almost by chance, a small American squadron – only 37 dive-bombers – found four of the six major Japanese carriers vulnerable as they refuelled and rearmed their aircraft. All four ships were destroyed. From this time onwards the United States had naval superiority in the Pacific.

One important consequence of this was a collapse in the colonies' almost completely agrarian economies. As more and more Japanese freighters were sunk by American submarines trade between them and Japan declined, and then virtually ceased. Burma and Thailand had too much rice, but people were starving elsewhere. Almost everywhere poverty followed unemployment, but actual food shortages caused famine in many parts of island south-east Asia. Malaria, substantially under control in 1939, became epidemic almost everywhere.

As the Japanese suffered defeat after defeat their attitude towards the Asian people in the colonies they had occupied changed significantly. Now these people became subject to forced labour and the usual pattern of Japanese brutality, and as a result any sympathy they had had for the Japanese disappeared. People fled their villages into the forests to escape the general decline of law and order and mass conscription into Japanese labour gangs. Resistance movements developed almost everywhere. These guerrilla bands, which attracted the support and assistance of the Allies, generally had a Communist element, deriving from the Communist parties established during the 1920s and 1930s. One such, in French Indo-China, was the Vietminh, commanded by Ho Chi Minh, who later would lead Vietnam to independence as a Communist state. Another was the Malayan Communist movement, led by Chin Peng, who marched in the end-of-war celebrations in London, but who would later lead his guerrillas through the long Malayan insurrection known as the Emergency.

The Pacific war ended with Japan's surrender in August 1945 after the cities of Hiroshima and Nagasaki had been destroyed, at an initial cost of 170,000 lives, by the first and only use of nuclear weapons in war. But the systematic pattern of firebombing ordered by American General le May had earlier turned Tokyo and 65 other cities into deadly infernos. This carpet-bombing with incendiaries exacted an even higher cost than the nuclear attacks – 260,000 civilians were burned to death and more than two million buildings destroyed.

The occupied areas in Asia had not fared much better. Invasion and the 'scorched earth' policies of the retreating European powers destroyed much of the already inadequate infrastructure. Burma, for instance, has still not recovered from the loss of at least three-quarters of its roads, bridges and railways. But one thing not in short supply was weapons, either left behind by retreating armies or air-dropped to resistance fighters. These were to serve, in some cases, bitter civil war, in others, the establishment of independence armies.

In most of the former colonies guerrilla movements set up interim governments as the Japanese occupation ended, and looked forward confidently to the rapid evolution of independent states. The Supreme Allied Commander in south-east Asia, Lord Mountbatten, warned the French and the Dutch they could not resume colonial government on pre-war terms. However, this advice was largely ignored, leading to major hostilities in both the former colonies. The Dutch did not persist long, but the French were more stubborn, fighting the Vietminh until they incurred a crushing defeat at a complex of mountain forts at Dien Bien Phu in 1954. Day after day, transport aircraft dropped paratroopers to reinforce the doomed forts. The Communists killed most of them before they reached the ground. Using only manpower, they moved mountain guns over what seemed to be impossible terrain until the French positions were at almost point-blank range. When Dien Bien Phu was forced to surrender, 10,000 French prisoners were taken.

This, the first defeat of a European power by an Asian resistance movement, had a tremendous impact throughout the former colonies. What could be done once might be done again. But early hopes that independence might come peacefully had been shattered in 1941. A historic meeting between British Prime Minister Churchill and American President

Roosevelt produced the Atlantic Charter, which declared 'the right of all people to choose the form of government under which they will live'. But within a month, speaking in the House of Commons, Churchill declared that the charter would not apply to any of the British colonies. France and Holland continued to fight the nationalists in their former spheres of influence.

The next decade was to be one of struggle, and at the end of it virtually all of the former colonies had become independent nations.

18 The South Asian Nations: Freedom, Partition and Tragedy

The south Asian nations, with almost one and a half billion people, are rivalling China to become the largest fraction of humans on the planet. They also face greater and more fundamental problems than other parts of Asia – an uncomfortably high rate of population growth, one of the world's lowest percentages of literate people, and one of the highest incidences of fatal or disabling diseases.

Their societies all have a small number of wealthy and middle classes, contrasting with an overwhelming majority who live in crowded, substandard housing, who lack clean drinking water and sanitation, who are not fed adequately and who can call on only the most minimal medical services. One would hope for signs of an eventual improvement in all these things, and the government at least in some parts of India is making efforts in this direction. However, a visitor to the region can see scant evidence of this, probably because of the sheer magnitude of the problems. The ramshackle slums that make up most of the larger cities seem to be more crowded, more broken-down, than they were 25 years ago. The industrial growth that has fostered a small but growing and moderately prosperous middle class has been ecologically disastrous – heavy blanketing of smog from factory chimneys and increasing motor traffic, choked roads and streets, and a constant clangour of noise. The beautiful Taj Mahal in Agra, surrounded by slums and a whole landscape of bleak industrial buildings from which a hundred tall chimneys belch smoke, eloquently characterizes India's urban problems.

The countryside is little better, made up substantially of arid fields in which the productivity of the soil is declining alarmingly and villages which every year have to house more people in the same wretched conditions, to share food resources which become more and more limited. Five per cent of village dwellers own as much as 40 per cent of the available agricultural land – in Pakistan four per cent own 36 per cent of the land. This represents close on a doubling of the alienation of land to the rich since

independence. Malnutrition oppresses about a third of the Indian population; around one in eight children die before they are five, and in Pakistan
the figures are as bad or worse. A UN survey in 2003 indicated that 47 per
cent of Indian children under five are underweight.

Another common characteristic of the region is that its people are more
influenced by their religions than many other human populations. The two
main religions, Hinduism and Islam, are similar to the extent that they
substantially control the individual and social life of most people. In other
respects they are antithetic, provoking violent reactions which have already
caused millions of deaths in the region. Recent political and social developments indicate, if anything, that these religious tensions are increasing, and
that the anger and violence they prompt are growing because of the misery
and frustrations caused by the lifestyle of the great majority.

Mohammed Ali Jinnah, a Western-educated lawyer, is sometimes considered the sole architect of Pakistan, but this is not borne out by the facts. The
vision of a separate Muslim homeland in India was that of Pakistan's
honoured poet-politician Mohammed Iqbal, who was president of the
Muslim League from 1930 until 1936. In 1938 the Muslim League actively
considered various proposals for a separate state, Jinnah agreeing to lead
personally a special committee to investigate what might be gained from
partition. The investigations appear to have convinced him. 'Pakistan is
inevitable,' he said soon afterwards. Gandhi's acid comment that the idea
was absurd served only to redouble the efforts of the Muslim leaders on its
behalf.

Meanwhile, war came to Europe in 1939, and Britain had little leisure to
consider the shaping of political forces in south Asia. Nehru had foreseen
the war, and had told the 1936 meeting of the Congress that 'it becomes
necessary for the Congress to declare clearly now its opposition to India's
participation in an imperialist war'. Congress demanded immediate self-
government on a basis to be decided by a constituent assembly of Indians.
In 1942 Britain sent a Socialist member of her War Cabinet – Sir Stafford
Cripps, long known as a supporter of Indian nationalist aspirations – to
Delhi. Cripps brought with him a plan for an independent India with
Dominion status with the right to secede from the Commonwealth, to be
established immediately after the war.

Congress turned down these proposals categorically, apparently at
Gandhi's initiative. He is said to have described Cripps's proposals as 'a
blank cheque on a failing bank' and wanted all Commonwealth forces out
of India so a possible Japanese invasion could be opposed with a passive
resistance campaign. The two words 'Quit India' suddenly appeared in

white paint, scrawled on walls and hoardings. A major campaign of civil disobedience was to be used to force Britain's hand. However, the British authorities acted at once. All the Congress leaders were gaoled and remained in prison until 1945. The Congress was declared an illegal organization. The first riots and sabotage began in Mumbai and quickly spread to other parts of India. Public buildings were burned down, railway and telegraph lines damaged, and there was some sabotage of military installations. British retaliation was violent and immediate.

So rose the sudden bitterness that was to cloud the last years of British rule – a sad blot on a record that contained much of value. More than 1000 nationalists were killed, 3000 injured, and 60,000 arrested before the 'Congress rebellion' was put down. But worse was to come. The year 1943 brought fresh horrors with a catastrophic famine in Bengal, the worst since 1866. The famine, little publicized at the time because of wartime censorship and, inexplicably, still ignored or understated by many modern histories of India and most standard reference works, killed at least two and a half million people (some estimates of the ultimate toll are as high as four million). It was one of the major tragedies of the Second World War. On any estimate, its death toll was far higher than British Empire military and civilian wartime deaths, which totalled around half a million.

The 1943 famine is the subject of a book, *Jane Austen and the Black Hole of British History* (1998). Its Australian author, G. M. Polya, speaking on a radio programme early in 1999, said: 'Although there was plenty of food potentially available, the price of rice rose ... driven by a number of factors including: the cessation of imports from Japanese-occupied Burma; a dramatic wartime decline in other requisite grain imports into India, compounded by the deliberate strategic slashing of Allied Indian Ocean shipping; heavy-handed government action in seizing Bengali rice stocks in sensitive areas; the seizure of boats critically required for food acquisition and rice distribution; and finally, the "divide and rule" policy of giving the various Indian provinces control over their own food stocks. Critically, cashed-up, wartime, industrial Calcutta could pay for rice and sucked food out of a starving, food-producing countryside.'

It is well documented that the Bengali villages were deprived of food by speculators, offered a ready market by the demand for rice to feed the Indian army, now two million strong. Gandhi fasted for three weeks in sympathy with the Bengalis, but his gesture, a considerable one for an ageing man, was ignored. The legal requirement to declare a famine under the Famine Codes was also ignored, with evidence that this was done to avoid the costs of alleviating mass distress and acknowledgement of the appalling total of deaths. Rather than sending relief stocks of food into rural

Bengal, the British administration oversaw a huge net export of grains and rice. Epidemics of cholera and malaria exploded through the weakened population, with high death rates in 1944. Lord Wavell, who became Viceroy in 1943, pleaded with British Prime Minister Winston Churchill to send a million tons of grain to Bengal, but Churchill seems to have hardened his heart. 'He hates India and everything to do with it,' Wavell comments in his diaries. Eventually less than half that amount was forthcoming. Wavell's successor, the Australian R. G. Casey, organized a major programme of cholera and smallpox vaccinations.

Several of the factors mentioned above suggest a British 'scorched earth' policy designed to deny assets in Bengal to an anticipated Japanese invasion force, at a monstrous human cost. Those consequences severely indict British policy makers of the time, in particular Churchill, and the failure to investigate and acknowledge them is to the discredit of all subsequent British governments.

So great was the output of new industries in India during the war, notably that of the huge Tata steelworks, that it not only cancelled out all Indian indebtedness, but actually gave India a credit balance in London of over a £1000 million. Consequently, the end of the war saw the disappearance of any economic justification for British rule. In July 1945 the wartime government of Winston Churchill was defeated and Labour, which had been critical of the India policy for some time, embarked on the task of making India free. The Labour prime minister, Clement Attlee, intended to grant independence without reservations and was little deterred by Churchill's comment that this would involve 'the clattering down of the British Empire with all its glories'. Even so, the task proved not so simple. In India strikes and demonstrations continued well into 1946.

Amid this confusion a dominant influence was the Muslim League, driven forward by Jinnah, its leader, who insisted on a separate Muslim nation. 'We will either have a divided India or a destroyed India,' he said. 'We have forged a pistol and we are in a position to use it.' Jinnah called for a direct action day on 16 August. It was to be an ominous and tragic occasion, resulting in the death of 12,000 people, 5000 in Kolkata alone, under conditions of appalling brutality. The year 1947 arrived with India on the point of civil war. The new British prime minister, Clement Attlee, admitted that Britain could no longer control events and urged Indians to 'sink their differences'.

Partition was now accepted as inevitable. New boundaries were drawn with little chance to consider local interests and loyalties with any care. Yet the line had to be drawn, and quickly. Inevitably it split village and clan groups, cut off irrigated land from its sources of water, among a myriad of other problems. This crude surgery led to another disaster, compared with which all the communal horrors of the past four years dwindled into insignificance. India and Pakistan became independent dominions within the British Commonwealth on 14 August 1947. At once both countries faced an explosion of communal violence on an unprecedented scale. In the border regions of the Punjab, which was partitioned, millions left their homes while Hindu, Muslim and Sikh fanatics preyed on them in a night-mare of butchery and destruction. Entire families died inside their homes as hundreds of villages were burned and the chaos prevailing on both sides of the new border cloaked every kind of atrocity – some barely imaginable. Crowded trains were found stopped on the line without a soul still alive in them.

No accurate estimate has ever been possible of the toll of this terrible disaster, but as many as a million people are believed to have perished. In what was probably the largest single shift of population the world has ever seen, seven million people crossed from India into Pakistan and slightly more migrated the other way.

Consideration of these events leads to a ready understanding of the bitterness and mistrust between the neighbouring south Asian states, which has led to war on a number of occasions, a host of minor military clashes, a confrontation along one of the most heavily militarized frontiers in the world, and an immoderate spending on weapons (by both nations) – including nuclear technology – money that is urgently needed to ease the poverty and deprivation experienced by the vast majority of their people.

Following the communal tragedy in 1947, Gandhi, at the age of 78, began a fast to exact a promise from the Congress leaders that the lives and prop-erty of the 40 million Muslims remaining in India should be respected. Five days later Nehru and his colleagues gave this undertaking. It was the last triumph of the man who, though he himself disliked the title, had become universally known as the *mahatma*, the 'great soul'. On 30 January 1948, as he walked out of a house in Delhi, an assassin fired three pistol shots at Gandhi. The killer was not some Muslim fanatic, but a *brahmin* member of the Hindu extremist party, the Mahasabha. Hindu orthodoxy thus at last exacted its penalty from the man who had fought so hard to free India from its ancient hatreds, superstitions and prejudices.

India's history since independence can best be summarized – and perhaps better understood – by looking at broad trends rather than a huge mass of political detail. The early decades after independence were difficult, with India able to feed its people only by dint of huge food imports and gifts from other countries. Gandhi's influence lived on in the person of his chief disciple, Vinoba Bhave, who walked through India persuading wealthy landowners to give more than a million acres of land to the poor. Useful though this was, it could have little effect on the huge and tragic mass of poverty.

It can be argued that the initial policies of the Nehru era, which indeed linger today, were wrong to the extent that they favoured capital- rather than labour-intensive industry – steel and cement works, coalmines, rather than the urgent measures so much needed to improve the lives of what now amount to more than half a billion rural poor. Nehru was, of course, not alone in this – the same situation resulted in major tragedy in China. Nevertheless, years of firm control by the Congress Party and a doubling of food grain production due to much higher-producing varieties in the two decades from 1965, brought improved conditions in which India became a food exporter. However, more recently new 'green revolution' plant varieties have proved less useful, and this, combined with losses of soil fertility in many places from over-cropping and the relentless growth of the population, has increased problems of poverty and disease, both in the villages and the burgeoning slum areas of the big cities.

There is one notable exception, the south Indian state of Kerala which, although very poor in terms of GDP, has better social indicators than apparently wealthier states, like the Punjab, due to a more even spread of available economic assets, especially land. In 1957 Kerala became the first state in the world to elect a Communist government, and has maintained a strong left-wing influence since. It was certified by the UN as completely literate by 1991 – a rate more than double the Indian national average – has a lower population growth rate than the United States, and a child mortality rate less than half the Indian average. Its advantages appear to be due to an extraordinary rate of community activism, a strong tradition of matriarchal hierarchies and a programme of land reform. Ninety per cent of the state's 30 million people own the land on which they live, while rural holdings are limited to 25 acres a family. This ensures sufficient food cropping to maintain a better nutrition rate than the average for India. Rural India's caloric intake declined an ominous five per cent between 1972 and 1994. The only states to record an increase were Kerala and West Bengal, which also has a strong left-wing tradition of government.

Kerala's governments appear to have concentrated on measures to improve the quality of life of its people rather than 'development' – a model which the rest of India might well study with profit. An example is organization of rice farmers to lend their land between crops to unemployed men to grow a vegetable crop, which is then available on the market at low prices. Kerala has comprehensive health services, including good hospitals, and schools well above national standards. However, in 2001 the Congress-led 'right-wing' UDF Party was elected with a sufficiently large majority to govern in its own right. Since then some pressure has been evident for Kerala to become a 'market economy', and to allow multinational agribusinesses to grow plantation crops there.

By contrast, India's poorest and most lawless state is Bihar, where caste enmities seem at their worst. The wealthy high-caste landowners have private armies, which they regularly use to attack desperate or even protesting peasants. One estimate, by the Kolkata *Statesman*, places deaths as high as 40 a week. Bihar, with 90 million people, has India's highest birth rate, with a population growth of almost 30 per cent in the 1990s. Most of these are landless poor, looking for work. There are frequent claims that many of the state's parliamentarians are criminals, and that official corruption is endemic. Perhaps unsurprisingly, Bihar has its home-grown terrorists, the Naxalite Maoists, and a record of steady decay of infrastructure.

There has been growth in the Indian industrial sector, resulting in a larger – although still very small – and relatively affluent middle class, and also a strident noisiness and very evident pollution in the cities. Nevertheless, while India has 17 per cent of the world's people, her economy amounts to less than 2 per cent of world GDP and 1 per cent of world trade. Manufacture actually declined in the 1990s, more than half of GDP coming from service industries. While 'outsourcing' of work to India, especially in the computer and telephone answering areas, has been much publicized, this employed well under a million people in 2004, compared with almost 10 million a year coming on to the job market.

Communal violence has continued in India between Muslims and Hindus, regularly causing more than 100 deaths a year and almost 400 in 1980. A more recent development has been conflict between advantaged and disadvantaged caste groups, incidents over five months of 1985 resulting in the death of 275 people in Gujarat State, with less serious conflicts in most other states. This violence recurred in 1998 and 1999, and extended to attacks on Indian Christians, who make up only two per cent of the population.

However, the worst communal violence came in 2002, when a train that had just left Godhra Station in Gujarat State stopped after someone pulled the emergency cord. Fifty-nine people, mostly Hindu women and children, were killed by Muslim slum-dwellers. Over the next few weeks more than 2000 Muslims were murdered, often in the most brutal circumstances; more than 20,000 Muslim shops and homes were burned and 100,000 people fled to refugee camps. While the killings were said to be organized with 'military precision', little effort was made to bring the perpetrators to justice. Ninety per cent of Gujarat's population is Hindu.

Politically, the tendency during the closing decades of the twentieth century was for greater regionalism, lack of strong national leadership and a gradual but definite increase in influence of Hindu nationalism. Especially after the decline of the Nehru dynasty – two prime ministers of that family, Indira Gandhi (not related to the Mahatma) and her son Rajiv, were assassinated – the influence of the Congress Party dwindled. Although it served a later term of office, the tide began to run against the Congress as a result of severe repression associated with a state of emergency imposed by Indira Gandhi in 1975, during which more than 30,000 people were imprisoned without trial. This followed a year of strikes, some of which involved as many as a million workers. A campaign against the union movement was widely seen as government support for the big industrial conglomerates, like Tata and Birla, that dominate Indian commerce and industry.

Congress was defeated in elections in 1977, and India was handed over to the uncertain leadership of a loose alliance, the Janata Party. By 1980 Janata had split into irreconcilable factions, and Congress regained power in elections that year. Mrs Gandhi was to survive only four more years. Late in 1984, following a bitter and bloody religious dispute with the Sikh community, she was shot down by machine-guns in the hands of two of her guards, who were Sikhs. This led once more to communal killings, directed against the whole Sikh community, whole families burning to death inside their houses. Perhaps 10,000 Sikhs died; 50,000 more retreated into secure camps around Delhi.

Indira's son, Rajiv, an airline pilot, succeeded her. The first year of his prime ministership brought to India an appalling tragedy – the world's worst industrial accident. Forty tons of a poisonous gas, methyl isocyanate, were released from a factory in the central Indian city of Bhopal, run by a subsidiary of Union Carbide. As this gas drifted through the densely populated residential areas around the factory, as many as 8000 people were killed. It was estimated in 2000 that as many as half a million suffered some after-effect.

Rajiv Gandhi took India in new directions – an era of technocrats rather than socialists – inspired by the new world order of economic rationalism. Business did well, but once again scant attention was given to the poor. However, as time passed his administration came to be seen as too closely associated with big business, too tolerant of tax evasion and kickbacks, especially in defence contracts. Support for him waned. He came to a sudden and dramatic end when he was assassinated in 1991 by a Tamil extremist, after Rajiv intervened in the bitter civil war in Sri Lanka.

An election in 1996 was inconclusive, necessitating another – in 1998. That election brought the Hindu nationalist Bharatiya Janata Party – the BJP – to power, but did not, however, give the BJP a clear authority. The party and others likely to support it held 19 seats short of the 272 needed for an absolute majority. However, the decision of the voters in the world's largest democracy confirmed a continuing downward trend in support for Western-style politics, as evidenced by the declining vote of the Congress Party, which won only 140 seats.

Instead the people appeared to prefer a party based on the Hindu traditions and ideas of the past, with strong organization and support at the grassroots level, and with a major commitment to local industry rather than multinationals. The BJP has been criticized because of past links with communalism, a criticism which extends to its leader, Atal Behari Vajpayee. Many of its members also belong to the Rashtriya Swayamsevak Sangh (RSS), a fundamentalist Hindu youth organization founded in 1925, which has been described as a cross between the Boy Scouts and Hitler Youth, and which has been implicated in past violence against the Muslim community.

In May 1998 India heightened regional tensions with five nuclear weapons tests, including that of a fission trigger hydrogen bomb. Within days Pakistan responded with a similar test programme. Both nations indicated their possession of missile delivery systems for atomic weapons, prompting worldwide fears of a dangerous nuclear arms race. Further testing, this time of launch vehicles, occurred in 1999. India's Agni II missile has a range of more than a thousand miles.

Early in that year a parliamentary vote of no confidence in the BJP succeeded by only one vote, resulting in the necessity for India's third election in three years in September 1999, at a cost to the nation of more than $200 million. The Congress Party, led by an unlikely candidate for the Indian prime ministership, Sonia Gandhi, widow of Rajiv (who is Italian-born and Christian), had its worst result ever. The BJP also failed to win a clear majority. Its dependence on an alliance of smaller parties and strong votes for regional candidates again raised the prospect of indecisive government in India. In a 1998 book, *The Idea of India*, Sunil Khilnani says: 'the presumption that a single shared sense of India – a unified idea and concept – exists has lost all credibility . . . the new politics of India are formed on regional race and caste lines'.

It could be hoped that the movement away from the legacy of the British *raj* might in time achieve government more closely linked to the most enduring element in Indian society – the villages. However, the reality is that India is governed by an educated elite, the Indian Administrative Service, which functions very much as the colonial civil service did. Its influence for conservatism has contributed substantially to the failure of all governments since independence to improve the lives of the vast majority of Indians. Perhaps only when those hundreds of millions can effectively influence events will the much-needed improvements come. This could well be the *sarvodaya* that Gandhi pleaded for at the time of independence – an abandonment of the confrontational trappings and terminology of Western-style democracy, and the disbanding of the Congress Party to make room for a political system of consensus based on the villages.

In an unexpected result, India's poor in 2004 did indeed cast their votes in protest against their unhappy lot, decisively defeating the BJP government, and significantly increasing support for the Communists (33 seats) and other left-wing parties, and those representing regional interests and 'the lower castes'. Nevertheless, the Congress Party, with the highest vote, won only 145 seats, far from a majority in the 545-seat parliament.

Sonia Gandhi, Rajiv's Italian-born widow, resisted strong pressure to become India's prime minister, perhaps because of the memory of the assassination of her mother-in-law and of her husband Rajiv. In comments made before her husband's death she had said: 'I was angry and resentful towards a system which, as I saw it, demanded him as a sacrificial lamb. It would crush him and destroy him – of that I was absolutely certain.' Instead, former finance minister and Oxford economics graduate Dr Manmohan Singh became prime minister at the age of 72. However Rajiv's 33-year-old son Rahul, a Harvard-educated economist, was elected to the parliament. When he has gained some political experience he will come under considerable pressure to perpetuate the Nehru/Gandhi dynasty.

Governing by permission of left-wing parties and those with narrow regional interests, the Congress administration faced many difficulties. However, the president's speech to parliament in June 2004 did indicate that overall policy will move away from commercial to social goals to some extent. Spending on education was to be increased 50 per cent to 6 per cent of GDP, with similar increases for public health. Measures like the extension of programmes to provide a free cooked midday meal in schools should result in healthier children, who also have an incentive to go to school. Ambitious employment guarantee measures proposed government-financed work to one member of perhaps 50 million of the poorest families at wages which are not much more than a dollar a day, but enough to avert utter destitution. Legislation to this effect was introduced late in 2004, and was estimated to cost as much as $9 billion a year. As general policy, government undertakings which are making a profit would not be privatized.

More than 5000 Indians were drowned when the 2004 tsunami struck the south-east, with major destruction of infrastructure along the coastal fringe. However, the Indian government shouldered the burden of reconstruction, as well as extending assistance to neighbouring Sri Lanka, which was much more severely affected.

19 Pakistan, Bangladesh and Afghanistan

While Pakistan is generally considered part of south Asia, geographically and culturally it is a borderland between the Middle East and Asia. It shares a frontier with Iran and the official language, Urdu, is closely related to Arabic and Persian. Pakistan has close ties with the oil-rich Middle East states, especially Iran, which provides economic assistance. However, the most important link is Islam. The large majority of Pakistanis are Muslims, and the country is an Islamic state. This means that the teachings of the Koran, including religious law, deeply influence all aspects of life.

Pakistan has remained poor and backward throughout its half century of existence, with some three-quarters of its people subsistence farmers, and at least the same proportion illiterate. The correspondence between these two figures is not a coincidence, since education is expensive and not compulsory. Most rural families need their children to work at home or in the fields and cannot spare them the time to go to school. There is a small but dominant privileged class, closely connected with business, administration and the armed services.

Many more boys than girls are in school, because it is widely considered that since women will go straight from virtual seclusion in their parents' home to the same condition in their husband's, there is no point in educating them. From an early age boys and girls are segregated. There is strict observance of the Muslim instruction that women should avoid being seen by men outside their own family. For this reason they must wear heavy clothing – the *burqa* – that covers the whole body except the face, whenever they appear in public. Most women emerge from their homes rarely, and there is strong orthodox religious feeling that they should not be trained in the arts and professions. Marriages are arranged, and the future husband and wife are not permitted to meet alone until after their wedding, although the *qazi*, the Muslim priest officiating at the wedding, is required to obtain the bride's consent at a private meeting with her.

In 1947 Pakistan consisted of two areas of territory separated by almost a thousand miles of India: the present-day Pakistan, and the preponderantly Muslim section of Bengal which is now Bangladesh. This curiously divided nation faced immediate problems. Because previous administration had been based on Delhi, there were no organized transport or communications services. Matters were not improved by the death from tuberculosis of Jinnah only a year after independence. In 1951 the prime minister, Liaquat Ali Khan, was assassinated before the basic principles of a constitution for the new nation could be established. An attempt at parliamentary democracy failed in conditions of growing political instability, and the army leader, General Ayub Khan, took over in 1958 after a military coup. He continued as president with wide powers for the next eleven years.

Hostilities with India over the state of Kashmir have been sporadic but regular, with armed clashes in 1948, 1965, 1971 and 1999. Kashmir became a part of India because it had an Indian raja, although most of the people are Muslim. Kashmir, effectively divided into two zones occupied respectively by Indian and Pakistani armed forces, remains an intractable problem, although actual shooting ended with a ceasefire late in 2003.

A short and hesitant renewal of parliamentary democracy ended with another military coup when General Zia ul-Haq imposed martial law in 1977. A devout Muslim, Zia committed Pakistan to a decade of authoritarian government that permitted little dissent or independent political activity. Zia arrested and, after a mock trial, hanged the former prime minister, Zulfika Ali Bhutto. Bhutto's family, including his daughter Benazir, were also arrested. She was later exiled. Initially the Western powers condemned Zia's coup, but outside events were soon to change this. This was the era of the Cold War, during which the United States and the Soviet Union sought every opportunity to gain an advantage. Russia invaded Afghanistan in 1979, the first step in a decade of war in which the Soviets and the United States supported opposing sides. The United States saw the conflict as a means of weakening the Soviets, which indeed it ultimately did. Like America, but basically to support his co-religionists, Zia backed the fundamentalist Islamic mujahidin, and so became respectable as a leading Asian anti-Communist. American support largely kept Zia in power until his death in an air crash in 1988.

Meanwhile, in 1986 Benazir Bhutto had returned to Pakistan and quickly gained public support. Immensely popular, she campaigned successfully in democratic elections and was elected prime minister. Oxford-educated, Benazir Bhutto is nevertheless a member of Pakistan's small privileged class, and a woman, in a country traditionally opposed to any exercise of power by women. She faced an almost impossible task to reform Pakistan's laws and society. Indeed it proved to be impossible, and the country drifted into a renewed phase of political and economic anarchy, directed by and to the benefit of influential groups of 'businessmen', who have not hesitated to intimidate and murder those who oppose them.

Attitudes towards women in Pakistan are as repressive as anywhere in the world. In 1999 Benazir Bhutto was sentenced to five years in prison on corruption charges which she insists are false and politically motivated. These convictions were, however, set aside by the Pakistani Supreme Court in 2001. Young women who have married without their father's consent, or who are otherwise seen as compromising family 'honour', are regularly murdered, often after torture. These killings are rarely investigated, and the killers even more rarely brought to justice. There were almost 500 such cases reported in 2002, but many more are believed to have occurred, but were not reported for fear of reprisals.

In 1999 a further military coup again ended the disorderly farce which parliamentary democracy had become. General Pervez Musharraf became the new strong man, and after an initial phase of international disapproval, like Zia two decades before him, achieved respectability for much the same reasons. He became an ally in the American 'war against terrorism' in Afghanistan, although a Gallup poll in 2002 indicated that only five per cent of Pakistanis approved of the US attack on the Taliban. America has provided massive economic and military aid to Pakistan, allowing Musharraf and the army to maintain control of the country.

Musharraf has nevertheless governed Pakistan more reasonably than its previous military dictators, and has taken at least initial steps to reform the economy, reduce corruption and moderate religious extremism. In 2002 a referendum to extend his term as president for a further five years attracted a 97 per cent 'yes' vote, although there were some objections to the way the ballot was conducted. Elections later that year for a new parliament were less in Musharraf's favour. His party failed to win a majority of seats even though the conduct of the poll was again questioned. Some leading politicians, including Benazir Bhutto, were forbidden to nominate. Anti-government rhetoric and violence has continued in Pakistan. Musharraf narrowly escaped death during two bombing incidents directed against him late in 2003.

Pakistan has intruded substantially in the affairs of its northern neighbour, Afghanistan, helping to arm and organize the fundamentalist Muslim organization, the Taliban. The young zealots of the Taliban were mostly trained in the *madrassas* (Muslim schools) in Pakistan. As the Taliban consolidated its hold, there were increasing signs of its extended influence in Pakistan, especially in the northern border areas. Pakistan's uneasy alliance with the United States came into further question when it was revealed in 2004 that the country's leading nuclear scientist, Abdul Qadeer Khan, responsible for the development of Pakistan's atomic arsenal, had passed on advanced nuclear technology to nations America regards as potential enemies – Iran, Libya and North Korea. President Musharraf pardoned Khan for these offences.

Bangladesh was born out of war. The Bengalis of East Pakistan found they had little in common with the far-off western wing of the country and, with Indian support, fought successfully for independence in 1971. With 150 million people, Bangladesh is one of the most heavily populated regions on earth. Located on the flat flood-prone delta of the Ganges River, much of its land is only a few feet above sea level, and subject to regular flooding as the Ganges, Brahmaputra and Meghna rivers are swollen by the melting snows in their headwaters. Flooding in Bangladesh has taken millions of lives. Late in 1970 a cyclone and tidal waves killed half a million people – the world's costliest natural disaster in recent times. A similar disaster four years later inundated almost half of the country, leaving millions of homeless and hungry people. Confined in camps outside the capital, Dhaka, they began dying in thousands. A virtual civil war ensued between these desperate, starving people and the police. Sections of the army turned against Sheik Mujid Rahman, the prime minister, who only three years before had been fêted as the nation's independence leader. In August 1975, he and several of his immediate family were murdered by elements of the army. Government by several military regimes has followed, with intermittent attempts at parliamentary democracy.

Flooding of record proportions, covering more than two-thirds of the country, drew world attention to the plight of Bangladesh again in 1988, in 1998 and 2004. The fact that flooding in Bangladesh continues, and even becomes worse as the decades pass, is a reproach to the world. The problem has been studied and it is known that the floodwaters could be controlled by reafforestation of the upper reaches of the major rivers, and by a series of dams and hydro-electric schemes, which would incidentally provide cheap power to the entire subcontinent. Such a development would save millions of lives, and improve the lives of tens of millions more. Its high cost, in the billions of dollars, is nevertheless only a small fraction of what the world spends annually on weapons of war. Bangladesh would be severely affected by even small rises in sea level as a result of global warming.

Other problems have emerged over the years. After Bangladesh became independent massive aid programmes were provided to deal with the almost universal incidence of waterborne disease. More than three million deep tubewells were bored. The water from these was for some years considered safe, but during the 1990s a further grave problem emerged – contamination of tubewell water with arsenic, causing skin keratosis, cancer and eventually death. The dimensions of this problem continued to increase into the new millennium, with no adequate solution by 2004.

Village life – that of 80 per cent of the people – is primitive and hard, with as many as a dozen people living in single-roomed mud houses with walls and a roof, but lacking other amenities. Life is a desperate battle to grow enough food and gain small amounts of money by labouring in export agriculture industries growing jute, sugar and tea. Most children must work at least five hours a day from the age of six or seven. There is little time, and few facilities, for schooling, hence the literacy rate is barely 20 per cent. As in Pakistan, girls are especially disadvantaged, for much the same reasons.

Even to refer to Afghanistan as a country and Afghans as a people is substantially illusory, since this is an area of many different tribal loyalties, many different languages and little common ground other than that of religion. Even this last is influenced by a division of the population between the major sects of Islam, there being a large Sunni majority and a significant Shia minority.

This territory on the roof of the world has for many centuries been a crossroads, through which a motley and diverse series of invaders has passed. Each has left its own distinctive imprint. Geography created this situation. Afghanistan is the natural invasion route to the rich north Indian plain, and it has been used this way for at least 3000 years. Persians, Greeks, Parthians and Turks, among others, have from time to time occupied parts of the present Afghanistan, usually only for relatively short periods of time. With them came their religions.

Afghanistan is a Muslim country now, but the huge Buddha statues on the cliffs overlooking the beautiful and fertile Bamiyan Valley, destroyed in 2001 when they were blown up by the Taliban, were carved in the third and fourth centuries during the expansion of Buddhism that reached as far east as Japan. Greek, Roman and Indian influences have all contributed to the culture of the Peshawar Valley in the south. In 1978, near the oasis town of Sheberghan in the northern region, Soviet archaeologists discovered, catalogued and put into safe storage more than 20,000 gold coins, ornaments and other objects. This region was once known as Bactria, where a Greek society existed for more than a century after the death of Alexander the Great in 323 BCE. This discovery, known as 'the Bactrian gold', shows a remarkable diversity of cultures ranging from Greek and Roman to

Siberian Altai. In spite of Afghanistan's turbulent recent history, it has apparently survived intact in a Kabul bank vault.

Persia – modern Iran – has left its mark on Afghanistan more than any other place. Persian is still the language of culture, and to some extent a unifying influence among at least 30 dialects and languages used by tribal groups. There are about 20 distinct ethnic groups, who claim origins from such disparate sources as Alexander the Great's Greek soldiers, Arabia, Mongolia and Turkey. To add to this confusion, Afghanistan's borders do not include all the people of these diverse tribal groups. Many of them live on both sides of the borders with the former Soviet states to the north. The Durand Line, the border imposed by the British *raj* between India and Afghanistan, is artificial, dividing the Pashtuns – once known as Pathans – almost equally between Afghanistan and Pakistan.

Nineteenth-century history repeated these earlier themes. As Britain tightened its hold on India, Afghanistan became a pawn in what Kipling called 'the great game' – intense rivalry for influence between Russia and Britain. The nineteenth century saw several Afghan wars, and battles against the fierce Pathans and the dangers of the Khyber Pass became standard themes in British fiction – especially books for boys. This was the place where the stiff upper lip was eulogized, and death in the service of the empire depicted as 'the greatest adventure'. However, these north-west frontier wars, in retrospect, achieved very little.

Afghanistan is essentially divided by the 7000-metre foothills of the Himalayas known as the Hindu Kush range. South of these mountains the land is mainly desert, to the north lies the great central Asian plain. The scarce areas of fertile land are mainly in the river valleys. Wheat and barley are the main crops supporting a subsistence agriculture.

During the first half of the twentieth century a very small Western-educated elite in the capital, Kabul, provided some appearance of modernity. However, little changed in the tribal areas, other than the evolution of a ferocious opposition to Western ways and values, which were and still are seen as decadent and anti-Islam. These tensions resulted in a series of mini-coups as the Pashtun majority struggled to maintain a hold on what passed for government – basically a military autocracy with little authority outside Kabul. This situation lasted until after the Second World War, when rivalry between the Soviet Union and the United States brought outright civil war and great hardship to Afghanistan. From 1955 onwards Russia made large money grants to Kabul, and by 1978 there were 2000 Soviet advisers in the country.

In the last days of 1979 Russia invaded Afghanistan, ostensibly to support an unpopular left-wing government. However, the real reasons were probably general Cold War paranoia and a desire to hedge a very considerable Soviet investment. Russia lost the war, which dragged on for ten years. As other invaders had done, it found the tribes difficult adversaries. This opposition came to be known as the *mujahidin* – the word means 'fighters for God'. However, this guerrilla movement should not be seen as monolithic – indeed its main problem was lack of unity. While attempts were made to organize it into seven factions, even these had numerous splinter groups within them. A major point of interest about the *mujahidin* was its recruitment of fighters from other Islamic countries, as far away as the southern Philippines and Indonesia, and insistence by the guerrilla groups that the war against Russia was a holy war in defence of the faith – a *jihad*.

The *mujahidin* was substantially but covertly provided with more than a billion dollars' worth of arms by the United States Central Intelligence Agency, pipelined via Egypt and Pakistan, in the Cold War interest of weakening the Soviet Union. Saudi Arabia contributed almost as much including the services of a young man called Osama bin Laden, who entered the ranks of the *mujahidin*. Much of this weaponry was sold off in village markets, creating a situation in which almost every man in the country possessed – and still possesses – an assault rifle. This war cost at least 200,000 Afghan lives. Five million people fled into exile, mostly in neighbouring Pakistan. The Russians, who had more than 100,000 soldiers engaged, lost 25,000.

The apparent victors – the *mujahidin* – reverted to banditry and fighting among themselves as soon as the Russians left. The 'moderate' Islamic regime in Kabul, itself riven by factionalism, proved inadequate. Conflict between the warlords from 1992 onwards led to widespread destruction of houses and public buildings in Kabul and the death of 50,000 people. Conditions in the shattered country, in which thousands were dying from starvation and cold in savage winters, and continued fighting between rival tribal groups, doomed the government from the start.

Out of this chaos came the Taliban, by processes that are far from clear. The Taliban, an extremist Islamic organization, appears to have emerged from the fundamentalist schools – the *madrassas* – in the refugee camps in northern Pakistan. Small in numbers at first, it gained recruits rapidly, finally coalescing as a major military and political force under the leadership of Mullah Mohammed Omar, a shadowy and mysterious figure whose title is Leader of the Faithful. When by 1996 it had control of the majority of the country, including Kabul, the Taliban attracted international disapproval, especially because of its rigid Islamic view that women should not work and should not be educated. It also commenced an intense campaign against Western ideas and values. However, the Taliban was able to bring a measure of peace and order to the areas it controlled, and introduced a ban on the opium industry, which had previously been a major supplier of illegal narcotics to the Western world.

When, on 11 September 2001, the World Trade Center towers in New York were destroyed, the Taliban became the first target in the United States' 'war against terror', although those who perpetrated the outrage were largely Saudi Arabian. The USA pursued the war by bombing from the air on a massive scale. Incendiary weapons and cluster bombs took a toll on the villages and people. Perhaps 5000 civilians were killed – on some estimates as many as 10,000. The Taliban fought some battles on the ground, but the majority appear to have simply melted away to regroup across the border in the quasi-independent Pashtun regions of Pakistan.

There was no clear-cut victory for either side. An American-sponsored and supported government in Kabul has gained little influence outside the capital, the rest of the country being controlled by warlords and 'bandits', in some cases regrouping Taliban. Opium is again grown and exported on a massive scale, causing the UN Office on Drugs and Crime to warn in a 2004 report that the nation was in danger of degenerating into a 'narco-state'. Poppy fields increased by 64 per cent in that year, and now produce 87 per cent of the world's opium. Even more troubling statistics show that much more of Afghanistan's opium is being processed locally into heroin. Ten thousand tons of chemicals are being imported a year to process three-quarters of the opium crop into heroin. According to the report, 'opium is the main engine for economic growth'.

Money from the international community needed to restore the shattered economy and infrastructure has been well short of what had been promised, and has proved inadequate. Prime Minister Hakim Karzai, after a year in office, pleaded with the international community for continued financial and technical assistance, especially to create a national army. Meanwhile a NATO-led coalition of 6500 troops from 35 nations, responsible for security since 2003, has attempted without much success to stabilize the country. While conditions have returned to normal to some extent in Kabul, the rest of the country is run by competing warlords. The south, bordering Pakistan, is particularly dangerous. Much of this area is poor, due to a chronic shortage of water. Military operations against 'bandits' and suspected Taliban, usually air strikes, continue to involve many deaths of innocent civilians. In one of the worst such cases late in 2003 two American air strikes killed 14 children. By 2004 insurgency in much of the south of the country was spreading north, with the motivators probably a mixture of *mujahidin* and regrouping Taliban.

In January 2004 the *loya jirga*, the political assembly to set in motion processes for Afghanistan's new constitution, renamed the country the Islamic Republic of Afghanistan. The new constitution provides for a president with executive powers, two vice-presidents and two legislative bodies. However, they may pass no laws contrary to the beliefs and practice of Islam. Of the 500 delegates at this meeting, only a fifth were women, and the majority of men represented regional and tribal power interests. The *Economist* commented (20 December 2003), 'If anything, the *loya jirga* confirmed one truth: Afghanistan will be rebuilt only with the acquiescence of warlords and drug pushers.'

Much Western feeling against the Taliban was due to harsh restrictions on the freedom of women. However, by 2004 the Taliban Ministry for the Promotion of Virtue and the Prevention of Vice had reappeared in the form of the Ministry of Haj and Religious Affairs, whose officers police 'un-Islamic' behaviour by Afghan women. Laws passed in 2003 banned co-educational classes in schools, prevented married women – who can be as young as nine – from attending school, and restricted women's freedom to travel out of their homes if not accompanied by a related male. Wearing all-covering clothing – the *burqa* – in public became mandatory at risk of severe penalty.

20 China: Two Revolutions

In 1896 there was a curious happening in England. A 30-year-old Chinese doctor, who had graduated only two years before from the medical school in Hong Kong, was kidnapped from a London street and secretly imprisoned inside the Chinese Legation. He was held there for 13 days, but before he could be spirited away to China for execution a warning note was smuggled to an English friend, and he was released by the British police.

The prisoner, on whose head the Manchu officials of the Chinese court had placed a price of £100,000, was Sun Zhongshan (Sun Yat-sen). An exile, a Christian, Western-educated, he was typical of the new class of Chinese looking for reform. The kidnapping episode did not deter him. In 1905 Sun formed in Tokyo a half secret society, half political party, which would develop in 1912 into the Kuomintang (Nationalist) Party, generally identified as the KMT.

In 1911 a plot against the government by officers of the military garrison at Wuchang, on the Yangzi River in Central China, was prematurely discovered. But the revolt was nevertheless successful and as the news of it spread more and more cities, especially in the south, declared against the Manchus. Sun, who was fundraising in the United States, returned to China as quickly as possible and in the first days of 1912 took the oath as president of a provisional republic. The following month an imperial edict announced the abdication of the emperor following pressure from the army commander, Yuan Shikai.

Sun held his office for only 44 days. In order to maintain the republic, he was obliged to hand over the presidency to Yuan Shikai, who had the confidence of the foreign powers and the substantial backing of the army. However, in 1914 Yuan, a man very much in the warlord tradition, disbanded the provisional government and declared the KMT illegal. His assumption of personal rule followed the classic pattern in which new Chinese dynasties have begun – even more so when Yuan announced he proposed to declare himself the new emperor. However, his imperial ambitions were forestalled by his death, apparently from natural causes, in 1916.

Virtual anarchy followed as the warlords – many of whom had been

Yuan's officers – and the KMT struggled for power. The infant Manchu emperor Puyi was suddenly restored, and as quickly deposed again. Sun renewed the declaration of the republic in 1917, but it controlled only a small part of south China when he died in 1925 of liver cancer. The warlords were generally cruel and rapacious. Their depredations were especially damaging to the Chinese peasantry, who were taxed into almost universal poverty and starvation. One important consequence was a meeting of twelve Marxists who, inspired by the Russian revolution, formed the Chinese Communist Party in 1921. They included a young man called Mao Zedong.

Jiang Jieshi (Chiang Kai-shek) became the next leader of the KMT with the support of the army, and, for the time being, the Communists. In 1926 he led the KMT army out of Guangzhou on the Northern Expedition, which was to unify China within two years and make the republic a reality. Jiang's task was to coerce or persuade the regional warlords into accepting KMT government. Some of these men controlled whole provinces, others little more than circles of ricefield bounded by the horizon as seen from the drum tower of a central walled city.

Jiang's Northern Expedition succeeded largely because the KMT army had a sense of discipline unusual in China at that time. But a breach with the Communists was not far off. Jiang was suspicious of them, and strong pressures were brought to bear on him – including a reputed payment of £3 million by Chinese and foreign interests – to break with those he came to be persuaded were dangerous revolutionaries. Jiang, after making a triumphant entry into Shanghai in 1927, suddenly attacked the Communists, who had assisted the capture of the city by paralysing it with a strike. Hundreds of Communists were killed in Shanghai, and the purge was extended to other areas. From Shanghai the Nationalists moved on from success to success, establishing their capital in Nanjing.

However, the Communist Party had not been destroyed. The more important leaders escaped, including Mao Zedong, a quiet, tall man of peasant antecedents from Henan Province. Mao had been trying to convince the other leaders that although classic Marxism, the revolt of an urban group, had succeeded in Russia, it was not appropriate in China. Mao's position in history depends considerably on his realization that China's essential problem was a rural one, that only a revolt based on the peasants could succeed. It is a curious irony that Jiang's purge of the Communists in 1927 brought Mao's ideas to the forefront. By eliminating so many orthodox Marxists, it diverted the Communist Party to a more realistic course that would deliver it government of China only two decades later.

Jiang was to find that he had no sooner resolved matters in the north than his old enemies, the Communists, had regrouped in the south. Mao and his ragged army killed landlords and redistributed their holdings to the peasants. Because of the extreme poverty of the peasants such methods quickly gained support and recruits. Mao, a military planner of ability and imagination, established a fundamental principle of Asian Communism with his insistence on guerrilla warfare, defined in his maxim: 'When the enemy advances, we retreat; when he retreats, we pursue; when he is tired, we attack.' However, in 1934 the Red Army allowed itself to be trapped into a disastrous 'set piece' battle in an 'encirclement campaign' by three-quarters of a million Nationalist troops. Towards the end of the year, when it had been reduced to half its former strength, the survivors slipped through the surrounding Nationalist blockade under cover of night.

So began the legendary Long March. The Communists' objective – more than 1000 miles away – was Yanan in a remote part of Shaanxi Province in the north-west. Here there was already a substantial Communist presence, and Mao planned to join forces with it. But since strong Nationalist forces stood between them and this possible refuge the Communists were forced to march around the borders of China for almost 6000 miles. The Long March took an appalling toll – of more than 100,000 people who set out, barely 15,000 reached Shaanxi. Almost every family, including Mao's, lost some members, for wives and children accompanied the men. The journey took 368 days, during which the Communists fought 15 major battles and 300 skirmishes. This epic of suffering and endurance has become Communist China's most important body of legend, well known to every schoolchild.

The years in Yanan saw a phase of experiment that set most of the patterns the new Communist government would use later throughout China. Membership of the Communist Party grew from 40,000 in 1937 to 1.2 million in 1945. The problem of land reform was tackled seriously, if, in the end, brutally. The party was carefully organized into a pervasive network of authority, leading and guiding even at the village level. Under Mao's control the Communist Party became a consistent, carefully woven thread in the fabric of Chinese society. It owes much of its present authority to the fact that it remains so today.

By the late 1920s China was in a parlous economic state, so much so that the 300,000 Westerners running industries there based on cheap labour were beginning to lose interest. Her foreign debt by 1924 was almost $800 million – a sum she had little hope of ever repaying. Meanwhile Japan had seen colonial opportunities in the divided China. She occupied Manchuria in 1931 and set up there a puppet state named Manchukuo, over which she recalled to the throne the deposed Manchu emperor, Puyi, much later to end his life as a humble gardener in Beijing.

Open fighting began between China and Japan near Beijing in 1937. The tide of invasion swept across China, marked by a series of brutal atrocities against civilians by the Japanese. The Communists did not escape these. They attempted an offensive against the Japanese in 1940, which led to severe reprisals – Japanese orders to its troops were to 'kill all, burn all, destroy all'. This became the fate of entire villages. Some who tried to escape this fury by digging underground refuges were killed when the Japanese pumped poison gas into these tunnels. The Communist Eighth Route Army was reduced by 100,000 killed, wounded or deserted; the population under their control halved to 20 million.

The Nationalists fared little better, and the Chinese people suffered yet again, with millions of deaths from drought and flooding. When in 1938 the Nationalists breached the dykes of the Yellow River in a useless attempt to stem the Japanese advance several hundred thousand peasants were drowned. The KMT eventually lost all of the coast and were forced back to Chongqing, west of the Yangzi gorges in the fertile and readily defended basin of Sichuan Province. Here they remained throughout the Second World War. Constantly bombed by Japanese aircraft, Chongqing's population was to inflate from 200,000 to over a million.

Jiang had done little to remedy China's poverty and despair. John Gunther's contemporary book *Inside Asia* (1936) claimed: 'About a million people die of starvation in China every year. In 1935, a normal year, 29,000 bodies were picked up off the streets of Shanghai alone, of men, women and children, dead of hunger. Many were female infants, left by their parents to starve.' Other accounts tell of seeing from the trains, running on lines elevated above the flooded surrounding country, people clinging in trees until they fell into the water, exhausted, and drowned. No attempt was made to save or help them. People trapped in flooded rivers were likewise left to drown, since it was traditionally believed unlucky to deprive the river gods of their prey.

Unfortunately, adversity did not improve the KMT government. It relied increasingly on terror and autocracy and its secret police came to be hated and feared. Men were conscripted to Jiang's armies who were so weak from malnutrition they could hardly walk. During the war over a million died before they could even reach the battlefields. Money and power was concentrated almost entirely in the hands of four families. One was Jiang's and another was his wife's. The ten years of Nationalist government were, on the whole, disastrous. The world depression and the huge costs of war, first with the Communists, then with the Japanese, made any general economic improvement impossible. Jiang Jieshi reinstituted Confucian values and while some economic gains were made, albeit from a very small base, these benefited only a handful of Chinese and foreign capitalists and did nothing to improve the poverty and despair of the vast majority of Chinese. More than $4 billion dollars in United States aid flooded in after Pearl Harbor, but this was largely swallowed up by corruption and maintenance of a huge inefficient army of five million.

The Communists awaited events in the north, in rugged country too remote and poor to interest the Japanese. However, despite difficulties they were able to replace the KMT as *de facto* rulers of much of north China, regions inhabited by 95 million people. They were also eventually able to fight back against the Japanese successfully, recapturing more than two-thirds of the Japanese-occupied regions by early 1945. By this time the Communist armies had grown to almost half a million men.

When Japan was defeated in that year Jiang emerged from his battered refuge in Chongqing nominally ruler of all China. However, his plans for a major campaign against the Communists were thwarted by the battle-hardened and expanding Communist armies, and the degree of support they had among the people because they had confronted the hated Japanese. Now more confident of his authority in north China, Mao took a more extreme line, confiscating property owned by landlords and rich peasants – these two classes now became automatically proscribed, no longer 'people'. The people in hundreds of villages met to indict the wealthy, and landlords were frequently beaten, tortured or killed by angry mobs.

The Communists continued to gain popularity because of harsh and inept rule by the KMT Nationalists in Manchuria after the Japanese had left, and their membership grew rapidly. They reacted promptly to an outbreak of bubonic plague in the city of Harbin, introducing immediate vaccination and quarantine measures. This plague, which killed 30,000 people, was caused by the deliberate release by the Japanese at the end of the war of rats they had infected with plague in biological warfare experiments. The nature of these did not become fully public until a suit was filed in the Tokyo District Court in 2000 by 180 survivors of Japanese atrocities. Unit 731, the biological weapons centre in Ping Fang, near Harbin, is estimated to have killed perhaps 300,000 Chinese in experiments between 1939 and 1945, during which it mass-produced bubonic plague, cholera, typhoid and anthrax organisms.

The Western powers and the Russians were anxious to see a peaceful settlement in China, but these efforts proved fruitless. In the spring of 1947 the war began in earnest. Jiang lost heavily in decisive battles in Manchuria in 1948 – more than half a million Nationalist troops surrendered, deserted, or were killed, handing over vast quantities of United States-supplied weapons to the Red Army. Barely 20,000 escaped.

Simultaneously the Communists thrust south and by February 1949 had assembled a huge army on the north bank of the Yangzi River, poised to invade China's heartland. In April nearly a million Communist soldiers crossed the river on a 300-mile front centred on Nanjing. The fall of the traditional Nationalist capital brought any organized opposition to an end. By autumn Jiang, with the remnants of his armies, had retreated to the island of Taiwan, where he was protected by United States naval forces.

Mao said, 'China will no longer be a nation subject to insult and humiliation. We have stood up.' But to the Western world, especially to the United States, the advent of a Communist government in the world's most populous state seemed a disaster. One reaction was the indefinite extension of the protecting hand America held over Taiwan; another, the virtual diplomatic isolation of the People's Republic from the Western nations.

21 Modern China: the Communist State

The Communist victory saw the world's most populous nation at one of the lowest points in its long history. The currency was worthless, the great mass of the people illiterate, only a shadow of internal organization remained, the exhausted soil was eroded and treeless, and everywhere profound social, medical and economic problems clamoured for solution.

The decades of struggle had hardened the new government to the pitch of discipline and ruthlessness necessary to attack these things. The Party's executive arm is its elite corps of full-time executives, the cadres, the effective successors of the mandarinate. Many of them are descendants of former scholar-officials, who were substantially the only group sufficiently educated for the tasks of government.

Indeed, after a phase of 're-education', the bulk of the intelligentsia and former 'upper classes' seem to have been able to accommodate themselves to life under Communism. Not all, however, were permitted to adapt so readily. Edgar Snow, in *The Other Side of the River* (1962), says that Zhou Enlai, himself of mandarin origins, had stated that 830,000 'enemies of the people' had been destroyed up to 1954. The KMT Nationalists put the figure at nine million dead. The draconic removal of these classes from their traditional influence and landownership permitted redistribution of their property among the landless. As early as 1952 almost half of China's cultivated land had been distributed to 300 million peasants.

Industry and business fared no better than the landlords. Banks and other major businesses were expropriated to the state, foreigners expelled and their property confiscated. Major penal sanctions, including the death penalty, were instituted to control criminal gangs and opium use. A new marriage law abolished polygamy, child marriage and the authority of families over women, and gave women the right to divorce. All this ran parallel with campaigns to raise the standards of health, education and overall prosperity and to create at least the beginnings of the industrialization the Communists saw as essential. Russian experts went to China to advise on the evolution of an industrial base that would provide the essential tools of a modern nation – good communications, cheap and plentiful hydro-electric power, and heavy industry, especially steel mills.

One of the most challenging tasks was to tame the Yellow River, long described as 'China's Sorrow' because of the flooding and drowning of millions of people when it regularly broke its levees. In 1954 the Yellow River Planning Commission began building 46 dams along the 2000-mile course of the river, a task undertaken, in a phrase popular in the Western media, by 'blue ants' – millions of blue-clad coolies using picks, shovels and wicker carrying baskets. A major afforestation scheme was started in north-west China to provide belts of trees that would hold back the sand and dust brought in by storms from the Gobi and permit the reclaiming of huge regions of semi-desert. This planting of tens of millions of trees was a remarkable achievement in world terms, and has created a 20 per cent forest cover again in a country that had been almost denuded of trees for fuel only 50 years ago. In 2002 China announced a $12 billion project to plant 440,000 square kilometres of forest – an area bigger than Germany – over the next ten years. The government requires every Chinese between 11 and 60 to plant three trees a year. In one year (1994) it is claimed that 490 million people planted 2.52 billion trees.

Mass immunizations were undertaken to control China's traditional scourges – smallpox, cholera, plague, typhoid and typhus. Leprosy and malaria control programmes were instituted where necessary. Since it was not possible to train fully qualified doctors quickly enough, a large corps of 'middle' doctors and nurses was organized into travelling teams to complete immunizing programmes as quickly as possible. These people later became known as 'barefoot doctors', although all I have seen were most correctly garbed, including shoes.

China was back at war again only five years after the successful Communist revolution. When the Second World War ended, the Soviet Union occupied the north of Korea. The Communist state established there launched a major attack on South Korea in June 1950. A United Nations force arrived just in time to save the south, driving the North Koreans back over the *de facto* frontier, the 38th parallel of latitude. The war was then continued into North Korean territory, although the Chinese had warned they would not accept this. A week later China launched a major offensive that drove the United Nations forces south of the parallel again. As more troops became involved – mostly Americans – the line was eventually stabilized at the parallel. Three million Koreans had been killed – about ten per cent of the population – and the infrastructure seriously damaged in both zones. Negotiations to end this futile and costly stalemate began in

July 1951, but Korea remains divided and the two halves of the country still face each other over one of the world's most heavily militarized frontiers.

There were other important consequences of the Korean War. One was a policy of neutralism adopted by governments representing three-quarters of the Asian peoples – the five principles of peaceful co-existence. A second was continued United States policy to support and guarantee the continued existence of a separate Chinese state in Taiwan. It is an intriguing possibility that another took place thousands of miles away on China's western borders when on the same day (7 October 1950) that the United Nations authorized its forces to cross the 38th parallel, the Chinese despatched a small army to occupy Tibet. The population then was about one and a half million, of whom perhaps ten per cent were Buddhist monks occupying some 3000 monasteries, the largest of which housed thousands of monks.

From the seventeenth century Tibet had been ruled by a line of Dalai Lamas, priest-kings perpetuated not by family succession but mysteriously 'discovered' as infants believed to be reincarnations of a previous incumbent. In fact the line was firmly established by a Chinese army which carried the seventh Dalai Lama to the capital, Lhasa, with much pomp and ceremony in 1720. The Dalai Lama governed from his remote capital with the assistance of a clique of Buddhist priests and officials, and a feudal class of nobles. Tibet, which had been virtually isolated from the world, was extremely backward by world standards, the society consisting of poor herdsmen and farmers supporting a large class of priests and nobles, who owned most of the arable land. The monasteries gained their wealth from taxes on their tenants, money-lending and trade, and law and punishment remained at a medieval level into modern times. Bands of huge 'warrior monks' – the *dob-dob* – terrorized the populace, using whips, knives and, according to some accounts, bunches of huge monastery keys as flails. When, in 1934, the respected and eminent Lungshar Dorje Tsegyal proposed a shift of power away from the inner circle of nobles to a national assembly, he was arrested. After his eyes were put out he was imprisoned for four years.

In 1951 China signed agreements with the Dalai Lama not to disturb his authority or the Tibetan way of life. For a time the Chinese maintained this conciliatory policy, but in 1956 the Khamba tribesmen of eastern Tibet rebelled. They were supported by other elements in the community, notably the monasteries, which provided them with weapons. The Khambas had had a long tradition of hostility towards the Chinese. They had harried the Communists at one stage during the Long March, and this, too, had not been forgotten by either side. There is considerable evidence of American CIA incitement of this revolt, the agency providing training and weapons to Tibetan militias for more than a decade before abandoning them totally in 1972.

The revolt spread throughout Tibet, reaching a climax in 1958. The Dalai Lama and his government fled into exile in India the following year. Chinese control of Tibet was now much more severely administered. The revolt was forcibly put down with a considerable loss of life, the lama (monk) class was proscribed, and the monasteries forcibly closed. The religious-feudal organization of Tibetan society was considered unacceptable by the Chinese government, who have taken all possible steps to destroy it and convert Tibet into a Chinese province like any other. To this end many thousands of ethnic Chinese have been resettled in Tibet and a major programme of 're-education' of the Tibetan people undertaken. Numerous deaths, imprisonment and incidents of torture were reported during this 'pacification' phase.

Tibetans suffered as much as Chinese during the 'great leap forward' in 1959 and 1960, with many thousands of deaths from starvation. However, there is now evidence that Chinese reform of agriculture and the establishment of industries and schools in Tibet have improved the lives of many people who were previously little better than slaves. Early in 2005 the Dalai Lama was quoted by the Hong Kong *South China Morning Post* as saying: 'Tibet is part of the Republic of China.' Saying Tibet was underdeveloped and materially backward, he added: 'So, for our own interest, we are willing to be part of the Republic of China, to have it govern and guarantee to preserve our Tibetan culture, spirituality, and our environment.' However, there have also been reports that China has been overexploiting Tibet's natural resources, especially its forests.

The Chinese Communist state was, then, consolidated by its redistribution of land, its establishment of a pervasive chain of authority, and its demonstration that it could improve the health and living standards of the people modestly. 'Correctness' – a severe Communist orthodoxy – became the dominant political virtue. There is abundant evidence of Chinese use of educational and psychological means to control the thought of their people; to implant hostility in their children towards outside nations regarded as enemies; and to correct 'wrong thinking' in individuals. These techniques, called 'brainwashing' by Western critics, were known by the Chinese as thought-cleansing. They were designed to alter the opinions of those with critical or independent points of view, and justified by the assertion that Communism as dictated by the state must always be right, so that all citizens are bound to give it not only obedience but acceptance without reservation.

The peasants continued to live together in families, each in its own

house with a small strip of land and livestock. It was nearly five years before
the government began to change this rural society. Then, from 1954
onwards, a series of policy decisions attempted to organize the people into
co-operatives and later into 26,000 'communes' – completely collective
societies in which private ownership of land and real property was abolished. This policy was in part motivated by China's rapidly increasing
population due to a falling death rate. Although heretical to Marxist theory,
an intense campaign for birth control began in 1956. This 'deviation from
orthodoxy' so offended many party members that it was soon discontinued, and another solution suggested. This was to be nothing less than a
rapid, sudden breakthrough to complete Communism, until then seen only
as an ideal to be achieved in the indefinite future. By late 1956 the government was calling for a much quicker rate of collectivization, and peasants
who resisted it were punished.

In 1957 the government apparently decided to test the loyalty of intellectuals by inviting free discussion of its policies – to allow 'a hundred flowers'
of opinion to blossom. There was a considerable volume of criticism; this
was the time of the first Democracy Wall in Beijing University, containing
posters critical of the Communist Party. When it was at its height the
government countered with a sudden and severe wave of repression. An
extensive purge of the public service followed. This was no small incident –
more than 300,000 intellectuals, including most of China's brightest and
most independent minds, were indicted as 'rightists', imprisoned, sent to
labour camps, or to unaccustomed manual labour in the countryside. This
unexpected blow was very significant, confirming the iron hand and severe
orthodoxy of the Communist Party.

When in 1958 the central committee ordered the complete reorganiza-
tion of Chinese society into 'peoples' communes', it was acting against two
long-standing bases of Chinese life: private property and the family. In
some places cottages were torn down and the materials used for communal
barracks. Children were cared for in crèches while both parents worked at
tasks assigned to them by the commune. Production quotas were fixed and
the whole system dominated by an almost military discipline. In some
instances the communes seem to have prospered, but in many the changes
were resisted. Three successive bad seasons in many parts of China, including a serious drought in the Yellow River basin, coincided with this planned
social dislocation and greatly aggravated its bad effects. Severe food
rationing had to be introduced and China was forced to import huge
amounts of grain.

The problems were worsened by the diversion of huge amounts of
labour to infrastructure development to make 'a great leap forward'. This

disastrous campaign collapsed in less than two years, even though the Chinese, tough and sturdy though they are, were driven to efforts almost beyond human endurance. Fourteen-hour workdays were common, and press reports told of 'heroes' collapsing from fatigue. The huge results claimed were later shown to be false. Much effort was dissipated on badly conceived projects, such as the creation of 60,000 'backyard furnaces' to make steel. These ten-foot-high earthen structures were fed with coke and iron ore and tended by hand – very labour-intensive processes that severely depleted the agricultural land force. The product of these furnaces was often so bad it could not even be used for simple agricultural implements.

It is impossible to estimate accurately the cost of these huge mistakes, but it is generally accepted that deaths, mainly resulting from starvation, may have been as many as 30 million, with China's population actually declining by two per cent in 1960 and 1961. In many places the hungry and despairing populace rioted, with some reports of armed revolts against the government emerging in spite of tight censorship. The retreats from the commune system and the 'great leap forward' were simultaneous and virtually complete by 1963, although the communes have been retained as an administrative framework, with most planning and day-to-day administration in the hands of much smaller production teams. Diversion of much industrial production to agricultural machinery like irrigation pumps, walk-behind tractors and fertilizer factories permitted a steady recovery in rural productivity from 1964. Nevertheless, grain production did not regain its 1955 levels until the early 1970s.

Then, in 1966, China was again plunged into chaos with a renewed struggle between moderate and extreme Communists – the so-called Cultural Revolution, in which the ageing Mao, crippled with Parkinson's disease, incited thousands of youthful Red Guards into a noisy and destructive campaign against traditional Chinese culture. This largely urban campaign, which was to affect China adversely for almost a decade, caused thousands of violent deaths, widespread dislocation of industry and education, and the wilful destruction of large quantities of China's art, writing and classical buildings.

In China in 1975 I saw ancient temples in which all of the Buddha images inside had been smashed; saw childish and ludicrous, yet still malicious, posters reviling Confucius; heard stories of eminent scholars forced to kneel on broken glass in public recantations of their 'errors'; heard how the staff of whole universities were compelled to coach politically acceptable factory workers to academic standards in circumstances where competitive examinations had been abolished. Disastrous subsequent results, including attacks on the Red Guards by exasperated workers, forced the ending of these excesses; and dramatic changes in policy ensued, especially after the death of Mao and his closest associate, Zhou Enlai, from stomach cancer, in 1976. The harsh conditions during these chaotic decades may have exacted a long-term toll on those not accustomed to them. This is suggested by a 2004 report from the official Xinhua News Agency of surveys showing that intellectuals were dying ten years younger than the general community, at an average age of 53.

There were many more tragic deaths in 1976. Almost half a million people died when a major earthquake, measuring 8.7 on the Richter Scale, struck the city of Tangshan. Nevertheless 400,000 people who had been trapped or injured were saved when a massive airlift from the city was organized at short notice. The earthquake destroyed 650,000 of the city's 680,000 buildings in two minutes. More than a million people were left homeless and China was forced to devote a massive effort to rehabilitation and reconstruction.

Rigid birth control measures were introduced in 1979, penalizing families with more than one child. This in itself has created an unprecedented situation in China, a generation substantially of only children who, it must be said, have been generally spoilt, cosseted and indulged by their parents as 'little emperors'. Once, at a state dinner in China, I sat next to an aged veteran of the Long March who with every course uttered dire predictions about the risks of spoiling only children, who, he averred, could not be normal because they have not experienced the complex network of family relationships so traditional in China. In 1985 this policy was relaxed to allow rural families two children, and in 2004 in Shanghai divorced persons remarrying were permitted a second child where one partner was childless.

Nevertheless, even now China remains only a few steps ahead of famine, and the population has more than doubled during the 55 years of the Communist state, to 1.4 billion. That approaches a quarter of all the people on the planet. To feed these China has only six per cent of the world's arable land – 26 per cent of the landmass is desert.

While recent decades have shown a liberalization, especially in the economic sphere, there is little indication that the rigid hold the Communist Party, with about 60 million members, has on the country will be relaxed. While there has been a considerable shift towards regional autonomy, the Communist Party and the army remain dominant in decision-making institutions at all levels of the community, and in all places. The Central Committee of the party, with several hundred members, elects a political bureau, or Politburo, of perhaps 20 people. But even this is not the ultimate leadership; that resides in a standing committee of the Politburo of around half a dozen members. The party has its own self-disciplining dynamic, regularly expelling lazy, corrupt or inefficient members, and demanding constant effort and self-criticism from its rank and file. A major purge of the lower echelons of the party appeared to have occurred in 2000, emphasizing political correctness and the avoidance of 'intellectual liberalism'.

Movements towards democracy have been decisively repressed, the most publicized example being the military suppression of student demonstrations in Beijing's Tien An Men Square and the broad boulevard that runs east from it, Zhangan Avenue, on 4 June 1989. Tanks and soldiers in armoured personnel carriers and trucks fired into the crowds, causing deaths variously estimated at between 200 and 2000. Thousands were subsequently arrested, with some initial executions for sedition, probably not more than 50 people. By standards of early Chinese Communist history, the reaction was moderate, with 18 people reported to have been given prison terms, some hundreds more 're-educated'. Nevertheless, the message was quite clear: 'Bourgeois liberalism', 'attempts to topple the Communist Party, overthrow socialism', were not acceptable.

While there was considerable support for the students in some major cities, especially Beijing, there is little evidence that the majority of Chinese had much sympathy for them. Most seem to have accepted the government's official line that the students were subversives, attempting to wreck the established social order. Since the Tien An Men Square 'massacre' has been the most talked about and written about event in China since the birth of the Communist state, its history is of some importance. The facts, reported by reputable Western journalists in Beijing at the time, are briefly these.

Demonstrations in the square began three weeks earlier, coinciding with a state visit to China by Soviet President Gorbachev, and subsequently turned violent, with hand-to-hand fighting and mobs throwing bricks, bottles and firebombs at the troops and police. On 3 June, 10,000 unarmed troops sent to the square to persuade the demonstrators to withdraw were forced to retreat. Later that day stone-throwing crowds attacked troops guarding the residences of the Chinese leaders, and seized an army bus loaded with weapons. Western reporters saw an armoured personnel carrier stopped by petrol bombs and its crew bludgeoned to death as they tried to escape. A pitched battle seemed to have occurred at Jianguomenwai, a large clover-leaf interpass, where reporters noted four burned-out army vehicles and a number of dead soldiers. There are other reports of soldiers cut down, hanged, disembowelled or burned to death, and burned-out army trucks, although there is no evidence these incidents were numerous.

Casualties on both sides were minuscule when compared with earlier events in China itself, or killings in East Timor by Indonesian soldiers, or even regular police actions by India against tribal minorities, and deaths in Afghanistan and Burma. The essential difference was that the Chinese allowed the Tien An Men events to be portrayed on world television – and they were shocking enough, including the crushing of young people under tank tracks and the shooting of young children.

However, the crackdown on 4 June plainly came after many misgivings. For instance, the 38th Army based in Beijing refused to move against the people and it was left to the 27th Army from Shanxi Province to make the assault. There are Western reports that they seemed frightened and on edge, and undoubtedly over-reacted. Rumours, promoted by the Western media, that there might be fighting between these two armies – effectively civil war with the attendant breakdown in Chinese society that must have ensued – may well have helped to push the Chinese leadership into final action. A factor was Deng's often expressed fear of *luan* (chaos), which he associated with the Cultural Revolution and the democracy movement.

Chi-chen Wang, emeritus professor of Chinese Literature at Columbia University, commented in the *New York Times*: 'The 40 years of Communist rule is the only period of stability in China this century. It might be one of the longest periods of effective government in all Chinese history, and it has been a period of unparalleled progress and comparative prosperity . . . The students called for democracy in vague terms and then demanded the resignation of Premier Li Peng. In effect they called for the eclipse of the government. They disrupted traffic, set fire to cars and buses and refused to disperse. When troops were finally called in, they resisted with fire bombs and rocks . . . It seems very unreasonable to expect the legally constituted government of China to yield to such lawlessness.'

The volume of criticism heaped on the Chinese government – far greater than that accompanying any other recent human rights matter in a very evil world, and repeated with monotonous regularity for more than 15 years – has had two consequences, which ought to have been foreseen by the world leaders concerned and their advisers: it has assisted in the eclipse of moderate elements in the Chinese leadership and perpetuated the continuing power of the hardliners. It has resulted in statements from Beijing that the Chinese government will now not listen to criticisms from the rest of the world, but will act only as it sees fit. Immediately after the Tien An Men conflict the Chinese media, previously achieving at least the beginnings of independence, were severely reined in, and contact with foreigners restricted. This continued until 1992, when a policy to attract more foreign investment and tourists led to a cautious and still restricted liberalization.

Meanwhile, the 11th Central Committee of the Chinese Communist Party, meeting late in 1978, had declared Mao's policies to have been mistaken and decided to 'correct the "leftist" errors committed prior to, and during the so-called cultural revolution'. The failures of the 'class struggle' era Mao had insisted on maintaining were observed. It was decided that management of farming would revert to families, who would also be given back the right to hold private plots. The economy was now to become the most important consideration and private enterprise and foreign investment not only tolerated but encouraged.

The driving force behind these reforms was the exasperation of the Chinese people with nearly three decades of hardship. Their architect was a tough, diminutive veteran of the Long March, Deng Xiaoping, who had been disgraced during the Cultural Revolution as a 'capitalist roader' and who spent years working in a tractor factory. Ultimately rehabilitated, his authority and iron willpower sufficed to turn China onto a new course – towards capitalism, but in the Chinese government's rhetoric, socialist capitalism. However, it was not enough to sustain his protégé and possible successor, the youthful and pro-Western Hu Yaobang, who was forced to resign as general secretary of the Communist Party in 1987 because he was seen by the party's hardliners as 'soft' on student demonstrations for democracy. Hu's eclipse – he died of a heart attack two years later – and the repression of the student movement triggered by his state funeral in 1989, must be seen as a significant victory for hardline elements of the government. Deng retired from public life in 1994 and died in 1997.

Jiang Zemin became president, leading an upper bureaucracy largely of technocrats, 80 per cent of whom were graduates. There was a further transfer of power in 2003, but not, apparently, a change of direction. The enigmatic, little-known technocrat Hu Jintao became president and Wen Jiabao premier. Both men are described as mild-mannered and conservative. During the next year they gave every evidence of continuing past economic policies and maintaining engagement with the outside world.

Confucius, violently derided during the Cultural Revolution, was officially reinstated in 1994 as the new leaders embraced traditional Chinese culture and nationalism. The sage's 2545th birthday was marked by the opening of Confucian teaching schools and the establishment of an international association of Confucian studies in Beijing.

In July 1997, the British colony of Hong Kong, with its seven million people, reverted to China on expiry of the original leases. One of the world's largest trading centres and a major tourist destination, Hong Kong appears to have settled down reasonably peaceably to incorporation within the mother country, although its prosperity has diminished and unemployment rates have increased. In 2004 there was, however, considerable protest at Beijing's restriction of democracy.

Major events in China in the new millennium were its 2001 entry into the World Trade Organization, and becoming only the third nation to put a man in space. In 2003 astronaut Yang Liwei was launched in space vehicle *Shenzhou* 5, went around the world 14 times, and was returned safely to earth.

Since Mao's death much has changed in China. There are now new styles of life and work which he fought desperately to forestall – what he called the 'ogres' of capitalism. Economic liberalization has again permitted private enterprise, both small businesses and joint enterprises, largely financed by foreign capital. It is significant that many of these are owned and managed by capitalists from Taiwan. There are once again very rich and very poor people in China, and the government, with some publicly expressed qualms, has accepted this, since the economic results have been impressive. A wide range of consumer goods is exported worldwide at highly competitive prices. Since 1978 there has been a steady growth in the gross national product of about ten per cent per year, with impressive increases in average wages and the virtual transition of urban China to a consumer society in modest terms.

The economy doubled in size during the 1980s, and again during the 1990s. Even though rural China is poorer than urban China, almost half of country households have colour TV, a third have washing machines, one in ten a refrigerator. China has favourable trade balances with a number of countries, including the United States, and in 2005 was holding a massive $610 billion in foreign-exchange reserves. Over the last decade it has progressed from being the world's fifteenth largest trading nation to the sixth. However, in spite of this apparent prosperity there has been a considerable cost – a pool of unemployed people variously estimated at between ten and 100 million, bouts of inflation and widespread financial corruption.

Nowhere is more typical of China's new capitalism than Shanghai. Its 630 square kilometre high-technology cityscape has a vast new 'market economy' area at Pudong, a complex of the world's tallest buildings, and modern centres for making almost anything the world might want or need, from construction steel to computer chips. In 2004 the world's first magnetic levitation train began to operate between the city and the airport, achieving speeds up to 250 miles an hour during its eight-minute journey. There are almost a million motor vehicles in Shanghai, while use of its main personal transport form only a few decades ago – the bicycle – is severely restricted. China has 20 million cars, with 2.5 million more going on the roads each year. The rapidly growing urban middle class who

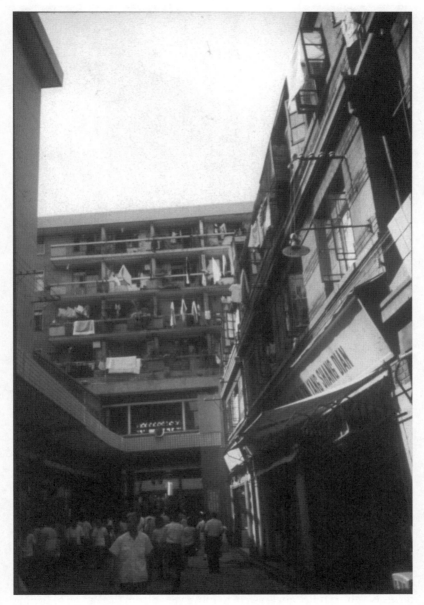

Figure 11 The landscape of the Chinese capital, Beijing, is being transformed by the construction of modern worker housing like this

Figure 12   In the Middle Ages probably most of the world's ships were built in Asia. The industry is now reviving, as in China, where this coastal trader is under construction

inhabit Shanghai and other 'high-tech' cities are showing signs of adopting many aspects of Western culture – another development Mao would have hated. According to a Chinese government survey, about a third of Chinese now celebrate Christmas – but only three per cent do so for religious reasons.

The Chinese leadership is committed to huge public works programmes – around $750 billions' worth in Keynesian solutions to problems of unemployment and hesitancy in some areas of the economy. Due for completion in 2009, the Three Gorges Dam project on the upper Yangzi River is the world's second largest engineering project, designed to control flooding, produce billions of kilowatt hours of electric power and to make the river navigable as far inland as Chongqing, more than 1000 miles from the coast. It began producing power in 2003, against the background of severe power shortages due to China's booming industries. The dam includes massive shiplifts, which will raise vessels of up to 10,000 tons from the lower river to the huge lake behind it. A second major works programme in global terms is a 2000-mile canal system to move water from the Yangzi to Beijing and the north of the country at a cost of $60 billion. This is claimed to be the largest engineering work in the world. Other projects are a 2000-mile pipeline to bring natural gas from Xinjiang to Shanghai, and a nuclear-powered desalination plant in Shandong Province to produce 52 million tons of water a year.

By late 2004 China faced considerable energy shortages, as well as major urban pollution. Three-quarters of the nation's electricity is produced by burning coal, involving dangerous levels of air pollution and carbon dioxide emissions. Coal consumption almost doubled to 1.7 billion tons a year between 2000 and 2004; a Harvard University study estimated 100,000 premature deaths a year due to pollution, and the Chinese Ministry of Health announced a doubling of lung cancer incidence in the last decade. With production from its four major oilfields declining, Chinese oil imports have more than doubled over the five years to 2004.

One of the more interesting and significant manifestations of the new economic freedom are the collectives – trading and manufacturing businesses owned and controlled by the people who work in them. These new and rapidly expanding businesses, in such areas as transport, clothing manufacture, packaging materials, bricks and other building materials and farm machinery repair and manufacture, are turning thousands of Chinese villages into small industrial towns. The collectives are being encouraged by the government and may well represent in the future a massive industry which is neither capitalist nor state-owned and managed – indeed, a socialist capitalism.

Meanwhile, the state-owned enterprises still dominate much of the economy, especially heavy industry, and employ around 20 per cent of the workforce. Many are inefficient and uneconomic, but the government has had difficulty phasing them out because this involves mass unemployment of workers who have become used to regarding their jobs as absolutely secure – the 'iron ricebowl', meaning one that could not be broken. Nevertheless, state enterprises are being closed or sold to private enterprise, at considerable social cost.

Agricultural productivity has improved since the inception of contracts with families. These mostly cover general farming, but they can be specific, allowing individual households to become specialists in such things as animal breeding and fish farming, or even the production of handcrafts. However, the Chinese countryside retains many problems, and its peasants are generally worse off in money terms than city workers. Girls who have left home to work in the urban factories might earn ten times as much as their father still on the land. There is also a massive labour surplus in agriculture. Tens of millions have deserted the land to seek work in the cities, with varied success.

The new millennium has seen the first of the single-child generation entering on their responsibilities. This has been associated with a dramatic and significant rise in the educational standards of many young Chinese. In 2004 almost three million graduated from university – around double the number in 2002, with further increases expected in 2005.

Hopes that China's authoritarianism might give place to Western-style democracy look very much like wishful thinking. In the last weeks of 1998 the authorities arrested the leaders of the fledgling China Democratic Party when it sought to register as a formal opposition to the Communist Party. The charge, the serious one of subverting the state, resulted in a sentence of 13 years in prison for the party's leader, Xu Wenli.

Nevertheless, there have been recent signs that reasonable non-political dissent might get some sort of hearing. In 2003 millionaire farming entrepreneur Sun Dawu, speaking at Beijing University and the China Agricultural University, made some forthright criticism of official policy, saying that the government must direct more money into helping the rural sector rather than pouring money into grandiose plans in the cities – in effect, there must be a third revolution. He also attacked what he claimed was a culture of bribery and embezzlement at the state administrative level. Mr Sun was arrested and gaoled for six months. Speaking early in 2004, after his release, Mr Sun seemed unrepentant. 'The public will know who is right and who is wrong,' he declared. He was interviewed on state television, supported by other businessmen and academics and, paradoxically, praised by an important Communist Party body, the Central Party School in Beijing, as a business leader helping to bring economic growth to the rural sector.

When in China on official delegations and the like it is possible at times to talk privately with the cadres who are always in attendance on 'foreign friends'. I asked perhaps a dozen Chinese the same somewhat dangerous question – dangerous to them, that is. Around half angrily refused to respond. The question was: 'You are expected to obey the government in all things, give up your personal freedoms more than just about anyone else in the world would be prepared to do. How do you feel about that?'

The answer generally was something like this: 'China has been poor and weak for generations. We must all agree to obey the government, if China is to catch up. Of course in many ways I don't like that, but on the whole I believe it is what we all must do, we must all pull together for China.' Impossibly idealistic? Government-dictated propaganda? Maybe. But my own impression was that many Chinese really do see it this way, a variation on 'Shut up and I'll let you get rich.' Perhaps, 'Shut up and I'll make us all great.' But as more people get rich and great, the time may not be far off when their opinions, dissenting though they may be, begin to influence Chinese policy.

Meanwhile, who are the new rich of China? Many are cadres, members of the Communist Party and the army, and their families. The People's Liberation Army, which makes and sells arms, is a major player in international finance and controls at least 20,000 profit-making businesses in China. This, perhaps, is yet another way these two organizations, the power monoliths of China, are seeing they remain just that in the new era of socialist capitalism.

'The dogs have gone. The pigs are here.' Such was the wry utterance current in Taipei, the capital of Taiwan, when at the end of the Second World War the defeated Japanese left and Jiang's Nationalist troops occupied the island.

In 1945, under the terms of the Yalta Agreement, Taiwan was handed back to China, then still under Jiang's governance. General Chen Yi, the Nationalist military governor sent to the island, proved so incompetent and corrupt that by 1947 the people were driven to major riots. Between 15,000 and 30,000 people were killed by the military when these were repressed, with the utmost severity. Martial law instituted then would endure for 38 years.

When the Communists took over China late in 1949, more than one and a half million Nationalist supporters, including 600,000 soldiers, fled to Taiwan, increasing the population by a quarter in a few weeks. The demands of this huge influx of people on food supplies and the economy generally were a heavy enough imposition; even worse was the use of martial law to compel the Taiwanese people to provide for an army of invaders determined to behave like conquerors.

Jiang considered his plans to use Taiwan as a base from which to attack the new mainland government sufficient justification for his harsh authoritarianism. But as time passed an invasion of China seemed increasingly less likely. The United States recognized the legitimacy of the Communist government in Beijing, and the United Nations seat bestowed on Jiang's regime was transferred to China. Most nations followed the American lead and recognized Beijing. Nevertheless, the United States still considered Communism a major enemy, during the phase of uneasy peace known as the Cold War. China was warned that America would resist any attempt to invade Taiwan. However, China has continued to regard Taiwan as a Chinese province which must be incorporated into the Chinese state, and has said it will invade the island if any attempt is made to declare it an independent nation.

In spite of martial law, a modern industrial economy has developed, largely through American technical and financial aid. This, together with a land reform programme, saw Taiwan develop into one of the most prosperous states in Asia. Nationalist domination of the government survived Jiang's death in 1975, but not for long. In 1986 the Democratic Progressive Party was founded, and two years later the first native-born president, Lee

Tenghui. took office. In 1991 he persuaded a 'rump' of 460 Nationalist members of Parliament of doubtful political legitimacy to retire. Taiwan's first free election brought the DPP to government, and this was confirmed in later elections for the assembly and presidency in 1995, 1996 and – by the narrowest of margins – in 2004. However, later that year it lost power in the assembly to the KMT and coalition partners, who by this stage were opposed to the idea of Taiwanese independence. This indicated more support than had been expected for the KMT attitude: 'we don't want war, or the road of provocation and tension'.

In 1995, when Lee had made a highly publicized visit to America, China began a series of intensive military exercises on the Fujian coast opposite Taiwan, together with a no less intensive verbal campaign warning that any attempt to declare independence would prompt an attack on the island. Similar warnings were issued in 2003, and during the run-up to the 2004 elections.

Nevertheless, since the end of Nationalist rule there has been a low profile but very real rapprochement on practical levels, including personal travel between China and the island and trade and commercial initiatives, among them a $30 billion investment in China by Taiwanese businessmen. However, Taiwan's position in the world remains an uneasy compromise, with most interested parties urging continuance of the status quo, while publicly agreeing that sooner or later there must be only one China.

Can the island's past history justify China's claim to Taiwan? The archaeological record indicates that Taiwan has been occupied by people for a long time. Its first inhabitants, arriving perhaps 6000 years ago from the mainland, were possibly the same Austronesians who spread through south-east Asia and the Pacific. Their descendants now make up rather less than two per cent of the present population of Taiwan.

According to the classic *History of the Three Kingdoms*, the Chinese state of Wu may have sent a military expedition to Taiwan in the third century, and the Ming Admiral Zheng He noted that the island existed. However, significant migration seems not to have occurred until late in the fifteenth century, when Chinese from neighbouring Fujian Province began to take up land on the western plains, forcing the aboriginal tribes into the central mountains and to the rugged east coast. There was, however, considerable intermarriage between the aborigines and the Chinese, a mix still giving the Taiwanese population a distinctive nature.

Portuguese mariners established a foothold in 1517. It was they who named the island Formosa – meaning beautiful – the name by which it was known to Europeans for the next several centuries. The Dutch and Spanish also established colonies there. The Dutch brought in Chinese migrants to work on sugar and rice plantations. Many of these stayed on, creating what seems to have been the first significant Han Chinese presence.

During the last years of the Ming Dynasty in China an adventurer named Zheng became a general. His son Zheng Chenggong, known in the West as Koxinga, continued the struggle against the Manchu until 1661, when he was forced to retreat to Taiwan with an army of 35,000. He campaigned successfully against the Dutch colonizers, who were forced to leave after 38 years on the island, and established what was in effect the last Ming outpost. This Chinese kingdom is regarded as a high point in Taiwanese history. However, it did not long survive Zheng's sudden death, probably from malaria, in 1683 at the age of 38. The Manchu Qing Dynasty took the island only a year later, and incorporated it as a prefecture, or county, of Fujian Province, which it continued to be until 1887, when it was restyled a Chinese province.

During these 200 years Chinese governments took little interest in Taiwan. It became notorious as a haven for pirates. For a time there was a Japanese colony on the eastern side. However, continued Chinese migration, driven by a series of famines in Fujian, brought the population to perhaps two million by the end of the nineteenth century. A Fujian farmer is credited with having brought tea plants to Taiwan in about 1800 – the establishment of what is still a thriving tea industry. John Dodd used clipper ships to export Formosa Oolong tea to the United States from 1867 with considerable success.

When Japan defeated China in 1895, Taiwan became a Japanese possession until the end of the Second World War. The Taiwanese initially resisted Japanese occupation, establishing an independent republic which, however, endured for only a few days before Japanese troops arrived to occupy the island. Thousands of Taiwanese conscripts were killed in the Second World War, and Japanese control was severe, even brutal. Nevertheless, there was considerable infrastructure development such as, roads, railways, schools and hospitals, which provided a basis for the island's present prosperity.

Taiwan's 23 million people represent less than two per cent of China's population, her land area less than three per cent. In the larger, more practical, aspect these figures seem almost insignificant. But behind the very considerable – and dangerous – level of rhetoric Taiwan generates are two barely submerged issues of huge significance: China's insistence that what she sees as her national territory must be integrated within the larger nation; and Taiwan's geographic position, with an unsinkable aircraft carrier almost within sight of the Chinese mainland, controlled by what Beijing regards as a client government of the United States.

22 Indonesia: Sukarno and After

Indonesia's first decades of independence were stormy and chaotic. The acute shortage of trained people caused grave inadequacies in administration and failures in the everyday necessities of a modern state. Telephones, electric power, the railways, the ports, customs – these and many other public services came close to collapse for want of expert control.

Actual bankruptcy at this point was averted partly because of Indonesia's grassroots prosperity, and because of continued control of the bulk of her export-earning industries by foreigners. The key industry – the oilfields – paid royalties which provided the bulk of government revenue. The Chinese, as they still do, owned most of the other industries and retail outlets, including the important rice distribution system, and, by and large, contrived to keep these things going.

Apart from overcrowded problem regions in central and east Java, most of the villagers were protected by a bountiful natural endowment that automatically provided self-sufficiency without too much work. Much of Java looks like a well-kept garden. The small, brown houses, often set high up on stilts, are almost lost in the lush growth of fruit trees that surrounds them, and the warm, even climate demands only simple housing and clothes.

Other than the opportunity to buy such things as a bicycle, a sewing machine, a television or radio, little of the modern technical world touches most of these villages. Hence the political froth in Jakarta affects national life less than people who do not know Indonesia realize. However, rapid population growth, partly caused by lack of finance for birth control programmes, have greatly increased Indonesia's problems of poverty and disadvantage. As villages become overcrowded and arable land less available, millions of young people flock to the cities to seek work, which as often as not is unavailable.

Industries in Indonesia have often been basically uneconomic, state-subsidized to the benefit of the country's military leaders and their families, and financed by huge loans obtained overseas. Corruption seems endemic at all levels of government. The financial chaos exacerbated by these excesses in 1997 and 1998 has had major repercussions. The fall of the *rupiah* to a fraction of its former value made it impossible for hundreds of businesses to meet their obligations. Widespread bankruptcy and unemployment of factory workers resulted in rioting in many areas, especially in the slum-like shanty towns around the major urban areas to which country-dwellers shifted to find work in the city. Unemployment and rising prices of basic necessities such as rice, cooking oil and kerosene have created a desperate situation for millions.

In 1901 a son was born to an impoverished Javanese schoolteacher of aristocratic *priyayi* origins and his wife, who was from a Balinese raja's family. This child, named Sukarno, is said to have exhibited early a lively, charming and intelligent personality. An influential friend, the early nationalist leader Tjokroaminoto, made it possible for him to enter Surabaya High School, where he studied for five years. During the 1920s Sukarno was an impassioned advocate for Indonesian independence. He was arrested in 1929 by the Dutch and gaoled. After two years in prison he was briefly released, then arrested again in 1932 and exiled to the eastern island of Flores. He read a great deal – Abraham Lincoln, Emerson, Jefferson, Nehru, Lenin, Marx – all were absorbed during this phase of development of his political thought. As time went by he became a legend in his own time, immensely well-known and popular among the people.

When Japan surrendered in 1945 British troops, sent to the city of Surabaya to bring out British and Dutch prisoners, became involved in a major conflict with Indonesian nationalists. During three days of major street fighting 6000 Indonesians were killed, and the fledgling independence army had its first experience of real war. Before long they also encountered Dutch troops, sent to reimpose colonial rule.

In 1949 the Indonesian government published a book called *Illustrations of the Indonesian People's Revolution*, designed to capture, in words and more than 2000 drawings and photographs, the spirit of the years of struggle. There is a fascination in the seemingly endless succession of pictures, nearly all of people.

However, the most significant was taken on 17 August 1945. It is ten o'clock in the morning outside a house in a Jakarta street – 56 Pegangsaan Timur, which was then Sukarno's home. Sukarno stands before a microphone, reading from a small slip of paper held in both hands. On the same page is a close-up of the paper, half a sheet of ordinary writing paper, somewhat dog-eared and containing some 30 words of writing in Indonesian, with some deletions and crossings-out under the heading, written in a firm hand and underlined twice *Proklamasi*. The photograph is of the actual declaration, read out by Sukarno in these words: 'We, the Indonesian people, herewith proclaim the independence of Indonesia. All matters pertaining to the transfer of power, etc, will be carried out in the shortest possible time.' Some hours later the declaration was broadcast from behind locked doors in the studios of the national radio in Jakarta.

The Dutch would not accept Indonesian independence and as a sporadic war dragged on international sympathy, notably from Australia and the United States, inclined to the independence movement, especially after Sukarno was arrested and deported to the island of Bangka in 1948. In that year a major push by the Communist Party to establish itself in central Java resulted in fighting between the Communists and other elements of the army. The climax came with a battle for the town of Madiun, in which the Communists were defeated. The 'Madiun affair' does much to explain subsequent hostility between the Indonesian Communist Party and the military. On 28 January 1949, the United Nations called for a transfer of sovereignty 'at the earliest possible date'. Dutch rule ended in December of that year, bringing the Republic of Indonesia into effective existence.

Sukarno now became the first president of the new nation. One of his first acts was to abolish 'The United States of Indonesia' – the federal form in which independence had been achieved – because of his mistrust of Dutch 'divide and rule' tactics. It could be argued, and strongly, that for Indonesia, with its thousands of islands and diverse ethnic patterns, a federal form of government would be most suitable, and that indeed appears to be evolving. Nevertheless on 17 August 1950, Indonesia became 'a unitary state' based on central rule from Jakarta. In the same year the 1945 'revolutionary constitution', which had given such wide powers to the president, was replaced by one which made Cabinet responsible to a national parliament, not to the president. So Indonesia began a disastrous experiment with Western-style parliamentary democracy.

There were already signs of disunity between Jakarta and the outer regions, which were less enthusiastic about the unitary state. The Dutch-sponsored Republic of the South Moluccas proclaimed its independence, but this dissident 'government' later became one of exile in The Hague, and has never had much influence. The extremist Darul Islam movement, which wanted an Islamic state, turned terrorist and fought the government from mountain strongholds in West Java and Sumatra. A major revolt began in Aceh in north Sumatra in 1953, aimed at creating an independent state, and has continued sporadically ever since.

Inexperience in administration began to tell increasingly as the months and years passed. In order to obtain revenues the government increased customs duties to a level that made smuggling really worth while. No resources existed to police the huge sweeps of coastline, and soon more goods were coming in over the beaches than through the ports. Also the government refused to devalue its currency, the rupiah, and the black market became a flourishing illegal business. By 1956 rupiahs could be bought on the streets of Djakarta with foreign currency at a quarter the official price and by 1960 this had fallen to a tenth.

In 1956, my first experience of Indonesia, it was no longer possible to get a telephone connection from one part of Jakarta to another, although one could still ring up within suburban exchange areas, at the cost of much time and patience. The capital's streets became narrow, muddy tracks full of deep potholes and ruts, partly due to the army's habit of running tanks over them to the detriment of the bitumen. Cars and spare parts, subject to duties of up to 500 per cent, were so valuable that everyone removed such accessories as hub-caps and wiper blades before venturing out, because these were frequently stolen if left on the vehicle.

There were grave difficulties in achieving coherence in the political system, divided as it was between four main influences – Sukarno, the parliament, the growing Communist Party and the armed services. Sukarno had fallen out with the army chief-of-staff, General Nasution, dismissing him in 1952. The following year Nasution published a book, *Fundamentals of Guerrilla Warfare*, which had such important implications for Indonesia's future that it deserves attention.

'The Indonesian National Army,' Nasution wrote, 'has been taught many different and often contradictory things. Things such as "The army should not engage in politics" . . . "The army is a tool of the country, an instrument of the government." All these expressions are merely slogans, and the person who suggested them used them for his own needs.' Nasution argued next, at some length, that because the Indonesian Army was a guerrilla, not a professional, force, its members must involve themselves in politics. 'They are different from a permanent army or a professional army whose soldiers carry a gun because they are instructed to do so by their master. The people's army is an army which defends the ideology of those people. The guerrilla soldier and partisan . . . is not merely a tool to be ordered about. He must be taught the country's ideology and policy. He must not be isolated from politics. He must have both feet firmly in the middle of politics.'

Nasution was back in charge of the army again only two years later, restored as chief-of-staff by the parliament while Sukarno was absent on a pilgrimage to Mecca. The Communists warned of a possible military dictatorship. When Indonesia's first democratic elections were held in 1955 six million people voted for the Communists, who had campaigned on a major 'land for the landless' theme which appealed to the poorer people. However, three other parties, Sukarno's PNI and two Muslim groups, the Masjumi and the NU, had each polled somewhat better out of a total vote of 37 million.

Sukarno spent a good deal of 1955 out of Indonesia. He visited the United States and China, and seemed oblivious to the mounting problems at home. He spent money freely on this foreign travel, refusing to listen to advice about the country's financial problems. 'Economics,' he is said to have remarked, 'make my head ache.' On his return he expressed impatience with the political parties and gave notice of a new concept he had in mind called 'guided democracy'. Early in 1957 it became a reality – a kind of national consensus based on traditional village government.

An attempt to assassinate Sukarno that year shocked the Indonesian nation deeply. He survived the bombing of a school, but of ten killed, six had been children, and this had a tremendous impact in a country where children are virtually worshipped. The four men arrested turned out to be Muslim extremists of the Darul Islam movement, who reiterated their hatred of Sukarno even in the court that finally condemned them. Sukarno and those who guarded him were fully aware of the danger of a further assassination attempt. The president moved with considerable fear along the narrow ribbon of road linking Jakarta with the presidential palace at Bogor. One morning when I was driving with an Indonesian friend to a picnic spot at Puntjak, he swung the car off the road onto the grass verge for no apparent reason.

'What is it?' I asked.
'Bung Karno.'

Then I heard the sound of motor horns in the distance and within minutes the leading motor cycles were in view, lights full on in the bright sunshine. There were four of them, followed by a white jeep, then a long, black car, which seemed to be empty but for the driver, and finally, more armed motorcyclists. In the front of the jeep stood an army officer, wearing dark glasses, his hand resting lightly on the windscreen. In the black car Sukarno crouched down low on the seat even though the doors were lined with sheet steel and the windows fitted with armoured glass. The white jeep became something of a legend in and around Jakarta and a host of stories, persistent, if of no verifiable authenticity, grew up around it. It was said that the officer in sunglasses used a bicycle chain, with which he lunged out to smash the windscreen of any vehicles obstructing the convoy.

In 1959 Sukarno ordered a return to the 1949 constitution, thus returning executive power to himself and weakening the other areas of government.

Parliament was further debilitated by the addition of more appointed members than elected ones. But behind this apparent dominance by Sukarno a bitter and intense enmity was developing between the army and the Communists.

By 1961 Sukarno felt strong enough to demand transfer of the western part of New Guinea – West Irian – which had been a Dutch colony, to Indonesia. He entrusted a tough regular soldier, General Suharto, with the task of readying a 25,000-strong invasion force. In April the first guerrillas were dropped into the jungles of West Irian (also known as West Papua). The Indonesian military performance in this sporadic war was no better than indifferent. However, there was no stomach for the war in Holland, and this, combined with strong United States opinion that Indonesia should have West Irian, carried the day.

In 1963, as Sukarno knelt in prayer at a religious meeting, a fanatic took out a pistol and fired a full magazine at him. Again he was untouched, but five people around him were wounded. Now even more elaborate measures were taken to guard him, including an elite palace guard all of the same blood grouping as the president. Its men tasted his food and drink before he touched it, and searched visitors for concealed weapons. Largely isolated from his people, Sukarno became a myth in his own time and some curious stories circulated about him. His interest in women and marital problems were expanded to give him a reputation as a great user of women in the tradition of the rajas of the past. He was said to go out at night, embrace trees, and walk barefooted during thunderstorms. He appeared at a formal function barefooted, explaining that he wanted to pick up electricity from the ground. Such things, and the extravagance of his daily life, served only to make the common people love and revere him all the more. This adulation was not so much towards Sukarno as a person as to his position as ruler. This tradition of obedience to the ruler simply because he or she is the ruler must be considered a continuing and significant political force in Indonesia.

When the federation of Malaysia was formed late in 1963 Sukarno opposed it – first with words and then by sending armed forces into Sarawak. In 1964 he announced 'the Year of Living Dangerously', a confrontation with what he saw as the forces of capitalism and neo-colonialism. There was increasing speculation about his health. Already an old man by Indonesian standards, he was plagued by a liver complaint that needed surgery. This he refused because he had been told by a fortune teller that steel would cause his death. Rumours that he might die at any moment may well have been the cause of a confused military coup in September 1964.

The first action seems to have been a rebellion by left-wing elements in the army supported by armed Communist activists at Halim Air Base. They claimed they had acted to prevent a planned coup by the generals to depose Sukarno. Armed bands of soldiers surprised leading members of the Council of Generals in their homes during the night. Six were murdered, at least one after being subjected to torture. A warning telephone call allowed General Nasution to escape over the back fence of his house in his pyjamas at 4 a.m. There was some shooting there – his six-year-old daughter died from her wounds.

General Suharto, the leader of the elite strategic reserve of the Indonesian army, became prominent at this stage, rallying loyal troops to break the 'revolt' by force of arms. There was fierce fighting with young Communist guerrillas at Halim Air Base and in central Java. The Communist leader, Aidit, was killed. His death was only the first of many in a massive campaign, said to be against the Communists, but actually against many others, especially the Chinese. This huge bloodletting is perhaps the greatest stain on the Indonesian nation, and was an ominous portent for the future. Research teams from Indonesian universities reported 800,000 deaths in Java, 85,000 in Bali and about 100,000 in Sumatra. Large numbers were identified as ethnic Chinese.

Independent eyewitnesses in Indonesia during December and January reported that not only men, but also women and small children, who could not possibly have ever had a political idea, were butchered by mobs of Muslim extremists. While army units stood by and watched this happen, and in some cases took part in mass executions in the villages, the carnage aroused horror and revulsion among the majority of the people, and within much of the armed services. Terrible though the death of the generals had been, the scale of the retribution seemed beyond all reason.

There is considerable evidence that the American Central Intelligence Agency and the British and Australian governments were involved in this campaign to 'destabilize' the Sukarno government. Much of the violence involved the *marhaen*, the proletariat, landless and uneducated peasants who have drifted to the cities in the hope of improving their fortunes. Often unable to find work even for a pittance, they joined one of the large aimless bands that loitered in the streets, always ready to undertake any activity, from a political demonstration to beating up a Chinese shopkeeper and looting his home. This group, one of frightening potential for irresponsible destructiveness, without aim, and without any real hope of legitimate employment, is often enough the vehicle for violence in Indonesia.

A restless, drawn-out struggle for power between Sukarno and General Suharto continued for a year. Sukarno's policies were steadily reversed.

The confrontation with Malaysia ended, Indonesia rejoined the United Nations. Sukarno was placed under house arrest. In February 1967, Suharto assumed all real powers of government, and a year later became Indonesia's second president, *bapak*, the father of the nation. Sukarno died in obscurity in 1970.

A stocky, slow-moving man, Suharto was born into a peasant family near Jogjakarta in 1921. During his youth he was strongly influenced by traditional Javanese beliefs, including that of the sacred person of the leader. After a primary education at a village school he enlisted in the Dutch colonial army at the age of 19, not long before the Japanese occupation. He was a regimental commander when the republic was formed, a colonel in 1957, and a brigadier-general and deputy-chief of the army staff three years later.

His 'new order' government continued to be anti-Communist and brought Indonesia into much closer orientation with the West and, in particular, the United States. The 350,000-strong Indonesian army became a vast administrative machine with the weapons to support its demands, controlling businesses ranging from huge corporations to village brothels, often in partnership with wealthy Chinese. By 1998, the end of the Suharto era, more than 12,000 soldiers held administrative jobs at all levels, including almost half the provincial governors and district controllers. Many army officers did not hesitate to use this dual role, known as *dwi-fungsi*, to their own advantage. The army owns three billion dollars' worth of land, as well as almost 300 businesses, ranging from department stores in Jakarta to resort hotels in Bali. In some areas police and the army fight gun battles for control of lucrative protection rackets.

Newsweek (16 June 1969), in an article about General Ibnu Sutowo, the then head of the state-run Pertamina Oil Corporation, commented: 'When he married off his daughter in March, the general threw a party that was truly sultanic in splendour. In a week-long festival of dances and ceremonies city streets were blocked for miles around to accommodate the 1000 guests who poured in each night to pay their respects. Closed-circuit television was installed so all could see and be seen and Jakarta's largest electrical generator was commandeered to provide power. Among the reported wedding gifts: 18 cars and a yacht.' In 1976 Suharto dismissed Sutowo as a result of one of the most massive defalcations in modern history, leaving Pertamina $10.5 billion in debt.

However, the huge wealth accumulated by the Suharto family – estimated as much as $40 billion – became the principal scandal. Official enquiries in 1998 estimated that a car-importing concession to Suharto's son Hutomo (Tommy) had cost the nation $1.5 billion. Hutomo was

Figure 13 These Balinese dancers, like many other girls, would have begun to learn their art in early childhood

allowed to import cars from Korea without paying tax, and sell them as 'the national car' in competition with all other importers, who had to pay tax. This was only one example of a complex pattern of fraud and dishonesty, involving major political figures and their families and friends, which came to be known as 'cronyism'.

Increasing repression by the regime also caused disquiet. At least 50,000 people arrested after the events of 1965 were still held without trial, although as a result of pressure from the United States some were released by 1980 into virtual house arrest. And there were more arrests of protesters, justified, not this time on the grounds of Communist subversion, but because of alleged radical Islamic conspiracies.

On the credit side for Suharto's New Order were an impressive growth in GDP in the 30 years to the early 1990s, a doubling of the manufacturing share of GDP to 24 per cent, increases in the rice yield, and predictable responses in international affairs. However, this wealth gain was unevenly distributed, and from a small base. Much of it derived from the huge increase in the world oil price in 1974, which quadrupled Indonesia's income from this source. 'Green revolution' gains in food crop production were mainly due to improved seed and the greater use of pesticides, but resulted in sharp disparities in wealth in rural areas between those controlling these new methods and the former smallholders, many of whom have lost their land to large agribusinesses.

While advances in industry and the raised GDP provided some general benefits, most went to the small minority of the wealthy and influential. New industry, almost always joint ventures with foreign capital, included labour-intensive manufacture like clothing and shoes, but also extended to glassware, electrical goods and motor parts. Indonesia became the world's largest exporter of plywood, although this industry eventually prompted a major scandal because of its rapid depletion of the country's timber resources and diversion of much of the proceeds to a few 'cronies'. Much of this logging is illegal, and is still continuing. The World Bank reported, in November 2000, that of 23 unlicensed sawmills in the Bukit Tigapuluh National Park in Sumatra, 12 were backed by the army, one by the police, three by the provincial forestry department and two by the local public works department. Losses to revenue because of illegal logging were estimated at over a billion dollars, and more than two million Dyak people in Kalimantan (Borneo) alone, are said to have been displaced by massive forest destruction. A further consequence has been the rapid depletion of orang-utan populations because of loss of habitat. Orang-utans – the name means 'man of the jungle' – are Asia's only great ape. Once existing in millions, numbers have now been reduced to perhaps 20,000.

On 7 December 1975, Indonesia invaded East Timor, using a large naval task force, aircraft and 10,000 troops, choosing a time of political instability in both Portugal, the colonizing power, and in Australia, less than 400 miles to the south. Australian public opinion was largely on the side of the Timorese because Australian commandos in Timor during the Second World War had been protected by the local people at considerable cost to the Timorese, who suffered greatly from brutal Japanese retaliation. However, in spite of this, the Australian government for two decades supported Indonesia's claim to the territory .

East Timor makes up roughly half of the island of that name, the western section, formerly a Dutch possession, having become part of Indonesia at the time of independence. Since Indonesia had no historic, ethnic or political justification to claim the eastern half, the invasion created widespread criticism within the United Nations and in communities and parliaments around the world. A civil war ensued following resistance to Indonesia from FRETILIN, a political party which had declared the territory's independence not long before the invasion. The Indonesian military contended they had invaded because FRETILIN was Communist, but the organization has denied this.

In November 1975 five Australian television journalists were killed by Indonesian troops in the small town of Balibo ten kilometres from the border of Indonesian Timor. Timorese spokesman, now foreign minister, Jose Ramos-Horta says they were simply taken prisoner by the Indonesian army and shot, and that 'the Indonesians were determined to "teach a lesson" to the Australians, as Radio Kupang (in Indonesian Timor) boasted that evening'. The Indonesian army claimed the journalists died when they were caught in crossfire. However, subsequent eyewitness accounts in 1998 indicate that they were shot and knifed by Indonesian troops in cold blood after no more than token FRETILIN resistance in Balibo had ended. Soon after the Balibo incident another Australian journalist, Roger East, was shot in particularly brutal circumstances by Indonesian soldiers on Dili wharf.

According to Ramos-Horta's book *Funu*, as many as 200,000 Timorese died between 1975 and 1981, partly due to acts of war, but substantially because of 'a deliberate strategy of starvation through destruction of food crops and continuous military operations that left the population unable to cultivate the land'. Thousands more perished later in the Indonesian occupation. However, a FRETILIN guerrilla army maintained the struggle. East Timor was returned to world attention by major television coverage of 'the Dili massacre' – an attack by Indonesian troops in 1991 on an unarmed assembly in Santa Cruz cemetery in the capital of the territory that resulted in an estimated 300 deaths – and the award of the Nobel Prize for Peace to Ramos-Horta and the Bishop of Dili, Bishop Carlos Belo.

After much negotiation the Indonesian government agreed to a vote of the East Timorese people in August 1999 to decide their future. When 78.5 per cent of the people of East Timor voted for independence, the pro-Indonesia militia and units of the Indonesian army shocked the world by visiting a terrible revenge on them, murdering, torturing, burning down almost every town and village before they were replaced by an Australian-led peacekeeping force. However, in October the Indonesian parliament decided reluctantly to endorse the East Timor vote, making way for the evolution of a new nation in Asia – Timor Leste. Its fortunes since have been varied. Lack of money and expertise have restricted development and repair of the country's ruined infrastructure, but this situation should improve as future revenues from offshore oil in the Timor Gap become available. In 2004 Australia's relationship with Timor Leste was strained by disagreement over how the income from these oilfields, in the sea between the two countries, should be shared.

Falling oil prices in the mid-1980s severely affected Indonesia's economy, dependent as it was on this single product. Corruption and cronyism seemed impossible to control – the more so because they were so often associated with the president's family and close associates. Banks were crippled or in some cases driven to insolvency by an increasing burden of bad debt, which by 1993 had doubled in five years to more than 15 per cent of all bank loans. The stock market index lost two-thirds of its value in the early 1990s, with an associated sharp increase in foreign debt to about $80 billion.

Community uneasiness at the very public corruption and extreme differences in wealth between the rich and the average Indonesian was to increase steadily from this time onward. Most Indonesians are Muslims, and the Islamic establishment, feeling itself isolated from the decision-making processes, became a leader of public protest. University students were also closely involved, using the Internet to co-ordinate their activities after the government muzzled or forced the close-down of independent newspapers. Suharto became increasingly unpopular, apparently maintaining his position only because of brutal repression by the army.

Following the shooting of five students by the army at a peaceful demonstration in Jakarta in May 1998, and major rioting in many parts of the country, Suharto was obliged to resign from the presidency after 32 years in office. Under his former protégé and successor, President B. J. Habibie, came limited signs of liberalization and the promise of fair elections within a year. Habibie ordered the release of some political prisoners, reversed the ban on the formation of new political parties and restored some freedom to the public media. However, although it was evident the army remained a major source of power, continued rioting, mob murders and burning of Chinese houses and shops and Christian churches made it equally plain that they were unable, or unwilling, to maintain law and order.

These events and the economic crisis from July 1997 served to bring many problems to the surface, but not to solve them. The bare facts of that situation were alarming enough. The Indonesian rupiah plummeted wildly from July 1997, seven months later stabilizing uneasily at 9000 to the American dollar, barely a third of its pre-crash value. With the private-sector foreign debt at around $70 billion, Indonesia immediately faced its worst financial crisis for 30 years. The value of shares in Indonesian companies fell in sympathy. The situation was not improved by the effects of a long drought, which had obliged Indonesia to import large amounts of food. The cost of imported rice rose more than three times and, even after government subsidies, was twice as expensive in the shops and markets.

Meanwhile the collapse of hundreds of businesses had increased unemployment by millions. Rusting steel skeletons in Jakarta's business centre were only too eloquent of the sudden cessation of work on high-rise building projects whose finance, loans coming from overseas, had dried up. Loss of income, combined with rising food prices, created a highly volatile situation, with food riots reported from many parts of the country. The numbers of 'middle class' people, earning between $600 and $1500 a month, was estimated to have fallen from 20 million to 10 million.

A disquieting aspect of the situation was regular violence against the Chinese. Although barely five per cent of the population, they controlled well over half of Indonesia's wealth. The early weeks of the campaign to make the Chinese the scapegoats for unemployment and rising prices brought some evidence that the government and the courts were encouraging it. More rioting, bringing thousands on to Jakarta's streets, came with a meeting of the People's Consultative Assembly in November, called by President Habibie in an effort to resolve some of the nation's problems. An announcement that elections proposed for May 1999 would be delayed until July increased the wrath of protestors. Hundreds more people were killed in these riots, often under the most brutal circumstances. That month also saw the revelation of a major killing campaign, including women and children, by the Indonesian army on the island of Biak, part of the former West Irian, and evidence of further army killing in the Aceh region.

Habibie, increasingly revealed as verbose and inconsistent, had by late 1999 little support among the people or the army. However, elections that year were relatively peaceful. Sukarno's daughter, Megawati, achieved the highest vote, 34 per cent. An Indonesian commented: 'They voted for the father.' Even so, in a surprise decision of the parliament Megawati was defeated by 373 votes to 313 for the presidency, the frail, almost blind leader of the largest Muslim party, NU, Abdurrahman Wahid, becoming Indonesia's fourth president. Severe rioting followed the decision. Although Wahid was a widely respected religious leader, he failed to cope with Indonesia's apparently intractable problems. He seemed unable to prevent the training and arming of the extremist Islamic Laskar Jihad militia, nor its transport from Java to the Maluku Islands, where it played a major part in a campaign that killed 5000 Christians and burned down hundreds of villages and churches. Corruption among his staff and associates also diminished Wahid's influence. He was dismissed by the People's Consultative Assembly and replaced by his deputy, Megawati, in July 2001. She became Indonesia's fourth president in four years.

It cannot be said that she was a strong president, nor was she able to solve the nation's severe economic problems. If anything, she appeared to have moved closer to relying on the army, which has continued to dominate the nation and now seems virtually as powerful at all levels of the economy and the society as it was in the Suharto years. Under her presidency civil war has continued to plague Indonesia, killing thousands in the Maluku islands, West Papua and Aceh, and driving many more thousands from their homes. An ominous aspect of this has been conflict between Muslim and Christian communities, which are roughly equal in numbers in the eastern islands.

A decision early in 2001 to delegate many functions, including health, education, water supply, mining and forestry to the country's 364 regencies – local areas – has tended to decentralize corruption rather than authority. This has been a considerable deterrent for foreign investment, creating even more complicated hierarchies which must be bribed by those seeking to do business in Indonesia. There was a direct outflow of $1.7 billion in foreign investment in 2002.

On 12 October 2002, a firebomb made from the fertilizer nitrate of ammonia and fuel oil killed 200 people in the nightclub strip of the popular tourist destination of Kuta Beach, Bali. This atrocity, committed by Islamic extremists, became linked into the worldwide 'war against terror' resulting from the World Trade Center attacks in New York. As with Pakistan, the United States and Australia softened their previous hard line against the Indonesian military, resulting in a significant increase in army power.

Four major influences on the present and future Indonesia can be identified. One is the hold the army and the financial elite from the Suharto era have on the community, which they seem able to maintain regardless of the decisions of the elected government. Closely associated is the second – the apparent inability of that government to control the country and its affairs. Government more and more is being exercised regionally, as often as not by local elements of the army. Third must be the continued poverty and economic inequality. According to an Indonesian Manpower Ministry statement, 36 million people, 17 per cent of the population, were unemployed in 2002, a problem 'we will not be able to overcome in the next five to 10 years'. Fourth is the growing strength of extremist Islamic groups in the society, and the tacit support of them by both the government and sections of the military. As elsewhere in the Islamic world, Indonesia is opposed to United States intervention in Iraq, which many people there see as a direct attack by the West on Islam.

Will Indonesia survive as a single, united state? The risk of balkanization is real enough. In a number of regional areas, especially in Aceh and Indonesian Papua, it is being suppressed only by force or the threat of force from the army. Aceh has demanded autonomy and control of its oil and gas revenues from the time of Indonesian independence. This has led to open conflict and the loss of perhaps 5000 lives during and after the Suharto years, with no signs of a peaceful solution at the time of writing. There has been a similar, if less well organized demand for independence in West Papua, especially since credible evidence emerged in 2001 that a referendum of the people there was 'just a whitewash', in which only 1022 handpicked supporters, overseen by the army, voted unanimously for integration with Indonesia, while a million more had no choice at all. In 2001 President Abdurrahman Wahid offered the Papuans a considerable degree of autonomy, but President Megawati appeared to have withdrawn from that position, proposing instead to, in the opinion of Papuan nationalists, 'divide and rule' by splitting the territory into three provinces. Dialogue with the Papuans effectively ended in 2003, to be replaced by harsh military rule. The army's special force, Kopassus, which has been involved in several well-documented atrocities over the years, was again operating in Papua, as also was the extremist Islamic militia Laskar Jihad.

Whatever happens to Indonesia is of major importance to the world. It is, after all, the fourth largest population on the planet, with 230 million people. Most of these people live precariously. One or more bad seasons could result in actual shortages of basic foods, even of starvation for millions of people. In such a case Jakarta's tenuous political authority could become even less effective, the army's control might be stretched to breaking point. Public exasperation increased in 2004 when the chairman of Golkar and the Parliamentary Speaker, Akbar Tanjung, was acquitted of embezzlement charges by the Supreme Court – one of a considerable list of big names cleared by the court. One judge, Abdurrahman Saleh, dissented, saying that the findings of two lower courts were right, and that Tanjung had engaged in 'corrupt practice and shameful conduct'.

Elections for the parliament and the presidency in 2004 delivered a sharp rebuke to Megawati and her administration for their failure to improve the lives of the huge army of the poor. Her Democratic Party for Struggle gained only 18.5 per cent of the vote for the parliament, running second to the wealthy and highly organized Golkar, the party of ex-Suharto supporters, with more than 21 per cent. Perhaps the most important result of the vote was its fragmentation, with no single party able to govern in its own right, and with most of the vote split between seven parties achieving more than 50 seats in the 550-seat legislature. The party that governs will need a complicated coalition, threatening an era of uncertain government. This could result in the army and the very wealthy again running the country.

Nevertheless, the elections resulted in a voter turnout of 87 per cent – 128 million – one of the highest in the world for nations with optional voting. It compares with, for instance, 50 per cent in the United States, around 55 per cent in India and Japan. An election for the presidency later that year, in which only Megawati and two ex-army generals were candidates, brought one of the latter, Dr Susilo Bambang Yudhoyono, to power with 60 per cent of the vote, compared with 39 per cent for Megawati.

Within weeks he faced a difficult challenge when the December tsunami killed more than 200,000 coast dwellers in Aceh, the northern section of the island of Sumatra. This death toll was tragic enough, but added to it was the uncertain future of as many as a million survivors who had lost almost everything – entire towns and villages destroyed, fishing boats smashed, wells and almost all arable land polluted with salt water. The Indonesian government could find only $50 million towards reconstruction costs assessed at over a billion dollars. However, massive international aid was pledged, including a billion dollars from Australia over a five-year period.

But beyond this localized disaster the seemingly intractable problems of the economy remain the most significant issue. Continued poverty can only become increasingly dangerous, breeding violence and instability. As Sukarno once said: 'The stomach will not wait.'

23 Malaysia, Singapore and Brunei

Malaysia is a new nation in more ways than one – her development as an organized community has taken place almost entirely within the last century and a half. Kuala Lumpur, the capital, and now the major centre of population and industry, was settled only after tin was discovered there in 1860. In the late nineteenth century the total population was a small fraction of the current 23 million, probably well under a million people. They were mostly seafaring tribesmen who lived in wood and *attap*-thatched villages straggling along the muddy banks of river estuaries. Apart from the brief and limited traditions of Malacca and Johore there was little sense of nationhood.

Peninsular Malaya, the central state of today's Malaysia, was important to the British East India Company in the first half of the nineteenth century because of three settlements along the west and south coasts, established as staging posts on the trade route to China: George Town on the mountainous island of Penang, Malacca and the island of Singapore.

Britain was uninterested then in the jungle-clad, largely mountainous and lightly populated interior. Here were no large, fertile delta areas, significant mines of gold or precious stones, no developed societies that might provide sources of raw materials and a market for manufactures. The climate was hot, humid and enervating, most of the soil poor. There were no roads, much less railways, and except for a few miles on either side of the river estuaries, the bulk of the snake-, tiger- and leech-infested country was inaccessible. It swarmed with the deadly mosquito *Anopheles*, as yet not identified as the carrier of malaria. Most of this country had never been explored, and there seemed little incentive for either Malay or European to do so. There was no land traffic between the east and west coasts, which are divided by ranges of high, steep and rugged mountains, to this day largely unexplored.

The opening of the Suez Canal in 1869 brought Malaya into much greater strategic and economic prominence. In 1867 the passage from London to Singapore was 116 days. Three years later a passage of 42 days was recorded.

In spite of the forbidding death rate from malaria, rural poverty in their home country drove tens of thousands of Chinese to Malaya as indentured coolies, mostly to work in tin mines in the northern states of Perak and Selangor. Up till then Malay mining had been small-scale and intermittent. Chinese labour and Chinese methods developed the industry so that by the end of the century it was the world's largest producer. The biggest migrations of Chinese were in the 1860s, when tens of thousands crowded into the shabby, lawless camps that grew up around the mines.

With scant law in up-country Malaya other than the knife and the gun, individual miners were more than willing to swear oaths of allegiance to a number of competing Chinese secret societies. These societies soon became rich and powerful, their rivalry bitter and violent. Pitched battles were frequent; members of one society boasted that their shirts were dyed with the blood of their rivals. Initiates were bound, as they still are today, to obey orders without question and to reveal absolutely no information about the society, on pain of death.

These circumstances laid the foundation for Malayan society as it is now, with a wealthy and influential Chinese minority numbering about a quarter of the population, within which secret criminal societies like the Triad still prosper, exacting 'squeeze' from shopkeepers, running brothels, engaging in illegal smuggling. They beat up opponents with bicycle chains, kill with the knife. Generally speaking, there is a deep underlying mistrust between the Chinese and Malay peoples.

During these formative decades struggles for power, plundering of neighbours and warfare were almost incessant among the Malay princelings. As new and productive tinfields came on line, so also did disputes as to who should get the royalties. Piracy off the coast became more impudent and common, with armed guards on merchant shipping regularly having to fight off attacking boats. General lawlessness in the end persuaded British authorities to intervene in 'up-country' affairs. In 1873 the authorities in Singapore were required 'to employ such influence as they possess with the native princes to rescue these countries from the ruin that must befall them if the present disorders continue unabated'. The provision, from 1874 on, of residents to advise local rulers led to an extension of British rule throughout the country. Dynastic squabbles were skilfully exploited by British diplomats to this end. The Malay rulers were obliged to accept British 'advice' in all matters except those relating to Islamic religion and custom.

By this time British interest was increased by two events that must be considered milestones. The first was the identification of *Anopheles* as the vector of malaria, and the development of measures to control it. The second was the introduction in 1888 of the rubber tree from its native Brazil and recognition that here was one export crop that would thrive on Malaya's poor soils, and for whose service there was an adequate pool of cheap labour. The mass production of the car made all the difference to the infant rubber industry. It boomed from 1906 onwards, and by 1937 there were more than two million acres of rubber plantation, exporting nearly three-quarters of a million tons a year.

For the first time, it became practicable for British planters to make a life for themselves and their families in the interior. Roads and railways were built, the coastal plain west of the mountains was cleared and cultivated and inland cities like Kuala Lumpur and Ipoh grew and prospered. Kuala Lumpur acquired a curious collection of public buildings, like the Jame Mosque, in the north Indian Mogul style, because in most cases the architects were Englishmen trained in India. An agreement with Thailand in 1909 resulted in four northern states, Perlis, Kedah, Kelantan and Trengannu being transferred to British Malaya. This event almost doubled the area of Malaya at the expense of its neighbour, although the Thais were happy enough to get rid of much of the troublesome Malay/Muslim minority in the south.

Although a Communist party was founded in 1930, largely among the Chinese, no independence movement evolved comparable to those in India or Indonesia. The multi-racial nature of the society was partly responsible for this. There was also by now a large minority of Tamil labourers from India, who had been imported to tap the latex sap from the rubber trees, and whose descendants now make up almost ten per cent of the population. Although the world depression of the 1930s caused some setbacks, life and progress continued in an orderly way – the Malaya of Somerset Maugham's novels, a placid plantation life made up of the casual social round in the Europeans' bungalows, with their wide verandahs and slow-moving ceiling fans. By 1940 the population had grown to four million.

In 1941 the Pacific war burst on this peaceful scene without warning. The Japanese landed in Kelantan only the day after the United States fleet was destroyed in Pearl Harbor and quickly extended their bridgehead. Early in 1942 Singapore fell. The Japanese failure to maintain preventive health services resulted in a major flare-up of malaria. The invaders treated Malaya's people with the same brutality they exhibited elsewhere in occupied south-east Asia, but reserved their especial vindictiveness for the Chinese.

A resistance movement, largely Communist, grew up among the Chinese, and continued in jungle hideaways during British reoccupation of

Figure 14   Rubber was one of the main labour-intensive crops during the colonial phase in Asia, and still exists as a cash crop. This picture shows how the tree is tapped, the raw latex flowing into a ceramic bowl

Malaya. In 1948 the Emergency, a bitter, protracted war between the Communist independent platoons and the colonial government, began. Soon the countryside took on a wartime aspect. The villages were surrounded by eight-foot-high barbed-wire perimeter fences, closely guarded and floodlit and under curfew at night.

Working in Malaya during the last years of the Emergency, I shared the stringent conditions imposed on everyone driving a car – the order to be inside a wired perimeter by nightfall or be fired on, not to stop between villages, not to carry food, money, canvas, plastic sheeting, writing paper, typewriters, arms and a host of other things that might be useful to the Communists. We were supposed to join convoys, trundling along behind a 'coffin' – an armoured personnel carrier – but this proved so likely to attract attack that it was safer, and faster, to travel alone. I recall ending up just on dusk in a village in which a tent was an officers' mess of the King's Own Scottish Borderers.

'Ye'll have a whisky, lad? Soda or water?'

'Water, thanks.'

A grin.

'Just as well now. Ask for soda here, we put ye outside the wire for the night.'

The Emergency dragged on largely because it was as much a Chinese as a Communist initiative. I was once a guest at a dinner of a number of wealthy Chinese in Penang, where several of the company drank so much they literally fell off their chairs, female staff of the restaurant discreetly carrying them off to bed in specially prepared rooms. One of these, a Chinese banker, after considerable brandy remarked to me: 'Ah . . . it is *our* army in the jungle.'

Political events were finally more effective in ending the Emergency than the very costly and attritional military ones, which had included herding much of the population into concentration camps. Whole villages were forcibly depopulated, a melancholy sight as one drove through the country. The misery and poverty caused by this British army policy did much to ensure that the Communist independent platoons had so many willing recruits they were able to keep up their numbers throughout the Emergency.

All three major Asian communities formed political associations dedicated to the task of achieving independence as a parliamentary democracy. The coming of internal self-government in 1955 was unexpected. The intention of the British government was that only limited powers be given to those chosen in Malaya's first general elections in that year. However, the Alliance Party, representing all three racial groups, won 51 of the 52 elective seats, a result so eloquent that its leader, Tengku Abdul Rahman, was able to get an undertaking for full independence as soon as possible. On 31 August 1957, Malaya became an independent dominion within the British Commonwealth. Malaya was fortunate in its first leader. A Malay prince, an educated, kindly man very aware of the risk of communal violence, one of his most eloquent acts was the adoption of Chinese children into his family.

Since independence deprived the Communist rebellion of any rationale, only isolated trouble spots remained and the state of emergency was officially ended in 1960. Nevertheless, the Communist leader, Chin Peng, and a small army of his most loyal and fanatical followers retreated to the jungle-clad hills at the Thai border, finally announcing the end of their armed struggle in 1989.

A major step forward was taken in 1963 with the inclusion of the British colonies of Singapore, Sarawak and Sabah with Malaya in an extended federation, called Malaysia. Oil-rich Brunei declined to become a member. Because it is mostly Chinese, the city-state of Singapore eventually, however, also elected to become an independent republic, leaving Malaysia in 1965.

Modern Singapore is an extraordinary testament to what its architect, Lee Kuan Yew, calls 'Asian values'. Not only do three and a half million people live on this tiny island of only 250 square miles, they do so in economic and social conditions that are among the best in the world. Life expectancy at birth is 76.6 years, the literacy rate is 92.2 per cent and population growth a low 1.1 per cent. All this is the more remarkable because the island lacks natural resources. The soil is mostly poor, and Singapore relies for more than half its water on neighbouring Malaysia, to which the island is connected by a causeway. Almost all food is imported.

During the 1950s the Foreign Correspondents' Association of South-east Asia had regular lunches at the Hotel de l'Europe (the Cockpit) in Singapore. Here I saw and occasionally exchanged a few words with a young, smartly dressed Chinese lawyer whom everyone knew as Harry Lee. You would not call him Harry now. In 1955 Lee Kuan Yew achieved the highest vote of any individual candidate in an election for an assembly in Singapore, although still with limited powers. He was one of three members of the left-wing People's Action Party (PAP) to be elected. The PAP now developed as a party in which two major factions struggled for control. One was the moderates under Lee Kuan Yew and the other a Communist 'front'. Britain gave Singapore full internal self-government in 1959. Lee Kuan Yew's remarkable charisma and political acumen were demonstrated when he attracted enormous applause by speaking to a large audience of Singaporeans in Malay after some less well-received speeches in English.

A general election later that year gave the PAP a landslide victory. The PAP, however, split, giving Lee's moderates a majority of only one, and for a time the new party, the Socialist Front, seemed likely to take over the government. However, Lee again distinguished himself as a shrewd, pragmatic leader. A general election in 1963 gave his party 37 seats out of 51. Lee undertook to provide 'performance, not promises. The millions of the dispossessed in Asia care not and know not of theory. They want a better life, a more equal and a more just society.' The task facing the new government was far from easy. There were serious communal riots in that year. Beyond this the former colony was ethnically divided, and short of modern infrastructure and adequate housing for most of its people.

A remarkable combination of ruthlessness, efficiency and, on the whole, benevolent intent enabled Lee to continue to dominate Singapore, and to become a world figure during the next three decades. By using actions in the courts and both subtle and not-so-subtle coercion to destroy opposition in the parliament, he came close to being a one-man government of Singapore. In 1968 the PAP won all 58 seats – 51 per cent of them unopposed. The PAP prides itself on its pragmatism. Its blend of parliamentary democracy and a deliberate restriction of the freedoms and political rights of the people gives it virtually unfettered power to mould the community in the ways it feels best. Families would be limited to two children, there would be no long-haired youth, 'decadent' music and dancing were forbidden, no one must spit in the streets, Confucian values like respect for parents and family solidarity would apply, very severe sanctions, including the death penalty, were introduced for drug use and trafficking. Efficiency, hard work, reliability became the established virtues.

On this basis Lee Kuan Yew transformed Singapore from a ramshackle Chinese provincial city on a south-east Asian island into a modern, wealthy and influential industrial power. Its former thatched shanty towns – so often the scene of horrific fires – and crowded terraces of Chinese shophouses were torn down and replaced by rows of modern high-rise apartments and a central business district skyline of tall office towers. Public transport and education facilities are among the best in the world.

A virtual obsession with hygiene transformed the city from one of many smells (it must be admitted) to a clean, aseptic metropolis, with the best-educated, healthiest and most prosperous population in Asia. For instance, it is an offence not to flush a public toilet in Singapore – a small detail of strict laws controlling air and water quality and public hygiene. Singapore has a severe and harsh legal system by world standards. Its government justifies this by pointing to the island's very low crime rate.

Singapore's economic miracle derives almost entirely from the intelligence, hard work and intense competitiveness of its people, three-quarters of whom are Chinese. Something of its nature can be deduced from the fact that almost three-quarters of GDP derives from services, mostly in the fields of finance, business, trade and tourism. All but a small fraction of the remainder comes from manufacturing. Much of this, especially electronics, is in the 'smart' category, with considerable attention given to information technology. In recent years there has been considerable emphasis on attracting research establishments with tax breaks and other incentives.

In spite of a check to Singapore's prosperity due to the Asian economic crisis, the PAP was elected for a further five-year term in November 2001, winning 82 of 90 elective seats. At that stage it had been the government for 39 years. Lee Kuan Yew's eldest son, Lee Hsien Loong, became prime minister in 2004 at the age of 52. Lee senior and the former prime minister for 14 years, Gho Chok Tong, remained, however, as the next most senior ministers in the Cabinet, the trio irreverently styled by some Singaporeans the Trinity – father, son and holy Gho. Lee Hsien Loong's wife, Ho Ching, is head of Temasek Holdings, a huge corporation through which the government controls much of the island's business and considerable overseas investments. Another son, Lee Hsien Yang, heads the big communications enterprise, Singtel.

One of Singapore's major problems, which it shares with many of the world's other prosperous countries, is a birth rate so low that it threatens a falling and ageing population. In 2004 women averaged only 1.4 children, well below replacement rate at 2.1. Characteristically, it was government that took on the job of coaxing young Singaporeans into a greater interest in the 'birds and bees' with a publicity campaign including steamy love songs designed to counter a lack of interest in sex (which an official survey claimed happens only once every five days, on average).

In 1841 the Sultan of Brunei gave the Borneo territory of Sarawak to an English adventurer, Captain James Brooke, in return for Brooke's help in subduing 'pirates'. The Brooke family ruled Sarawak from its *istana* (palace) in the river capital of Kuching for several generations; over the door of their home was the motto 'What I have I hold'. After some hesitation, the British government recognized this dynasty of 'white rajahs' in 1864 and granted British protection in 1888. After the Second World War the third rajah ceded it to the British Crown. The first elections were held in 1959 to establish a degree of self-rule under a legislative assembly called the Council Negri. Elections for the state government in this territory of two million people have since resulted in coalitions of parties representing the major ethnic groups.

Sabah, which was then called North Borneo, lies to the north of Sarawak and, like that territory, shares a wild mountain border with Indonesian Kalimantan. Most of this has never been explored. Sabah has almost two million people, of whom 200,000 are Chinese and the rest native tribes, the Murut, Kadazan and Bajau being among the most numerous. Like Sarawak, Sabah came under British protection in 1888 and, with the small island of Labuan off its coast, became a Crown colony after the Second World War. Like Sarawak, Sabah has an essentially agricultural economy, exporting timber, rubber, copra, pepper and some tobacco.

In this substantially rural scene Brunei stands out in vivid contrast. The total population is around 350,000, occupying some 2000 square miles of the Borneo coast. But Brunei does have rich oilfields, and for its population size is one of the wealthiest states in the world.

Brunei's era of glory was the sixteenth century, when the sultanate is believed to have controlled most of Borneo and many islands in the Sulu Sea which are now part of the Philippines. It became a notorious haven for piracy until the middle of the nineteenth century, when the British navy destroyed the pirate fleets. Brunei's territory and influence had declined by then, and when it became a British protectorate in 1888, it was no more than a tiny, poor and obscure Muslim principality on the banks of a muddy estuary. Since oil was found near the coast at Seria in 1929, it has brought in so much money in royalties the state has difficulty spending it. A banker in Brunei once told me that the whole population could live comfortably into the indefinite future on the income from its overseas investments.

Whether this remains the case depends on how the royal family spends the oil revenues in the future. The sultan is one of the richest men in the world, with assets at one time of about $50 billion. His current wealth is estimated to be less than half that. A decline in Brunei's fortunes has been partly due to huge spending by the royal family, sometimes to the benefit of the people, but at times on luxury items for themselves. The town of Brunei has a huge marble mosque, completed in 1958 to look like the Taj Mahal, modern schools, hospitals, and roads. Education and health care are free, and there is no income tax. Rice and housing are subsidized.

However, with the oilfields due to run dry in 18 years at present production rates, Brunei was suffering from its first economic problems by the turn of the millennium. In 2000 the sultan's younger brother, Prince Jefri Bolkiah, who had been finance minister, faced a lawsuit to recover $15 billion he had spent on such items as luxury hotels, jewellery, cars, aircraft and gold-plated hairbrushes. The prince settled for an allowance of $300,000 a month, and left Brunei to live in Europe. The following year an auction of his possessions was held in Brunei, raising nearly $8 million. Items on sale included a 12-foot-high bronze rocking horse, grand pianos, mirrors, antique cannon and a marble factory. However, in spite of some financial troubles, Brunei still has a gross national income of almost $8 billion, with per capita GDP at $18,000 in 2002. Other social indicators are high, with literacy at 91 per cent.

Brunei became an independent state in 1983 after 100 years of British protection, and has close relations with Singapore, including training of defence forces. It has spent at least $2 billion on modern defensive weapons systems, such as Exocet missiles.

Earlier, in 1959, Brunei had achieved internal self-government, with three tiers of government. Of these, only the district councils were elective. The left-wing Parti Rakyat Brunei (PRB) emerged with policies for democracy and the unifying of the three north Borneo states, under the leadership of

Ahman Azahari. It became a major force after achieving a high vote in district council elections in 1962. However, when Azahari declared himself prime minister of a new state of North Borneo and announced an armed struggle, the sultan was able to retain power with the help of British forces from Singapore. The PRB was proscribed and its leaders imprisoned or forced into exile. From this time onwards the sultan ruled by decree, Brunei thus becoming one of the world's few remaining absolute monarchies. Not surprisingly, it has one of the most restrictive immigration policies in the world.

Severe racial rioting in Kuala Lumpur in 1969, in which 200 people were killed, led to a suspension of the Malaysian parliament for two years and a general tightening of law and order procedures. But when parliament resumed in 1971, democracy became 'controlled'. The constitution was amended to stress Malay dominance. Malay would be the national language and Islam the official religion. The media, even parliament and the law courts, became subject to government control. There is an echo here of the concept in traditional Malay kingdoms of *derhaka* (treason) as the ultimate crime. A consequence of such evident racial tensions has been government preoccupation with the ethnic issue, especially a continuing situation in which most business and money is controlled by Chinese and Indians, with considerable poverty among the Malays. In 1970 over half of the Malays were estimated to be below the poverty level, but as a result of government intervention to admit Malays into occupations formerly dominated by non-Malays, this has now been reduced to under 20 per cent. There was a further outbreak of communal violence in Kuala Lumpur in 2001, in which at least 12 people were killed.

Successful offshore exploration for oil and gas after 1970 greatly assisted the economy. Reserves are estimated at 5 billion barrels of oil and 80 billion cubic feet of gas, and hydrocarbons make up nearly 10 per cent of Malaysia's export income. Palm-oil plantations began to replace the less profitable rubber estates. Manufacturing had become the most important area of export income by the mid-1990s.

Malaysia's initial democracy had hardened into authoritarianism by the late 1980s. The fourth prime minister, Mahathir Mohamad, who took office in 1981, used Malaysia's draconic internal security laws – a hangover from the Emergency – to close down four newspapers and arrest 119 political opponents and independent-minded journalists in 1987. More were to follow during the next decade. People arrested under these laws could be and were imprisoned without trial. Since that time Malaysia has had a syco-phantic and compliant press, and political opposition has been severely discouraged. Mahathir, the first Malaysian leader to challenge continued British economic patronage, made vigorous attempts to reduce the dominance of British companies in the rubber industry by acquiring their shares and placing them in a state-owned corporation, Permodalan. Foreign ownership of the modern sectors of the economy, more than half in 1970, is now well under a quarter. However, by 1995 policy again tended to favour privatization of major industries.

The government has worked steadily to increase both the wealth and the status of the Malays and other indigenous peoples, who make up almost 60 cent of the population. There is now a numerous and visible Malay middle class.

The collapse of the economy in 1997 and the attendant hardships caused increasing discontent with government authoritarianism. As elsewhere in Asia people were prepared to tolerate it as long as they were modestly prosperous – what has been succinctly described as 'Shut up and I'll let you get rich.' In 1998 this discontent coalesced around the person of the dismissed deputy prime minister, Anwar Ibrahim, leading to extensive demonstrations and pitched battles between the 'rioters' and the police. There was widespread criticism of members of the government said to be involved in 'crony capitalism'.

Anwar, who had attracted worldwide respect for his moderate and enlightened attitudes, had been expected to succeed the ageing Mahathir. Instead Mahathir dismissed Anwar. Anwar was immediately charged with a variety of offences and imprisoned. When he appeared in court with head injuries inflicted by the arresting police, many world leaders – even those of some other Asian countries – spoke out in his support. Anwar was not alone in this predicament. Hundreds of the thousands who regularly took to the streets to support him were beaten or arrested.

Early in 1999 Anwar was sentenced to six years in prison, following a bizarre trial which raised considerable doubts about the integrity of the Malaysian system of justice. However, Dr Mahathir was returned to power in an election later that year, although with a reduced majority. He stepped down late in 2003. In an election early the following year his successor, Abdullah Badawi, achieved a resounding victory. The government won 198 seats of 219 in the parliament, and the Islamic party, PAS, retained only seven of the 27 it had won in 1999. This was widely interpreted as a vote for the status quo and an indication of public fears of Islamic fundamentalism, but the result must also have been influenced by the considerable restrictions imposed on opposition parties in conditions of 'controlled' democracy. Anwar was released from prison in 2004, but under Malaysian law cannot occupy any political office again until 2008.

Malaysia's prosperity had revived substantially by 2000, following a temporary isolation of its economy from the international system and the injection of millions of dollars into industry in the form of low-interest loans. An advanced high-technology industry in electronics earns more than half of export income.

24 Japan: the Iron Triangle

The opening of Japan to trade with the rest of the world after almost three centuries of isolation, and her rapid progress from a seemingly rigid feudalism to a Western-style capitalist economy, made her a major world power within a single generation. This was without doubt a revolution, although quite different from those in colonial Asia. Even so, the transformation of Japanese society after she concluded the first trade treaties with the West in 1854 was not as sudden as it seemed. Feudalism, already far into decay, was ready to collapse at a touch.

In the decade after the 'opening of Japan' the society became even more fluid. Western merchants took advantage of Japanese inexperience by exploiting the *bakufu*'s unrealistic exchange rate between gold and silver, more than twice that on world markets. Foreign traders made huge profits and there was a tremendous, destabilizing drain on Japan's gold reserves. This, coupled with similar manipulation of other exportable commodities, caused disastrous rises in the cost of living (rice increasing twelvefold, raw silk trebling) in eight years.

As a result, the decision to admit foreign traders provoked widespread and increasing hostility. In 1863 the large and powerful Choshu clan fired on American, Dutch and French ships from its shore batteries dominating the narrow and strategic Straits of Shimonoseki. The next year a Western fleet retaliated by destroying the batteries. Choshu, a clan traditionally opposed to the *bakufu*, now placed themselves firmly behind the emperor. Armed with 7000 modern rifles bought from the West, in 1866 they defeated a *bakufu* army easily. The following year the *shogun*, making a realistic assessment of the facts, abdicated voluntarily.

In 1868 the 16-year-old emperor, advised by a *samurai* clique largely consisting of Choshu men and their allies the Satsuma – both clans with a higher proportion of *samurai* than the average – announced his assumption of full authority. Choshu were later to lead development of a modern Japanese army, Satsuma a modern navy. This elevation of the emperor to lead the nation was confirmed by important changes in the state ethic. Confucianism and the various cults of Buddhism, which had been popular during the Tokugawa period, were officially displaced, and Shinto, the animist religion of the ancient Japanese, restored to primacy.

However, Shinto now became more than a religion. It was carefully modelled into a national cult, designed to promote belief in the virtual divinity, infallibility and invincibility of the emperor and the duty of every Japanese, if necessary, to die for him. The state machine insisted that everyone believe the myths of Japanese creation, asserting divine origin of the imperial line and the uniqueness and purity of the Japanese people. Even to question this 'emperor system' invited severe punishment. Archaeologists whose work indicated quite different conclusions about Japanese prehistory were thus effectively silenced until after the end of the Second World War in 1945. In such ways the new clique in power sought, as the Tokugawa had done, to stabilize the new order and ensure the obedience of the people.

The fact that the Western powers, with their modern weapons, had been able to force Japan into trade, and their own inability to resist, made a deep impression on the Japanese. Envoys sent out to study the outside world recommended that Japan adopt Western science, trade methods and industry as quickly as possible. The feudal system was officially dismantled, and the *daimyo* ceded their lands to the emperor, who moved his court to Edo in 1868. The city was renamed Tokyo, which means 'eastern capital'. The new era, called Meiji after the reign name taken by the emperor, led to the transformation and modernization of Japan at a breakneck pace. However, there was nothing democratic about the new order. Japan became effectively a police state, in which the police saw themselves as substantially occupying the position previously held by the *samurai*. Universal conscription was introduced for the armed services.

In 1871 the *samurai* lost their notorious right to 'kill and go away' and in 1877 30,000 of their number died in a rebellion that was put down by an army consisting mainly of commoners. Torture as a routine legal practice was abolished in 1876. Farmers were permitted to ride horses on public roads, and to own, buy and sell land, but were required to pay a third of the yield of their crops in tax. Japan was linked to the outside world by cable telegraph. Gas lit the streets of Yokohama in 1872. Railways spread across the country and urban complexes, complete with steel mills, power plants and other appurtenances of the modern industrial state, grew rapidly.

All this was achieved with money wrung from the heavily taxed peasantry and young women and men who worked in textile mills and coalmines for long hours on very small wages – almost as slaves. Infanticide became common, many families killing all but the first boy and girl at birth. There are contemporary accounts of peasants who decapitated their starving children, unable to bear their suffering. But among the wealthier urban classes Western styles of dress, Western methods and designs and Western manners were carefully studied and imitated. The Japanese word for a Western-style business suit, *sevilo*, derives from Savile Row.

But to attribute all this to a mere passion for copying is to miss the point. The motive was astute appreciation that only by change could Japan survive as an independent nation. The Japanese did not copy the West so much because they admired it as from a desire to put themselves in a position to compete with it in material terms. The carefully restored Shinto cult was a conscious rejection of Western, indeed all foreign, cultural ideas.

Japan's new leaders were determined she should be strong. A powerful modern navy was built in British shipyards and trained by British officers, and an army was developed on the German model. A major difficulty was the position of the two million *samurai*. Eventually the class was dispersed as such, although much of its tradition was carried over into new occupations, such as police and military officers, teachers and bureaucrats. This term, rather than 'public servant' is used, because the Japanese bureaucracy did not see itself as servants of the people. There is a saying, *kansom minpi*, which means 'official exalted, people despised'.

And, indeed, conditions of life and work for the ordinary people were appalling. Impoverished peasant families virtually sold their daughters into indentured labour in cotton mills and weaving sheds. Ninety per cent of workers in these 'sweated' industries were women, 13 per cent of them under the age of 14. They normally worked 12 hours a day, but work days of up to 19 hours were not uncommon. Living in crowded and unsanitary dormitories, they fell victim to tuberculosis in millions – one 1913 statistic puts death from this disease as high as 40 per cent of factory workers, and 70 per cent among those who later retired to their villages.

The Mitsui Company's coalmines were effectively a hell on earth. Failure to meet unreasonably high work quotas in the dangerous and hot, humid conditions incurred beatings or even worse punishment, including torture. And these conditions did not just apply to men. Women and children were sent down the mines – some as young as 10. Women were defined by law as second-class citizens and exploited in every possible way, including the sale of girls from impoverished peasant families into the public brothels found in every major city. Women were educated and trained to be 'docile and modest' and to subordinate themselves completely to their husbands and their families.

Decisive land and sea victories over China and Russia established Japan as a world power – moreover, as an imperialist power, conquering and assuming control of Korea, Manchuria and Taiwan. The Koreans opposed Japanese occupation vigorously – 12,000 resistance fighters were killed in 1907 and 1908. Although the forms of parliamentary democracy had been established in Japan in 1890, they had little effect until in 1925 universal male suffrage was introduced. However, by then two major catastrophes were affecting Japan. One was the world economic depression, the other Japan's worst natural disaster – the 1923 earthquake and fire that destroyed most of Tokyo and Yokohama and killed more than 150,000 people. Because of a rumour that Koreans had started the fire, almost 3000 Koreans were killed by lynching mobs. These economic and natural disasters brought in a period of harsh repression of such people as labour leaders and socialists, many of whom were executed.

By the middle of the decade militarism, which had seemed to be in decline after the First World War, was again on the ascendant. From May 1925 every school of middle grade or upward had a military officer on the active list attached to it. To the new generation educated to a fanatical nationalism, moderate policies appeared only as weakness. During the 1930s the army acted as a force above and beyond the law. A series of brutal assassinations of senior Japanese statesmen by young army officers occurred in 1932, with more such murders four years later. From then on the army, led by General Tojo, took over Japan.

Open war and invasion of China in 1937 involved atrocities that brought protests from around the world. The sacking of the Nationalist capital, Nanjing, was especially brutal. Japanese soldiers killed civilians, including women and children, mostly by the sword, and the Yangzi River, which passes through the city, was said to have literally run red with blood. The Chinese claim there were 300,000 dead. Eyewitnesses told of groups of up to 20 young people being tied together and thrown into the river to drown, people buried to the waist in the ground then torn to pieces by Alsatians, bizarre biological research, including injections of plague, anthrax and cholera. The refusal of Japanese Prime Minister Keizo Obuchi to apologize for these atrocities during a visit to Japan of Chinese President Jiang Zemin in 1998 led to a breakdown in talks designed to improve relations between the two nations. However, three years later Premier Koizumi did offer 'heartfelt apologies'.

In 1940 Japan placed herself on a complete war footing. The political parties were disbanded, making Japan totally subordinate to the military. Responsibility for the loss at Hawaii's Pearl Harbor of eight American battleships, three cruisers and at least half the effective air power of the Pacific Fleet brought Japan into four years of war that would ultimately prove disastrous. In spite of fanatical resistance, the Japanese were forced back from their initial Pacific conquests, which had brought them to New Guinea, the very doorstep of Australia. Damage to Tokyo was so great from aerial bombing, including probably the most severe fire bombing in human history, that its population fell from seven to three million due to casualties and evacuation. In July 1945 the Western Allies called on Japan to surrender unconditionally.

On 6 August 1945 an atomic bomb that would ultimately cause 200,000 deaths was dropped on the Japanese city of Hiroshima. Three days later a similar weapon destroyed Nagasaki. Five more days brought Japan's surrender. In the words of Emperor Hirohito, 'we have resolved to pave the way for peace for all future generations by enduring the unendurable'. Many people, including prominent national leaders and their wives, killed themselves. Thousands knelt outside the Imperial palace to beg forgiveness for their insufficient efforts. Yet as a result of the war almost two million people alive in 1940 were now dead, almost nine million homeless.

Japan was ruled for seven years from 1945 by a military occupation force – virtually personal rule by the Supreme Commander for the Allied Powers, General Douglas MacArthur. Japan seemed amenable to changes in direction and its military clique became hated and despised, not so much because of the misery and damage of the war, but because Japan had been defeated.

Basically, occupation policy was to guide Japan into new and democratic ways of government, and to reshape the education system and the economy. The big industrial conglomerates, the *zaibatsu*, were dissolved because of their close association with the military. The emperor became a constitutional monarch, but the popularity of the institution grew rather than declined because of efforts to 'democratize' his position. Many Japanese saw these as attempts to humiliate him, and this increased their feelings of loyalty. When the occupation ended in 1952 he visited the shrine of the Imperial Ancestors at Ise and reported to them that Japan was again free.

The permanent effects of the MacArthur 'shogunate' were few indeed, since most of its reforms have been reversed. In fact the reconstitution of the *zaibatsu* and the limited restoration of the armed forces began before the Americans left, and with their concurrence. Land reform was perhaps the most valuable and lasting result of the occupation. Peasant ownership of land doubled to almost four million, the beneficiaries being former tenant farmers.

However, there was nothing temporary or illusory about the regeneration of Japan's economy, which began during the occupation and was no less impressive than that of the Meiji restoration. Japan rapidly became the world's biggest shipbuilder, a major car manufacturer, and evolved through heavy industry to become a world leader in information technology. This 'great leap forward' was based substantially on a policy of ploughing profits back into development, rather than dividends. Typical of this was the Sony Corporation, which had humble beginnings in a small Tokyo shed with an initial capital of $500. Riding on the flood tide of demand for transistor radios, it was selling over a billion dollars' worth of its products annually by the 1960s. Japan built the world's largest ship, a tanker of 276,000 tons, and the world's fastest train, the Tokaido bullet train. In 1960 Japan had only 3.5 million cars and most people used an adequate public transport system. Thirty years later there were 65 million cars choking the roads, creating an urban nightmare of pollution and delays. This motor explosion quickly demanded more and better roads – thousands of miles of highways were built, a major element in what has become known as the concretization of Japan.

An early symptom of this was the destruction in 1967 of Frank Lloyd Wright's Imperial Hotel in Tokyo, internationally regarded as an architectural masterpiece, and so well designed that it was one of only a few buildings to survive the 1923 earthquake. A characterless 17-floor hotel replaced it. The pressure on land became enormous, leading to massive reclamation projects from the sea, such as the new Osaka airport on a wholly artificial island. Tokyo has no natural coastline left at all, and the areas adjacent to it only a few miles. There are also staggering plans to go upwards – buildings as much as a mile high are on the drawing-boards.

During the 1970s heavy industry began to run into trouble due to pollution and the sheer lack of suitable sites. The Tokyo–Kobe–Osaka region, the Kansai, in the words of one Japanese environmentalist, was rapidly becoming uninhabitable. Japan commenced a switch to post-industrial, high-tech industries. Strenuous efforts to decentralize these to regional technopolises – entirely new cities – have had varied success.

The massive infrastructure growth in Japan has not been driven by demand so much as by corrupt links between the government, the construction industry and the bureaucracy. This collusion, *yuchaku*, led to several public enquiries, and became so blatant that in 1994 a number of politicians and high-level businessmen were gaoled. The investigations revealed that as much as three billion dollars a year were being stolen from the frugal and long-suffering Japanese people – much of it going back as contributions to the Liberal-Democratic Party (LDP) government which had authorized the expenditure in the first place and channelled it to 'suitable' contractors. These would then kick back funds to 'feed the troops', that is, to the vote-buying system of Japanese politics.

This remarkable people, the modern Japanese, have over a trillion dollars stashed away in the one financial institution they trust – and the world's largest of its kind – the Post Office Savings Bank. By the 1980s, their hard work, obedience and skills had produced an enormous river of money that spilled over from Japan into all parts of the world, but especially into Asia and Australia. Billions of dollars were used to buy land, property and golf courses; new resorts and ski-slopes, burgeoned in Japan itself. Huge sums went into overseas investments, mostly in Korea and south-east Asia. When this bubble burst at the end of the decade property values in Japan fell heavily, and had not recovered as late as 2004.

The corruption scandals in the construction and finance industries contributed to loss of office by the LDP in 1993, after 38 years continuously in power. Hopes that this might presage genuine reform of Japanese politics dwindled as four uneasy coalition governments became necessary over as many years, during which Japan's financial situation caused increasing concern. Elections in 1996 brought the LDP back to government, which it retained comfortably in elections in 2000. In both of these polls barely half of the electorate voted.

However, the *tetsu no sankakukei*, the 'iron triangle' of politician, bureau-crat and big business, appears to have survived intact, as able as ever to resist change, especially if this would threaten its common interest. Fourteen of Japan's 17 major banks stood in need of a financial bail-out because of bad debts incurred during the four recessions of the 1990s. The rescue package cost the government $50 billion. Continued heavy expendi-ture on often unnecessary infrastructure made Japan the most indebted nation in the world by 2000, with a public debt of almost three trillion dollars, 120 per cent of GDP. In 2001 industrial production figures dropped almost eight per cent, as a result of Japan's fourth recession in 11 years.

In 1995 an earthquake struck the Kobe area, killing 6000 people and destroying 20 per cent of the houses in the city. It also revealed elements of the construction industry as being more than financially corrupt. Some of the collapses of freeways and bridges were found to be due to bad building and skimping on specified material such as reinforcing steel and concrete. Assistance to the stricken city was much less than adequate, especially since offers of assistance from the outside world were refused. Kobe's expe-rience, tragic enough in itself, also caused a further anxiety: What would happen to the Tokyo area if a similar earthquake occurred?

In 2001 a more flexible and charismatic man than was usual became prime minister. Junichiro Koizumi took over leadership of the LDP govern-ment with promises that he would end the party's faction system and revive Japan's economy. However, by the time of the next election at the end of 2003 little seemed to have changed, and the LDP lost support significantly.

The main opposition, the Democratic Party, won 177 seats compared to the LDP's 237. The Democrats actually won two million votes more than the LDP, but the result was skewed by a long-standing gerrymander favouring rural voters heavily against city dwellers.

Contrast is the essence of Japan. In the great, brightly lit shopping centre of Tokyo, the Ginza, Westernization seems complete. People wear Western clothes, the music systems in the big stores play Beethoven, Bach, Mozart. Yet just around a corner in a quiet street, behind an unobtrusive entrance, a traditional inn provides an environment and service largely unchanged from the Tokugawa.

In the industrial city of Osaka, under its pall of smoke, a whole region is given up to concrete, tall chimneys, noisy machines, construction cranes and the urgent clattering through a vast railway junction of the wheels of a score of over-crowded electric trains. Yet as one looks out of the carriage windows, there, between the points of two converging lines is a little plot of rice-growing, brushed by the bogies of every passing train. On the quiet shore of Lake Hacome, in the mountains not far from Tokyo, one may watch hundreds of Japanese reverentially looking out over the water at the cone of the sacred mountain, Fujiyama. An hour later one struggles to keep one's feet in the dense crowding of a railway carriage, rowdy with a hundred shouted conversations, the floor strewn with the debris.

In 1988 the Takeshita government gave a million dollars to each of Japan's 3000 local government areas to spend as they saw fit to invigorate their communities. The results showed a remarkable diversity, in many cases going back to traditional crafts and industries: making charcoal, straw sandals, growing mushrooms, nurturing older varieties of plum trees, attracting fireflies, eliminating bright lights in a place traditionally noted as being the best for looking at the stars. This regional diversity contrasts with a depressing uniformity of lifestyle in the Kansai cities. Those who live there nevertheless tolerate the ever-present throng of people and cars, the unnatural heat generated by so much concrete, with remarkable stoicism. Families live in tiny apartments, the breadwinners travel, usually standing, up to four hours a day in commuter trains. Many get home only at weekends, sometimes using tube hotels where the 'rooms' are not much larger than coffins – just big enough to lie down in.

In spite of this severe restriction of the natural advantages of life, such as space, fresh air, peace and quiet and untroubled leisure, the Japanese people are affluent in material things, with every imaginable form of technical gimmickry available to them. Efficient, fast cars clog the roads, regularly able to average little more than a walking pace, restlessly redirected by huge signs over the motorways warning of traffic jams ahead.

Numerous restaurants offering a wide range of foods are usually crowded, because most Japanese homes are too small to entertain in. Men buy the best in golf clubs and accessories, but mostly use them alongside hundreds of others inside driving ranges. Access to real golf courses is so expensive it can only be afforded occasionally. There is a lavish range of 'theme parks' available to the public, but little natural countryside or seaside. Food is abundant, but also often artificial and most of it has to be imported – indeed, Japan imports more of its food than any other country. The Japanese like seafood and the world's oceans are scoured for it.

The health and general welfare of Japanese has improved vastly. In 1920, one in eight children died as infants. That figure is now four in a thousand. Life expectancy, over 80, is the highest in the world. Like many other industrialized countries, Japan has an ageing population. The present 127 million is predicted to actually decline from 2005, to perhaps 100 million in 2050. The number of people of working age – that is, between 15 and 64 years – has been falling steadily from 87 million in 1995 to a predicted 54 million in 2050, with those over 65 rising from a fifth to a third of the population. On government estimates by 2020 there will be barely two workers to support each retiree, as against three now and four five years ago. Because of this pensions were reduced by five per cent in 2000, and the age of eligibility increased from 60 to 65.

Will Japan revert to the worst aspects of the 'emperor system', with its overtones of military aggression, absolute obedience of the mass of the people to an oligarchy and insistence on the myths of Shinto? Probably not, if only because so many young people are well enough educated and influential enough to resist it. However, the physical means are there – Japan is one of the world's biggest spenders on weapons for its 'self-defence force', a large and modern army, navy and air force using mostly American matériel. There is some evidence of revival of Japanese nationalism, also considerable pressure on the people and the academic community to believe in the purity and uniqueness of Japanese society. A major Japanese motion picture, Pride, the Fatal Moment, was produced in 1998 which presented a picture of the Second World War idealizing the wartime prime minister, General Tojo, who was executed for war crimes in 1946. This film, which showed to capacity audiences in Japan, rewrote history in several important ways, justifying Japan's actions and derogating those of the United States, while ignoring atrocities like the carnage in Nanjing. When the Mayor of Nagasaki publicly acknowledged in 1990 that Emperor Hirohito must bear some responsibility for the war, he was shot in the back in an assassination attempt. Considerable controversy resulted in 2000 when Prime Minister Yoshiro Mori described Japan as 'a divine land with the Emperor at its heart'.

In 2001 Japan's neighbours criticized a visit of Japanese Prime Minister Koizumi to the Yasukuni Shrine as provocative, and some Japanese politicians accused him of encouraging a dangerous nationalist trend. The shrine, which honours the war dead, was central to development of the 'emperor system' in the 1930s. In 2003 the Board of Education ordered that the Rising Sun flag be raised and the national anthem sung at all school assemblies 'without fail'. Several hundred school staff were punished for failing to comply. *Kendo* – the way of the sword – is still taught to young people in Japan, just as it was during the Tokugawa. However, *The New History Textbook*, compiled by a group of right-wing academics in 2002, and widely criticized because it glossed over much of the Second World War history, has been rejected by a majority of Japanese schools. An updated version was, however, again approved in 2005, resulting in another wave of protest from Japan's neighbours, including large demonstrations and attacks on the Japanese Embassy and businesses in China.

Japanese society remains hierarchic. The most important element is the group – the *dantai* – the least important the individual person. Almost all decision making is collective – innumerable meetings and conferences are characteristic of Japanese business. Social relationships are rigid and complex, with set forms of language, especially for greetings, to be used between people of different social levels. This is the basis for the generally observed politeness and formality of Japanese people – also the absolute necessity for a *meishi*, a business or calling card, so the social position of a new acquaintance can be established on first meeting.

Something called *nakama*, the cement that holds together the groups to which all Japanese are attracted, be it a workplace, a club, a school, an office, must be permitted to operate smoothly. *Nakama* means 'insider' and in its broadest sense, involving the whole country, includes Japanese and only Japanese. Foreigners, even though they will be treated with formal politeness, are *yosomono*, a mildly derisory term meaning 'outsider', and will remain so no matter how long they live in Japan.

Discrimination does not apply only to foreigners, of whom Koreans are the most substantial group. There is a minority of three million Japanese who are the equivalent of India's untouchables. These, the *burakumin*, are the descendants of hereditary low-caste groups who butchered animals, worked with leather, or dealt with the dead. They live in segregated communities in most larger Japanese cities, and suffer severe educational, social and economic disadvantages.

25 Thailand: Two Hats – the Struggle for Democracy

Thailand, as Siam came to be renamed, is in many respects the most advanced state in mainland south-east Asia, in spite of the fact that the succeeding authority to its absolute monarchy has been, effectively, the army. Army officers frequently wear 'two hats', meaning they have another job in the nominally civilian administration. Parliamentary democracy there has been regularly punctuated by military coups, although the 'managed' democracy regime of Thaksin Shinawatra, elected in 2001, still governed four years later. An increasingly educated and assertive middle class has, over the last decade, become less tolerant of military influence. The Thai armed forces, numbering more than 270,000, nevertheless remain a significant force in the community – even, in the last analysis, the decisive one.

King Mongkut's son, Chulalongkorn, carried on his father's policies of reform with enthusiasm when he inherited the Siamese throne in 1868. At that time there was no proper code of law, no public education system, no organization of state revenue, and no comprehensive road network. During his reign until 1910 Siam acquired these things and more. This was due in part to close relations with Britain as a result of a treaty signed in 1855. While this 'unequal treaty' regulated import and export duties at low levels, it nevertheless guaranteed Siam's status as an independent nation and was the basis of a continuing and, on the whole, progressive British influence.

Chulalongkorn sent his own children abroad to be educated and, with the help of his numerous brothers and sisters, energetically imposed on the nation a veneer, at least, of modernity. Although the nation's quasi-colonial dependence on Britain obliged him to use British advisers and encourage British investment, he was careful to recruit advisers from other European nations, such as the French and Belgians who helped devise the legal code. Two reforms were typical of him. He ended the custom that obliged subjects to crawl into the royal presence on hands and knees, and abolished slavery. Nevertheless he used the army to enforce Siam's authority within what are its modern boundaries. Revolts in the Muslim south led by the raja of Pattani, in the Chiengmai region in the north, and in the north-east, resulted from the diversion of revenues from local leaders to the state. In 1873 a modern revenue system replaced 'tax farming', and local lords became salaried provincial governors. Chinese migration grew rapidly, reaching ten per cent of the population at the end of Chulalongkorn's reign.

He is otherwise notable for the adroitness with which he kept his country out of the hands of any one of the great powers. Even so, it lost more than 200,000 square miles of territory. French gunboats steamed up the river to blockade Bangkok, forcing Siam to return all territory east of the Mekong River to the French colonies of Laos and Cambodia. Five years later it surrendered what are now the four northern provinces of Malaysia in return for a British loan of £4 million to extend the Siamese railway system, in spite of a protest from the Sultan of Kedah that his state 'had been bought and sold like a buffalo'.

However, Chulalongkorn refused overtures from a group of 11 Siamese, including four princes, who had been abroad, to introduce cabinet government. By the 1930s the absolute monarchy was the last in the world in any country of consequence, and increasingly appeared an absurd and repressive anachronism. In 1931 the king, Prajadhipok, had to go overseas to be treated for failing eyesight and, when he returned, retired to his seaside palace at Hua Hin to convalesce. Prince Paripatra acted as regent. It was a time of considerable interest in the dynasty, because Rama I had predicted it would last only 150 years. That anniversary, however, passed without incident on 6 April 1932. Then, early in the morning of 24 June, tanks rumbled into the grounds of the royal palace in Bangkok and Prince Paripatra, still in his pyjamas, was taken away to join other members of the royal family being held hostage by the leaders of a coup d'état.

This 1932 coup, which was almost bloodless, was the work of a group of 114 mostly Western-educated people. Economic problems, compounded by the effects of the world depression, were a major reason for the move. Siam insisted on staying on the gold standard when the rest of the world had abandoned it, and as a result was pricing herself out of the world export market for rice and timber. A National Assembly, designed to make Thailand a modern democracy, was instituted, but it was soon to be subverted. Although the country was introduced to representative government with apparent ease, it proved difficult to make it work. It became necessary to invent words hitherto unknown in the language for such concepts as revolution, politics, constitution.

The hoped-for democracy never came. One of the coup leaders, a young

Figure 15 People in many parts of south-east and south Asia have lived in houses like these, built out over the sea on stilts, for thousands of years

army captain named Pibul Songgram, who was an admirer of European Fascism and Japanese militarism, took over the country in another coup. It was he who changed the name of the country from Siam to Muang Thai, which means the land of the free people.

Thailand granted the Japanese free movement over her territory to invade Malaya during the Second World War, although later the Thais found the Japanese occupation unpleasant. Pibul, briefly ousted after the war, was back in charge by 1947. Elections were held ten years later at the insistence of the United States, but were so unashamedly rigged that they led to a major public outcry, and another coup, the declaration of martial law and another phase of military rule from 1958.

I was in Bangkok at that time. Near the airport and at street junctions soldiers had dug into foxholes from which machine-guns peered, belts of ammunition in the breeches. In the main streets tanks and armoured cars dominated major intersections, although the coup remained bloodless. Soldiers manning the tanks sat out on top of them, regarding the passing crowds in good-natured idleness, or reading newspapers. As for the public, so used were they to this kind of demonstration they took no notice at all.

General Sarit Thanarat, who thus came to power, did do some useful things. A native of the grossly underdeveloped Isan (north-east), he diverted public funds to what had been a forgotten region, and made an attempt to curb the opium trade. He liked to walk around the streets handing out fines to people he found throwing fruit peelings on the pavement. However, like those of other Thai strongmen, Sarit's reputation did not long survive his death in 1963. It was disclosed he had acquired a huge personal fortune, and in 1964 his estate was required to repay most of this to the national treasury.

Military rule continued more or less continuously for more than half a century. A coup in 1971 that brought another military leader, Thanom Kittikachorn, to power led on to student demonstrations in Bangkok in 1973 that introduced the first civilian government in 20 years. A proliferation of new political parties and trade unions seemed to promise a significant move towards democracy, but the military took over again in 1976. A short-lived civilian phase ended with yet another military coup in 1991. However, an attempt to install the army commander-in-chief, General Suchinda, as premier after elections the following year led on to ugly and tragic consequences. In what has been called 'the protest of the middle class' thousands of people took to the streets of Bangkok and other major cities. Army units opened fire on the unarmed, largely peaceful, demonstrators. At least 50 were killed, hundreds more injured and 34 declared 'missing'. The king finally intervened, and an election in 1992 led to the installation of a popular civilian leader, Chuan Leekpai, as prime minister.

Nevertheless, the power of the military effectively remained. Elections in 1996 involving the usual vote-buying and intimidation brought to the office of prime minister Chavalit Yungchaiyudh, a former army commander. However, public disquiet at the corruption and cronyism that contributed so much to Thailand's economic difficulties of 1997 again brought Chuan Leekpai to the prime ministership in November of that year, with a mandate for reform. The Thai constitution was rewritten in that year to provide for a Human Rights Commission, but its ability to influence events seems doubtful. Amnesty International noted in 2002 that none of the soldiers responsible for the 1991 killings had been brought to trial.

Thailand, like much of Asia, was overwhelmed by the financial crisis. In mid-1998 the government announced the cost of the economic collapse in a single year: a recession of the economy by nine per cent, heavy losses in the value of real property and stocks, and a million unemployed.

Thaksin Shinawatra, a former police officer, an ethnic Chinese from northern Thailand and an American-educated Ph.D., gained control of a huge financial empire, mostly in telecommunications. He was reputed to be the nation's richest man when he became prime minister as a result of

elections in 2001. His Thai Rak Thai (Thais love Thais) Party won 248 seats
in the 438-seat House of Representatives and with its coalition partners has
a commanding majority in both houses of parliament. Its grassroots
campaign appealed especially to rural voters, offering cheap hospital treatment, a three-year moratorium on debts, and micro-credit schemes in
Thailand's 70,000 villages. By 2003 Thaksin had instructed Thai banks to
lend $13 billion in a major pump-priming exercise. Much of this money was
loaned to small farmers and businesses outside the capital, and resulted in
steady increases in GDP – rising from 1.8 per cent in 2001 to 6.7 per cent in
2003. Farm income grew a significant 11 per cent in 2002. Thaksin,
described as confident, engaging, quick-witted and amusing, is said to be
very popular with the people.

However, the government has increasingly restricted the Thai media and
foreign correspondents it sees as critical of the regime. Thaksin appointed
his cousin commander of the army and his brother-in-law deputy police
chief. By 2003 his family controlled all of Thailand's television stations and
more than ten per cent of all stocks on the Bangkok exchange. Thaksin has
been quoted as saying 'democracy is a means to an end', and is an admitted
admirer of former Malaysian leader Mahathir and Singapore's Lee Kuan
Yew's mixture of democracy and autocracy.

Thaksin has used the army and the police in Draconian exercises said to
be necessary to maintain law and order and the cohesion of the nation. In
February 2003 he undertook to break the illegal drug trade in three
months. By the end of April thousands of people had been shot outside any
legal process as 'suspects' in a campaign to control the drug trade. Some
estimates put the number of dead at over 2500. Thailand rationalized its
1909 land cessions to British Malaya as a convenient way for the Buddhist
kingdom to rid itself of a troublesome Muslim minority. However, the
Muslim Pattani region, once a key entrepôt in Islamic maritime trade,
remains a part of Thailand, and in modern times has become the centre of
what the Thai government regards as a fundamentalist *jihad* army, dedicated to fighting for an independent Muslim state. Following considerable
unrest in the region, in 2004 the Thai army attacked the Krue Se Mosque in
Pattani, killing more than a hundred people, many of them teenage boys.
Later in that year 78 young Muslim men were suffocated or crushed to
death when they were 'stacked like logs', hands tied, face down, in army
trucks, an incident described by Prime Minister Thaksin as 'a bit rough'.

Thailand's controlled democracy was confirmed by a landslide victory
for Thaksin in general elections in 2005, in which his party won almost 400
seats in the 500-seat assembly, The Democrat Party, the main opposition
and the voice of the educated middle class, came in with less than a hundred

seats. *The Economist* (5.2.2005) commented: 'Thaksin does not seem over-exercised about democratic niceties . . . Thailand is quickly becoming a one-party state.' Nevertheless this was a personal victory for Thaksin, due to his popularity, the thriving economy, and a reduction in those below the poverty line from 14 per cent in 2001 to less than ten per cent in 2005.

Thailand provides free, compulsory education, and the literacy rate is a high 93 per cent. Around 300,000 students are enrolled in tertiary institutions, with as many again in open universities. The position of women is favourable by Asian standards, with equal access to men for education and work opportunities. Women are heavily represented in the professions and in business management. More than half the workforce is employed on the land, mostly growing rice, but there is a growing manufacturing industry which has absorbed about 15 per cent. Food processing, textiles and clothing, and electronics are the main industries, which are mostly centred on the capital and only large city, Bangkok.

Outside Bangkok Thailand consists mostly of a dozen or so large market towns and thousands of small villages. Almost half of these are on the immensely productive river plain of central Thailand. This fertility ceases abruptly at the sharply defined line where the lush, green ricefields, like a calm sea, meet a range of rugged, dramatic hills, full of peaks and cliffs of weathered limestone. Beyond these ranges is the north-east, comprising about a third of the nation's area.

Until the successes of Vietnamese Communism made it 'strategic', this region was allowed to remain neglected, virtually medieval, approached by only a single horrific road with tottering wooden bridges. When the first medical surveys were made, it was estimated to have almost a quarter of a million lepers, now being treated in a World Health Organization programme. Other diseases, like malaria and liver fluke, were widespread. Even as late as 1998 liver fluke, a debilitating and life-shortening parasite, affected at least a third of the population.

My work in the north-east took me to hundreds of villages, many of them so remote they had never before been visited by Europeans. Here – other than from savage dogs, many of whom might be rabid – one meets an unfailing courtesy, a placid calmness of demeanour, and a social pattern than seems successful in spite of the absolute lack of many facilities Westerners take for granted. Life in this arid region is especially difficult during the six months of the dry season. However, one finds a bleaker picture at the fringes, the poorest most remote land to which young people have been forced because of overcrowding in their home villages. In these hamlets of the crudest shanties there is a very evident lack of hope, humanity forced back on to the ropes, existing in a narrow margin only just on the living side of death. In spite of an appalling rate of infant mortality here there are plenty of children, most with the bulging bellies that tell of acute malnutrition. There are tens of millions like this throughout village Asia. Their tragedy – and the world's – is that they don't make news, nobody does anything for most of them, and there is little indication that most people even know they exist.

Early in the mornings a file of barefoot, yellow-clad, shaven-headed monks would pass through the town. The mistress of every household waited smiling at the gate to put a spoonful of rice into the begging-bowl each of these men carried. But as with much else in Thailand this appearance of humble, impoverished mendicants was deceptive. The apparent poverty, the need to beg for food are things are chosen voluntarily by the Buddhist monkhood, many of whom are highly-educated men and who willingly shoulder the burden of being the social cement, and running the schools, even in small villages. Almost all Thai men enter the monkhood for a period of weeks or months. There are estimated to be 140,000 Buddhist monks, occupying nearly 20,000 *wats* (monasteries), a feature of even small villages.

From time to time when I got home from work two or three would be sitting patiently on the floor of my house waiting for me. They spoke excellent English and were versed in the European humanities. They would have some questions for me, and after a discussion – it might be about anything from nuclear weapons to birth control – they would rise quietly and leave without a farewell. This tradition of knowledge dates back to King Mongkut, whose reforms to the Buddhist establishment stressed intellect rather than ritual, and firmly established education by the monks at village level. This extensive influence of the monks and their connections with the royal family is an important counterbalance to the power of the military in Thailand.

Thailand has a population of 64 million, growing at around 1 per cent a year. While this is not a high rate of population increase, pressure on rural land, as elsewhere in Asia, has encouraged an organized trade selling young girls into prostitution, both within Thailand and overseas. There has been some growth in Thailand's industry, provided with cheap labour by peasants flocking to the capital in search of work. However, working conditions are often dangerous, with hundreds of deaths in recent years from factory fires. Bangkok has become heavily polluted, its narrow streets unable to accommodate some of the heaviest and most congested motor traffic in the world, even though most of the city's characteristic canals – *klongs* – have been filled in to make room for cars.

26 The Philippines: Trouble in Paradise

Like Indonesia, the Philippines is a chain of islands, of which Mindanao in the south, and Luzon in the north, are the largest, between them making up rather more than half the total land area of the republic. The central part consists of eight larger and thousands of smaller islands, collectively known as the Visayas. Most of the others are tiny islets – some 4000 of them so small they are not even named. Off to the east is the long, narrow Palawan, grouped around which are 200 more islets, many no more than barely visible coral reefs.

Most people live near the sea. The interiors of the larger islands are lonely, mysterious regions of smoking volcanic cones and forest-clad mountains, in which cinnamon, cloves and pepper still grow wild. The coastlines are idyllic. Atolls and islands, strands of dazzling white sand, brilliant corals, clear lagoons of placid green water, are all exactly like the standard dream of a tropical paradise. There is a rich natural endowment – gold, copper, nickel, coal, uranium, and offshore natural gas fields.

Regrettably, this paradise is flawed. Population pressures are now becoming extreme, impelled by one of the highest rates of increase in the world – 2.1 per cent, more than a million additional people every year. Over the last decade the population has grown by one-third to 84 million. There is also one of the world's largest gaps between the minority of the very rich and the great mass of the very poor, with more than half the population living on less than $2 a day, and more than three million unemployed – around 13 per cent of the workforce. This has led to a high crime rate, and heavily guarded new suburbs like Forbes Park in Manila for the affluent. They are typically surrounded by walls as high as 12 feet, topped with barbed wire and broken glass. Night and day armed guards watch the barricades at the only entry and exit points. These are fortresses built against the surrounding sea of poverty and lawlessness.

During the ice age glacials, land bridges connected the Philippines with Borneo and the Asian mainland. The first Filipinos whose origins can be assessed with any accuracy moved in at that time. They were small-built people of the type anthropologists call *negrito* and were closely related to the pygmies of Africa. A few thousand of them can still be found in the Visayas, where their presence gave one of its islands – Negros – its name. However, the majority of Filipinos are of Malay type, closely resembling Indonesians and Malaysians. They were seafarers who settled on the islands and established *barangays* – loosely organized autonomous states which fought one another whenever they came in contact. They had a feudal type of social organization based on family and clan ties which can properly be regarded as the origin of the strong family loyalties of present-day Filipinos.

One of the more common misconceptions about the Philippines – indeed, about many parts of Asia – is that Europeans 'discovered' it, and that trade and development began with their coming. In fact the major cities of the Philippines were thriving trading centres long before then. The cotton textiles for which the Ilocano people of north-west Luzon are still famed were prized by the Chinese, whose big trading junks plied regularly to Luzon with the monsoons to buy cotton. During the fourteenth and fifteenth centuries the southern part of this varied, busy world was also reached by the trader-missionaries of Islam.

It was 40 years before Magellan's landings in the Philippines were followed up by Spain, with the establishment in 1564 of trading posts, which were eventually consolidated on Manila in 1571. The main initial importance of the Philippines to the Spanish Crown was the Manila entre-pôt, for it was here that the trading of silver from the Spanish Mexican colony for Chinese goods took place. Chinese ships brought silk and a wide range of artefacts – carpets, ornaments of jade, pearl and ivory – which became fashionable and hence valuable in Europe. Spain controlled the galleon trade between Acapulco in Mexico and Manila.

Meanwhile the missionary friars were operating in their own interests in the rest of the country. Village chiefs who agreed to become Christian became exempt from tax and their authority was deemed hereditary provided they saw to it that the rest of their village paid tribute and provided corvée labour. Large areas of what had been communal land were taken over into vast estates, the *encomienda*, owned by the Church and later by individual families.

In most cases the people of Luzon and the Visayas were receptive to Christianity, partly because they had no formal religion with which the new faith must compete. They were animists, believing in nature spirits, but there was no definite body of doctrine and no organized church with a vested interest in their religious devotion. By the middle of the seventeenth century there were half a million Filipino Christians, almost all Roman Catholic. The Dominican friars established what is now Asia's oldest university, Santo Tomas, in Manila in 1611. Most Filipinos are Catholic today, and the Church's opposition to birth control is largely responsible for the rapid population increase. The southern island of Mindanao is almost entirely Muslim.

European trade with the Philippines increased considerably after the opening of the Suez Canal in 1869, bringing greater influence and wealth to a new and growing class of merchants. In many cases these families had Spanish blood. Possession of landed estates was such an important mark of social distinction in Spain that the Spaniards in the Philippines, both traders and priests, were anxious to acquire feudal grants of huge tracts of land and were given the right to administer and use the labour of the 'Indians' living on that land.

Spanish rule was cruel and oppressive. Laymen and priests alike regarded it as natural and proper that the Filipino peasants should labour for their support, and give them implicit obedience. The friars of the Franciscan order were particularly grasping in their ambitions to acquire more and more land, on which they lived in idleness. The people had no part in the government of the islands, although a form of democracy was kept alive in the villages – the *barrios* – which retained the village councils they had always had. However, rapid population growth was already causing increasing poverty and restlessness. Discontent centred on the repressive policies of the government and the continued alienation of agricultural land to the religious orders.

In 1872 about 200 Filipino soldiers and workmen mutinied at the arsenal in Cavite, near Manila. They killed three Spanish soldiers and seized the port. The rebellion was planned to coincide with another uprising inside the walls of Manila itself, but its timing was premature and the revolt was easily subdued. The Spanish authorities, alarmed by the growth of nationalist feeling, executed 13 of the rebels. While most Filipinos might have accepted this, they did not tolerate so readily the further execution, by strangling on the garrotte, of three Filipino priests charged with instigating the revolt – one of them a man of 85.

Among those deeply impressed by this incident was a ten-year-old boy named Jose Rizal, who was to become a man of remarkable achievement and personality, and the most honoured Filipino patriot. A product of the growing middle class and educated in Europe, Rizal was a competent author, musician and painter as well as a teacher, linguist and surgeon. He was also the first serious advocate of Filipino nationalism. When he formed the Liga Filipina in 1892 he was arrested and deported to a remote part of Mindanao, even though this nationalist association was, like Rizal himself, moderate and in the final analysis opposed to violent methods. However, there were other nationalists who were more extreme and, after Rizal was exiled, the cause fell into the hands of the militant Katipunan, an organization founded by Andres Bonifacio and some associates, also in 1892.

An emissary of the Katipunan visited Rizal in exile to seek his support for an armed uprising against Spain. Rizal, however, declined. He had given his word not to try to escape from exile, and believed the people were not yet ready for independence. Without his moderating influence the nationalist movement quickly developed from an organization of talk and pamphlets into an underground resistance dedicated to violent terrorism. Rizal, who felt he was wasting his life in exile, asked to be sent to Cuba as a surgeon to the Spanish garrison there. The authorities agreed, and he was actually on his way when he was arrested, brought back to Manila and executed by a firing squad in 1896. Spain had provided the nationalist cause with its martyr. Rizal's books were read as never before and his name became a rallying cry.

Rioting and terrorism flared up in many parts of the Philippines and within a year of Rizal's death Spain was forced to commit 50,000 soldiers to the task of pacifying the colony. The Spanish eventually came to terms with the rebels, paying their leader, General Aguinaldo, to go into exile in Hong Kong. Aguinaldo complied, but used his time in Hong Kong to negotiate arms purchases for a further rebellion.

Fourteen months after Rizal's death an event far from the Philippines broke the stalemate. Relations between the United States and Spain over the then Spanish colony of Cuba reached breaking point. When Spain refused an American ultimatum to leave Cuba, a war broke out in which Spain was easily defeated. General Aguinaldo, in Singapore when he heard of the war, hurried to Hong Kong to discuss co-operation with the Americans. Shortly afterwards a United States ship returned him to the Philippines. He was quickly able to raise a large revolutionary army, which mounted a siege on Manila and extended the rebellion into other parts of Luzon. The Filipinos believed the Americans were helping them to gain complete independence, since the United States was then regarded as a champion of oppressed colonial peoples.

The nationalists established a revolutionary civil government, with a constitution modelled on that of the United States. Although there were 13,000 Spanish troops inside Manila, the city capitulated after a two-month siege in which there had been little more than sporadic fighting. With this came the first nationalist doubts about American intentions. Manila was occupied by United States forces, whose commander unexpectedly refused to allow the Filipinos to enter the city. Nevertheless, most of the nationalist army remained outside the city while Aguinaldo and other leaders withdrew to the north to establish their seat of government in the Luzon provincial city of Malolos. There they proclaimed an independent Republic of the Philippines on 15 September 1898, the first such declaration anywhere in the colonial regions of Asia.

However, the day after the republic was established President McKinley of the United States privately told his envoys to the Paris talks ending the war with Spain that they must press for the cession of Luzon at least to the United States. A representative was sent by the republic to Paris to plead its cause, but the other parties refused to recognize it. So matters were finalized without reference to the nationalists. Spain agreed to renounce control of the whole of the Philippines which, with Guam and Puerto Rico, became colonies of the United States.

The acceptance of responsibility for the Philippines as a colony was unwelcome to many Americans and Filipinos. The fact that the United States, an ex-colony that had had to fight for freedom, was now becoming imperial master of another people was widely opposed in America. The Filipinos found it a cause for war. In a pitched battle outside Manila in 1899 the Filipino irregulars were defeated. Two months later, Malolos was occupied by the Americans. Aguinaldo and his men retreated northward. The bitter ensuing guerrilla war should not be underestimated, although some books dismiss it with a phrase. The civilian population, looted and oppressed by lawless elements of Aguinaldo's army, suffered most. Deaths probably exceeded 100,000. The war ended with Aguinaldo's capture in 1901 and acceptance of United States rule. It cost the lives of 4200 Americans.

Thereafter matters improved rapidly. The United States granted the first elements of limited self-government with an elected lower house of parliament in 1907 and more extensive powers in 1934, although complete independence did not come until 1946. This transfer of American-style political institutions was not without its problems. Election of officials such as police chiefs has become politicized and corrupt in the Philippines. Freedom to carry arms has contributed to a high crime rate, especially a high murder rate. It became quite usual to see notices at the entrance door outside Manila nightspots such as: 'Deposit your firearms here'.

However, the United States redirected many of its soldiers in the Philippines into peaceful projects. They acted as teachers in *barrio* schools, started road-building programmes, and organized such small but collectively important tasks as digging deep wells to provide the villagers with disease-free water. The importance of this work was emphasized by epidemics of cholera so severe they resulted in an actual decrease in the population. The Americans worked enthusiastically and effectively and conditions soon improved. The United States recruited and sent almost a thousand American schoolteachers to the Philippines, many of them Quakers. As none could speak the local language, Tagalog, they first had to make their pupils literate in English. A direct result is the present widespread knowledge of English, especially on Luzon. By 1921 there were a million children at school.

The United States paid the then considerable sum of $7 million to reclaim the huge estates held by the Franciscan order. The Filipinos had bitterly resented the alienation of land to the friars, and this action did much to reconcile them to United States rule. Nevertheless, American land reform programmes failed to solve all the problems. Many big church estates were left untouched, and the land bought from the Franciscans was not distributed to the farmers who worked it but usually sold to wealthy Filipino families, often of Spanish blood. Most of these proved harder taskmasters than the friars had been.

American policies also resulted in the alienation of huge areas of riceland to export crops like sugar, pineapple, tobacco and coconut, to the advantage of big American corporations, but at the cost of ending Filipino self-sufficiency for food. They did little to improve the serious underprivilege of the bulk of the people; indeed, the first president of the Philippines, Manuel Quezon, commented in 1939 that 'the men and women who till the soil or work in the factories are hardly better off than they were under the Spanish regime'.

The Second World War caused terrible hardship in the Philippines. The islands' dependence on exports caused almost universal unemployment when these were cut off. In spite of the relatively small population there were not enough food crops to feed the people, and widespread starvation resulted during the years of Japanese occupation. In 1942 the Communist leader Luis Taruc launched a resistance movement in central Luzon called 'The People's Army against the Japanese'. The first word of the Tagalog translation of this is *hukbalahap*, hence the resistance fighters became known as the Huks. By 1945 the Huks had established a well-organized soviet which redistributed the holdings of absentee landlords, levied taxes, dispensed justice and even ran schools.

Post-war politics were bedevilled by the fact that three-quarters of the pre-war Congress had collaborated with the Japanese. One such, Manuel Roxas, became president as a result of a highly corrupt election in 1946.

Among other things, Roxas refused to allowed Huk congressmen elected from Central Luzon to take their seats. He forced through Congress legislation pardoning all collaborators, and acts which confirmed United States economic dominance of the Philippines. Under these unfortunate circumstances the Philippines became an independent republic.

The Huks returned to their strongholds to wage war on the government. After some initial successes they were controlled by a more efficient government army trained and equipped by the United States. The young Filipino Defence Secretary overseeing this campaign, Ramon Magsaysay, became president in 1953 in what were said to be the first honest elections ever held in the republic. Magsaysay introduced liberal policies, including the first genuine attempt at land reform, until, one night in March 1957, he was killed when an airliner crashed on the island of Cebu. His liberal policies were largely abandoned after his death. There was widespread rumour – although no proof – that the air crash may have been deliberate sabotage. Whatever the truth of that, the political scene again became one of barely concealed corruption and self-seeking. The economy sagged, and the national rate of growth fell far behind in its race with an explosive population increase. By the end of 1966 more than a million Filipinos were unemployed.

Some hope for reform came with the election of a charismatic former resistance fighter, Ferdinand Marcos, in 1966, as sixth president. However, this was short-lived. During his 20-year presidency Marcos used his position to amass a huge personal fortune, exploiting and abusing the Filipino people mercilessly. Claiming that the nation was threatened again by Communism, Marcos declared martial law in 1972, and ruled thereafter as a dictator. In 1983 Marcos's military murdered his principal political rival, Benigno Aquino, shooting the popular Aquino in the head as they were escorting him from the aircraft returning him to Manila after medical treatment in the United States. More than a million people marched through Manila's streets in his funeral procession.

The government imprisoned people without trial, and there was increasing evidence of torture and murder by elements of the army to discourage opposition. Marcos's wasteful use of public money and the diversion of funds to himself and his cronies resulted in a huge foreign debt. Public unrest grew to an unprecedented extent. Two million people joined protest marches in Manila; more than a million petitioned the murdered Aquino's widow to run for president in elections in 1986. This led to the election of Corazon Aquino, the Philippines' first woman president. In spite of a 60 per cent vote in her favour, Marcos attempted to keep power. Intervention by military elements, led by the army deputy chief of staff,

Fidel Ramos, and massively supported by the people, proved necessary to dislodge him.

Again there were high hopes for significant reforms in the government and the economy. Sixteen military officers were brought to trial and convicted of the Aquino murder. However, Mrs Aquino, like most Filipino leaders since independence, came from the wealthy landowning class directly responsible for the nation's problems, and her influence proved disappointingly slight.

There was little significant improvement during the administration of President Fidel Ramos, who replaced Mrs Aquino in 1992. The rapidly growing population and the disinclination of governments to face the nation's basic and urgent problems made these beautiful islands a place of nightmare, with one of the highest crime rates in the world, major inadequacies of public services and utilities, massive unemployment, and a huge disparity of income between the rich and the poor.

Some progress was made, however, in 1996 in settling the long-standing rebellion against the Manila government by the Moro National Liberation Front in traditionally Islamic areas of Mindanao. The peace agreement, which provided for a special development zone in the Muslim areas, did not, however, bring peace, other rebel groups outside the liberation front continuing an armed struggle. Some believe these are now associated with global fundamentalist Islamic 'terrorism' opposing Western intervention in Afghanistan and Iraq.

Widespread discontent resulted in the election as president in 1998 of 61-year-old former movie star Joseph Estrada, on declared, if vague, policies to help the poor and disadvantaged. However, by 2001 he, too, was discredited, facing allegations of corruption and criminal associations. Public indignation supported by elements of the army forced his resignation and replacement by the vice-president, Gloria Macapagal Arroyo, a former university economics academic. She was narrowly re-elected president in her own right in 2004.

In that year 40 per cent of the population remained below the poverty level, with a large public debt, dwindling tax revenues and declining foreign investment offering the government little room to effect improvements. The wealthiest 10 per cent were earning more than 20 times the income of the poorest 10 per cent, many of whom live in squatter towns on the outskirts of the major cities. When, after five days of typhoon rains, a mountain of rubbish slipped on to the shanties of people living within a garbage dump more than 200 people were killed. It was impossible to know exactly how many people were missing because nobody knows how many live in the Manila squatter colony, called Lupang Pangako – the

Promised Land. However, it is thought to be the home of 80,000 slum dwellers, who live by picking over the rubbish for anything of value.

The Philippines economy remains stagnant – essentially agricultural, with a small electronics industry suffering from undercapitalization and competition from other producers, especially China.

27 Korea: Divided Nation

Communist North Korea and the southern Republic of Korea confront one another across one of the most heavily militarized frontiers in the world. To an extent this is a consequence of Korea's geography and her history – the north has long had ethnic and cultural associations with China and Manchuria, while the south, although also influenced by China, has tended to look outwards, with long-standing sea trading connections to many parts of Asia.

Korea consists of a coastal strip of Manchuria bordering China, a peninsula extending south about 600 miles, and more than 3000 islands. The north particularly is rugged, with high plateaux and mountains up to 9000 feet. This mountain chain continues into South Korea almost the whole length of the east coast, dropping into the sea in sheer pine-clad cliffs interspersed with coves at the mouths of short east-running rivers. Westward are larger rivers, with fertile plains, and formidable mountain spurs which divide the country into definite regions. These set the boundaries of independent states early in Korea's history.

According to the mythology, in the year 2333 BCE a bear was miraculously transformed into a young woman. When Hwanung, son of the Creator, came to earth and breathed on her she gave birth to Tangun, Korea's first king. North Korea, in particular, makes much of the Tangun myth in her modern ideology, asserting a continuous culture and nationalism going back more than 4000 years. The actual archaeological evidence indicates primitive neolithic societies, hunters and shell fishermen, during the fourth millennium BCE, with agriculture evolving perhaps 2000 years later. At about this time a distinctive style of pottery ornamentation spread to Korea from China, the first manifestation of a profound and enduring Chinese cultural influence on Korea. However, it was not until 109 BCE that Chinese annals record a successful invasion, after which four Han Dynasty garrison cities were established.

Wars against the Mongolian tribes during the first centuries of the common era forged a large and highly professional military class in the mountainous, largely infertile north of Korea. Their new state, Koguryo, became very powerful, and by the fifth century had extended into much of Manchuria. The Sui Dynasty in China saw this large and aggressive neighbour as a threat, and despatched four huge armies – one said to have numbered over a million men – to bring Koguryo under Chinese control. The first three were defeated at great cost – it was probably the enormous drain of these Korean campaigns that weakened and brought down the Sui Dynasty. The fourth fared little better, the hostilities ending in a truce. Thousands of captured Chinese soldiers were returned home and officials of the succeeding Tang Dynasty came to Pyongyang for the rites associated with the burial of the bones of the Chinese dead.

Tang influence nevertheless came to dominate most of Korea, especially the southern state of Silla, which became a maritime trader of consequence, dominating the sea trade between Korea, China and Japan. This was the beginning of the end for Koguryo, which was defeated by combined Silla–Chinese forces in 668. Pyongyang, the capital of a state of perhaps three million people, was almost totally destroyed. Koguryo should, however, be remembered, because it unified much of Korea for the first time, and because of the resolve and toughness of its people, who after all had withstood repeated invasions from their vast neighbour for 70 years. From the fourth century on it had been an important centre for *mahayana* Buddhism, which was taken on to Japan by Koguryo monks. There is evidence of a considerable Koguryo literature, written in Chinese, most of which was destroyed at the fall of Pyongyang.

Its heir to at least partial unification of Korea was Silla, which now expanded rapidly in a close association with Tang China, subordination being guaranteed by the despatch of Silla princes to the great Chinese capital, Zangan, as hostages. Thousands of Koreans studied there. Chinese medicine, astronomy, music, literature, administration and laws of landownership, were all transferred more or less intact to Silla.

Silla's capital, Kyongju, with almost a million people, was one of the world's largest and richest cities at that time, known and admired as far away as Arabia and India. The opulence of the Silla aristocracy was based on unlimited power over the peasantry as absentee landlords, and their possession of large numbers of slaves. The numerous Buddhist monasteries were also large landowners. As the Tang Dynasty in China declined, so did Silla in Korea. Weakened by regular and bloody disputes over succession to the throne, it fell in 936 to a revived northern state, Koryo. The name Korea derives from Koryo.

The pattern then is one of the client states of China, rising and falling in parallel with the fortunes of Chinese dynasties, nevertheless fiercely independent and following the Chinese example because they admired it rather than as a result of conquest; of a northern region of warriors and a more prosperous southern region of farmers and traders; and of efficient and ruthless oligarchies battening on a sturdy and resilient peasantry who were, however, far from compliant, rebelling regularly against their masters. It is tempting to see an echo of this in the hostility between late twentieth-century Korean workers and their employers, the huge family-based industrial conglomerates. Koryo was controlled by such an oligarchy, who nevertheless so admired the achievements of the Chinese Song Dynasty that they emulated, and even improved on them. Koryo celadon pottery, with its restrained ornamentation, sophistication and transparent blue-green glaze, was regarded as the finest in the world.

A warlord phase in the twelfth century brought unrest and banditry on a major scale, followed by a succession of Mongol invasions, a small part of the huge military campaign of Kublai Khan that subjugated China. Mongol savagery was no less extreme in Korea than elsewhere. The walled cities resisted bravely, attracting praise even from Mongol generals, but in the end fell to the relentless professional assaults, which included elaborate siege machinery and firecarts fuelled with human fat made from boiling down prisoners. Nearly a thousand Korean ships were used in Kublai's massive but unsuccessful attacks on Japan, sharing the disaster of the *kamikaze* – the divine windstorm that saved the day for Japan.

Mongol rule of Korea was firmly established by 1270. It was predatory to a disastrous extent, bringing fresh horrors of starvation and disruption to a society already on its knees. This occupation lasted for 130 years. By 1368 the new Chinese Ming Dynasty had driven the Mongols out of China. However, seven years before that a young Korean soldier, Yi Songgye, had been active in campaigning against the Mongols. He rose to be a general, and, after some bloody infighting among the Korean elite, became the founder of a dynasty that would endure into modern times. Its capital was Hanyang, the city now called Seoul, and the state was called Chosen, the Land of Morning Calm.

Hanyang became virtually a new city. A conscript labour force of over 100,000 built palaces and quarters for the ever-present bureaucracy, the tentacles of which now embraced the nation as never before. Every Korean was obliged to provide an identity tag bearing name and place and date of birth for verification with an official record. The material for these virtual identity cards ranged from ivory down to plain wood according to rank. Movement outside a person's home province was forbidden, and this was closely policed. Within the counties the maintenance of the law and collection of tax was led by officials called *yangban*, a hereditary ruling class whose performance was guaranteed by the despatch of their sons to the capital as hostages. Less fortunate were the next level down, basically policemen and tax-collecting clerks. They were conscripted into their duties, for which they received no payment other than what they could 'squeeze' from the peasantry.

The people actually working the land were closely supervised and controlled, five households being lumped together into a group jointly held responsible for the good behaviour and corvée responsibilities of all its individuals. Peasants paid 50 per cent of their production to the landowner, and both were liable to a ten per cent tax to the state. Other payments were exacted by regional government offices and a tax could be paid in lieu of compulsory military service. The state itself owned 350,000 slaves in 1484. They were often so much better off than the peasants that many free men actually sought to become slaves.

Agriculture, mainly growing *padi* rice, which was the occupation of the great majority of the people, was carefully studied and improved wherever possible. Thousands of water storage dams were built, and rain gauges were issued to the provinces in 1442. The land was carefully surveyed and mapped, allowing the imposition of tax to become an exact science.

Movable copper or bronze type, using Chinese characters and developed in Korea in the thirteenth century, was in regular use 200 years later. Books were produced in thousands, often beautifully illustrated in colour with woodblocks. Many of these books were designed to promote the neo-Confucian ethic then current in China; family values, the authority of fathers, the obedience and humility of children – all these 'virtues' became deeply inculcated at all levels of Korean society. An alphabet of 24 letters was evolved in 1444, far better suited to the Korean language than Chinese ideographs, but scholars considered it vulgar. It languished for many centuries, but is now widely used.

When the Japanese Shogun Hideyoshi conceived the unrealistic ambition of conquering China, the obvious stepping stone appeared to be Korea. Angered by Korea's natural reluctance to co-operate, he invaded the country with an army of 160,000 *samurai* in 1592, and pressed on to Seoul in spite of heavy losses. In the capital the invaders were helped by a revolt among the slaves, who set fire to buildings housing the slave records. A Korean appeal to Ming China brought a less than adequate response, but did involve China in the wars, which dragged on until Hideyoshi's death in 1598.

One of the curiosities of this war was the turtle ship of Admiral Yi Sunsin, an armoured barge propelled by a square sail and 20 oars, considered to be the world's first ironclad. These fast vessels, armed with 40 cannon, caused such destruction to Japanese supply ships that the Japanese ruler Hideyoshi demanded some proof of his army's valour. The bizarre response was the despatch to Kyoto of the ears cut from almost 40,000 Chinese and Korean dead, pickled in salt. The war caused enormous destruction in Korea, including the burning of many monasteries. But the chief victim was the old social order. Much of the opposition to the Japanese had come from peasant guerrillas, and in some cases bands of slaves. The leaders of these irregulars became powerful enough to enter the ruling classes, fighting their way into positions of influence.

In the seventeenth century Korea was again invaded as a consequence of a power change in China. In 1637 Korea became a tributary state of the Manchus, who, although deadly enough in battle, were indolent in administration. They left Korea much to itself to recover from half a century of war. Gold, silver, cloth and especially the small Korean cavalry horses were required as tribute, but the Manchus had little permanent influence on Korean society.

Even so, restoration of the old social order was next to impossible. The slave and taxation records had been destroyed, and the government found itself largely impotent from sheer lack of money. Recovery was slow and gradual, and involved important social and commercial changes. There was more private, rather than state, enterprise, and a wealthy commercial class developed. The number of slaves was greatly reduced. Their use in state enterprises ended in 1801, although private families and businesses continued to own slaves until 1894.

The centuries of Yi rule set an enduring pattern for Korean society, much of which remains today. A hereditary caste system which placed the scholar-official at the highest level made necessary accurate genealogical records spanning many generations, and quite complex rules determining who should marry whom. Of continuing importance, too, is the concept that only the 'first son' – the eldest – has *chong-che*, the mystic capacity and right to succeed his father. This, often perceived by Westerners as nepotism, extends from the control of family property and businesses through to politics. The succession in North Korea from Kim II Sung to his eldest son Kim Jong Il is typical.

The Korean caste system, by no means as pervasive as the Indian one, nevertheless had its equivalent of untouchables, among them those who butchered animals and dealt with the dead. There remain today different ways of addressing people in different social categories. The Confucian concept of respect for elders involves the use of special honorifics whenever they are addressed, and is basic to an elaborate system of family hierarchy with a distinct ranking position for every member: the father at the top, wife obeying him, daughters (and daughters-in-law) subordinate to the mother, younger children below older ones.

However, the superficial appearance that such a system must be oppressive, even cruel, is mistaken. Korean parents tend to indulge their children, and will extend themselves financially to an extraordinary extent to educate them. Obedience and loyalty to the family structure come not so much from discipline as from the deep respect children have for their parents. Children too, take their education seriously from infancy and make every effort to learn up to the limit of their capacity, to do their best in whatever they undertake. This is a significant driver of the remarkable economic growth Korea has achieved in recent decades.

By the late eighteenth century government was again destabilized by almost constant warring between factions of the ruling classes, typified by the murderous and lecherous conduct of a crazy prince, Sado. Since it would be a crime to kill royalty, Sado was persuaded to be shut in a wooden box which was left out in the hot sun. Thirteen days later he was dead.

The ordinary people suffered appallingly from flood, famine and especially plagues. A cholera epidemic in 1821 dragged on for two years, killing a million people. The impotence of central administration led the people to resort to mutual aid societies, and villages worked together in specialist co-operative enterprises. Banditry was widespread, as also were regional revolts against the central authority. One of these, in 1811, developed almost into civil war.

During a famine resulting from two years of drought in 1812 and 1813 an estimated 4.5 million people starved to death. As the countryside sank into deeper and deeper despair crime and rebellion became even more prevalent. Merchants and officials were slaughtered in 18 southern cities by bands of peasants, and in 1894 followers of a religious and mystic cult, Tonghak, began a revolt so serious that China and Japan once again intervened in Korean affairs.

As in China, the nineteenth century had brought increasing contacts with European ships. These were attacked and looted whenever possible. In 1866 an American ship, the *General Sherman*, was boarded and burned when she grounded in the Taedong River, following an incident in which American sailors fired into a crowd on the river bank. Reprisals were inevitable. In 1871 American warships fired on the batteries at Kanghwa Island, which guards the entrance to the river. When the marines landed to attack the forts the Korean defenders fought back ferociously, but ineffectively, since they lacked modern weapons.

Four years later a similar incident involved a Japanese naval vessel. These incidents prompted an official Korean policy of strict isolation from the outside world. However, gunboat diplomacy would not be denied. Following the arrival of a formidable Japanese fleet in 1876, a treaty was signed with Japan, opening three ports to international trade. Subsequent trade treaties were signed with Britain, several European states and the United States. The number of these treaties does not indicate any desire on the part of Koreans to 'open up' the country. Rather, it was hoped that by dealing with many contending interests outside influences would be kept at bay.

Such was the situation when the Tonghak rebellion brought both Chinese and Japanese expeditions to Korea. At that time Japan was modernizing itself rapidly. One of the last acts of the *shogunate* had been the establishment in 1865 of the Institution for the Study of Barbarian Literature, which two decades later became the Tokyo Imperial University. Those selected to study the ways of the outside world recommended that Japan adopt Western science, trade methods and industry.

In Korea a 'progressive' faction, sponsored by Japan, felt Korea should take this same course. The conservatives, centred around the monarchy, maintained their allegiance to China. Two successful Japanese wars – with China in 1894/5 and Russia in 1904/5 – decided the outcome. In 1905 Korea was placed under Japanese 'protection', and in 1910 it was formally annexed to Japan. Ironically, ideas of nationalism and freedom had reached young Koreans mainly from Japanese intellectuals, only to be crushed by Japanese military imperialism. The Koreans resisted strenuously. During this rebellion hundreds of villages were burned and perhaps 20,000 people killed.

Japan's colonial control of Korea, which lasted until the end of the Second World War in 1945, continued to be harsh – even brutal. Resistance movements persisted throughout the occupation, during which thousands of people were killed or imprisoned. In 1919, Korean protestors were burned alive in a church in which they had taken refuge at Sunron, near Seoul. As with the other colonizers, Japan did improve the infrastructure, creating an extensive rail network, chemical fertilizer plants, and major irrigation and land-clearing works to maximize the rice crop, needed to meet food crop shortages in the Japanese homeland, where the population was growing rapidly. Half the Korean rice crop went to fill Japanese stomachs, causing mass malnutrition and poverty in Korea.

Koreans were ordered to take Japanese surnames, and even the use of the Korean language was banned. Shinto shrines were built, at which Koreans were forced to worship. During the Second World War almost two million Koreans were conscripted as slave labour in Japan, much of it 12-hour days under appalling conditions in mines. Among these conscripts were well over 100,000 'comfort women' – young girls forced into prostitution to serve Japanese soldiers. Seven thousand Koreans were set to work in 1944 to build a retreat bunker near Mount Fuji for the Japanese Emperor, under conditions so harsh that over a thousand died. At least 10,000 Korean conscript workers died in the atomic bombing of Hiroshima and Nagasaki.

As the war ended, the Russians occupied the north of Korea, United States forces the south. Two states, Communist north and American-supported South Korea, resulted. Both were harshly authoritarian and corrupt. By June 1950 they were at war – a war that was really an expression of the zonal rivalry between the United States and the Soviet Union and China.

This war caused enormous suffering and loss to the Korean people – two million military dead, three million civilians. This created a whole genera-tion of widows and orphans and a massive infrastructure loss from which Korea recovered only slowly. A major American aerial bombing campaign began with General MacArthur in command, ordering the destruction of every aspect of infrastructure and human society, even village houses, in North Korea. The capital, Pyongyang, was virtually destroyed. The war solved nothing, achieved little except destruction, the two rival states at the end still facing each other after a ceasefire agreement across a border at the 38th parallel of latitude.

South Korea subsequently passed through a phase of remarkable indus-trial development, making it a major exporter of many commodities until this expansion was checked by the 1998 Asian economic crisis. By then it had become the world's twelfth largest economy. Most families had televi-sion sets, refrigerators and washing machines. South Korea became a major shipbuilder and exporter of motor vehicles. Education was actively encour-aged – now almost the whole population of 50 million is literate. The massively increased industry and urbanization resulted in major changes in Korean society, including a drop in the rural population to only 18 per cent, compared with 55 per cent in 1965. Per capita GNP, about $100 in 1983, was over $10,000 in 2003. Nevertheless these decades of growing prosperity were marred by virtually a state of war between the workers and the big industrial conglomerates, backed by a rigidly authoritarian government and a large and frequently brutal military, who did not hesitate to use mass killing, torture and imprisonment to put down opposition.

A military coup in 1961 brought Park Chung Hee, a former officer in the Japanese army, to power as virtual dictator. Although some of the trappings of democracy appeared in 1963, Park, by now president, continued as an autocrat. In 1972 he imposed martial law, with rigid suppression of any opposition, a situation which continued until his assassination in 1979. Little changed during the rule of several dictators who succeeded him.

However, the Korean people, increasingly unhappy with the corruption and authoritarianism of the government, took to the streets in millions in 1987 in protest. This pressure and others forced slow progress towards greater freedom. In 1992 President Kim Young Sam made vigorous attempts to control corruption and redress some of the wrongs of the past. Two former dictators were indicted and sentenced to gaol terms. Relations with North Korea, however, deteriorated, Pyongyang announcing in 1996 that it would no longer honour the agreements which had ended the Korean War in 1953.

In 1997 the much-persecuted democracy activist Kim Dae Jung was elected president of South Korea. During the previous two decades several attempts were made to murder him: a sentence of death on him for sedition was commuted only after American intervention in 1980; he was exiled in 1982; and on his return to Korea two years later, was placed under house arrest. However, his accession came in difficult times – the severe recession caused by the Asian financial crisis. It left Korea with debts estimated at more than $150 billion. It is typical of the Korean people that they made a gift to their government of gold jewellery and other family treasures which, when melted down, amounted to a staggering 220 tons of bullion. It is also typical that as unemployment mounted to almost 9 per cent, suicides of laid-off workers became numerous – so numerous that the government had to grease the framework of a bridge in Seoul to prevent people climbing it and jumping off.

These conditions eroded Kim's support, and in 2002 self-made lawyer and political activist Roh Moo-hyun narrowly won an election to become president. Mr Roh is anxious to improve relations with North Korea and has expressed concern at US actions in Iraq and Afghanistan. He survived an attempt to impeach him on a technicality in 2004, and gained considerable support when the liberal Uri Party gained a majority of seats in the parliament in a general election that year.

The Uri victory, which came only seven months after the party's foundation, sprang from considerable public dissatisfaction with the impeachment attempt and with the American alliance. At a party conference after the election 63 per cent of the parliamentary members decided that China should be South Korea's most important diplomatic and trading partner, with 26 per cent considering the United States should be. While the party has been categorized as 'left-leaning', it has a centrist faction said to be 'market friendly'. At the time of writing, Uri's detailed policies were unclear. There may be problems developing them in the light of the party's composition of several factions ranging from relatively conservative businessmen to young student activists.

Meanwhile, one of the world's few remaining Communist states persists in North Korea, its nature and policies readily identifiable with its past. For its population – 23 million – North Korea is intensely militaristic, with armed forces numbering over a million, the third largest in the world. This figure is maintained by compulsory conscription of adults, men and women, for three to as long as ten years. Almost a third of the country's GDP is spent on the military.

This regime has presided over a shattered economy, with poverty so extreme it had resulted in deaths from starvation in rural areas during the late 1990s estimated by some observers to be in the millions. United States Congressman Tony Hall, who visited North Korea in November 1998, put deaths at between one and three million, and quoted UN statistics indicating that 30 per cent of North Korean children under two were acutely malnourished. He brought out with him a bag of 'substitute food' being distributed at a government food station: 'Dried leaves and straw, so coarse even cattle would turn away from it', Mr Hall said. 'They grind it into powder and make it into noodles. The noodles have no nutrition and are indigestible, leaving people holding their aching stomachs.'

While the worst effects of the famine were controlled after 1998, a combined European Union/UN survey in 2002 assessed almost half of North Korean children as chronically malnourished, stunted, 10 kilograms lighter and 20 centimetres shorter than their age equivalents in the south. As much as a third of the population are dependent on international food aid. Dissent is severely discouraged, typically being punished by imprisonment in the *Kwan-li-so*, the political penal labour colonies, where conditions are so severe thousands die every year from starvation or ill-treatment. Many thousands of North Koreans attempt to escape across the border with China. It has been reported that when they are sent back to Korea they are also imprisoned in these concentration camps, in which as many as 200,000 people are said to be confined.

North Korea is reclusive and secret, shunning contact with the outside world as much as possible. Because foreign observers are discouraged and allowed little freedom of movement if they do get into the country, there is little accurate information about contemporary North Korea. However, North Korea is developing nuclear facilities capable of producing weapons-grade plutonium, and in 1998 test-fired a long-range ballistic missile into the Pacific. This Taepodong missile is said to have a range of 2000 kilometres – enough to reach all of South Korea and much of Japan. North Korea's nuclear programme was interrupted in 1994 when the US government, with Japan and South Korea, agreed to provide North Korea with two light-water nuclear reactors – a type not suited to extracting weapons-grade material – and 500,000 tons a year of fuel oil until the reactors were operational. However, the United States renounced this deal in 2002, on the grounds that North Korea was persisting in a nuclear weapons programme. Several large North Korean mines are exploiting reserves of about 300,000 tons of high-quality uranium.

North Korea does not deny its nuclear weapons programme, claiming it has enough fissile material for five or six bombs. It also has a thriving export business for missiles, one of the numerous trading, manufacturing and mining businesses run by the armed services. The country's president, Kim Jong Il, is so secretive and reclusive that his neighbours and the large powers find it difficult to assess whether he indeed has the weapons to start a nuclear conflict and, if so, whether he might actually do so. His own people know as little about him. A huge and pervasive public relations effort portrays him almost as a god who must be adulated – and from all appearances this seems to be what actually happens.

This propaganda campaign is carried to an extent and cost which seems bizarre, especially when it is put beside the country's abject poverty and hundreds of thousands of hungry children. Thousands of people dressed in colourful costumes regularly sing and dance in public performances in praise of The Dear Leader. Revering crowds file past the white marble statue and embalmed body of his father, Kim Il Sung, who died in 1994, within a mausoleum complex said to have cost at least $100 million, constructed when the famine was at its height.

28 Vietnam, Laos and Cambodia

As the world depression of the 1930s deepened, French exploitation of the Vietnamese people became extreme. Tens of thousands were herded into palm-thatched sheds in the rubber plantations and forced to work 12 hours a day or more tapping the trees. Plantation owners in France insisted on higher and higher work quotas until people dropped with exhaustion or even died. There is evidence that workers who failed to meet the quotas were punished by being beaten on the soles of the feet, after which they were forced to run.

In 1930, 8000 people set off on a march of protest to the provincial capital of Vinh. The march was peaceful, and to emphasize its pacific nature the front ranks were all women and children. It has been said that the first use of military aircraft against civilians was at Guernica, during the Spanish civil war. But six years before that Potez biplanes from the French Armée de l'Air massacred 700 of the Vinh marchers. The attack was made on a narrow section of the road, hemmed in on both sides by paddy-fields and trees. The first 22-lb bombs were dropped on the front of the march, among the women and children. After dropping their full load of bombs the three aircraft strafed the marchers with Lewis machinegun fire.

Following the discovery in 1916 of plans for a rebellion against the French, nationalist feeling had been effectively subdued by police measures for two decades. However, many of the 100,000 Vietnamese conscripts who fought for France during the First World War came back with nationalist and some with Communist ideas. These last looked for leadership to a man then known as Nguyen Ai Quoc, which means Nguyen the patriot. Later called Ho Chi Minh, this man formed the Indo-Chinese Communist Party in 1930, a year of widespread unrest resulting from the unemployment and poverty caused by the depression. The creation of large areas of rubber and rice plantation had led to massive alienation of land away from the peasants, who had no option other than to become plantation labourers or coolies. By 1930 three per cent of landowners held almost half of all land, while three out of four peasant families had none at all.

The Communists led uprisings and proclaimed two soviets – self-contained rebel states – in the north. French repression of these was severe to the point of brutality and again included the strafing of villages from the air and systematic torture. There was some liberalization in the second part of the decade – due mainly to Leon Blum's Popular Front government in France – but the economic and political scene remained substantially unchanged at the coming of war again in 1939. France, quickly over-whelmed by the German *blitzkrieg*, was subsequently governed by the puppet Vichy regime, which permitted Japan to occupy Indo-China from late 1940 onwards.

At this stage there was already a group of North Vietnamese patriots, partly Communist, known as the Vietminh, or League of Independence. They fled across the border into China following an attack on them by the Vichy authorities in 1941. One of the Communists among them was 30-year-old Vo Nguyen Giap, a teacher from humble origins who had achieved a doctorate at Hanoi University. He was later a teacher. When Giap fled to China his wife and her sister were both arrested by the French and died in captivity.

In 1942 the Americans saw the value of the Vietminh as a resistance movement against the Japanese, but it was thought that the name of Nguyen Ai Quoc should not be used because of its pre-war associations. This was why the Vietminh leader assumed the name of Ho Chi Minh, which means 'he who enlightens'. When the Japanese surrendered in August 1945, the Vietminh took over control of Hanoi. By the end of the month there was a Vietminh government claiming control of the whole of Vietnam. It was backed by a toughened partisan army of about 12,000.

The returning French at first offered independence within a French Union but ultimately negotiations failed because they refused to accept a government that included what was then a minority of Communists. Instead a Dominion government was set up that was virtually devoid of popular support. The result, quite the opposite of that sought by the French, was a significant increase in Communist influence within the nationalist movement which, by 1949, had become Communist-dominated. Alarmed, the United States government began to provide military equipment to France for use in Vietnam.

This did not happen without some misgivings. In the *New York Herald Tribune* of 4 April 1950, respected commentator Walter Lippman seriously questioned French motives and wrote the following prophetic words: 'The French army can be counted to go on defending south-east Asia only if the Congress of the United States will pledge itself to subsidise heavily – in terms of several hundred million dollars a year and for many years to come

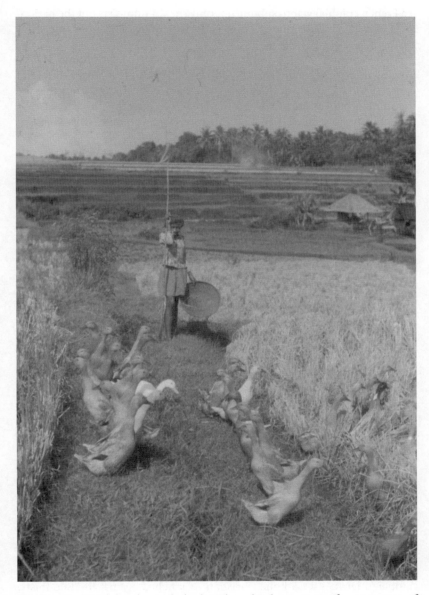

Figure 16 Duck herder with ducks. These birds are a significant source of protein in thousands of villages

– a French colonial war to subdue not only the Communists but the nation-alists as well.' This identifies accurately the beginning of the great tragedy of Vietnam.

The Vietminh quickly infiltrated the Red River delta around Hanoi, proving more than a match for 180,000 French troops in almost a thousand concrete forts. Unrealistic direction of the war from Paris and a fear that the Vietminh would invade Laos led the French to attempt the defence of a mountain hollow called Dien Bien Phu, more than 200 miles from Hanoi in wild upland country, in 1954.

A ferocious Vietminh assault destroyed the steel matting aircraft runways, cutting off Dien Bien Phu for good. In an attempt to reinforce it, day after day transport aircraft dropped paratroopers over the doomed forts. The Communists killed most of them before they reached the ground – the French surrendered after 56 days. Such was the bitterness of the struggle that the survivors who returned to France were described as 'like Christ off the Cross'. When Dien Bien Phu surrendered it represented the first defeat of a major European power by an Asian Communist army. It cost the French 16,000 dead or captured and ended their will to go on fighting. They had lost a battle, a war and an empire.

The United States accepted only with disquiet the Geneva agreements that ended the war, for they had created a new Communist state, North Vietnam, above the seventeenth parallel of latitude. Close on a million people, mostly Catholics, fled to the south. For several years, the northern and southern halves of the country devoted themselves to consolidation and recovery.

The first prime minister of South Vietnam, Ngo Dinh Diem, was firmly supported by the United States. The Geneva agreements had stipulated that elections be held in 1956 to determine who would govern the whole of Vietnam. When Diem, already unpopular in the south because of his autoc-racy and nepotism, refused to hold the elections four years after the agreed date, the Hanoi government decided to invade the south. The ensuing war was inconclusive for many years as the United States became increasingly involved.

In November 1960 Diem narrowly missed being deposed in a coup orga-nized by paratroops of his own army. In 1963 his government drew major opposition from the Buddhist organization. Around three-quarters of the people of south Vietnam are Buddhist. The world was shocked by the campaign Diem – a Catholic Christian – launched against the Buddhists, especially by the protest suicides of seven monks, who soaked their robes in petrol and set fire to themselves. Soon afterwards elements of the army arrested and later murdered Diem, with other members of his family.

During the phase of political instability that followed, ten prime ministers held office in 20 months. American military advisers had been assigned to Vietnam in 1962, and by 1968 half a million American troops were involved in a destructive and controversial war that seemed to have no ending and increasingly no point.

The death rate on both sides and the refusal of many young Americans and Australians to accept conscription to fight in Vietnam brought massive public opposition to the war, especially after the massacre by American soldiers of 400 unarmed civilians, mostly women and children, in the village of My Lai in 1968. That incident and a worldwide outcry at the devastation of huge tracts of forest from aerial spraying of a dangerous herbicide, Agent Orange, hastened the ending of the war and the reunification of Vietnam as a Communist state. The war took over a million Vietnamese and 67,000 American lives, and cost the United States $150 billion. The 8 million tons of bombs dropped amounted to almost four times those dropped in all of the Second World War – probably the heaviest weapons assault in human history.

So deep was the trauma of the war that Vietnam was not assisted by the Western world to recover from the damage caused by the heavy aerial bombing. Only in the late 1980s was it able to approach normalcy, with moves away from doctrinaire Communism towards a free market economy and enhanced relationships with the outside world. Economic reforms implemented by the Vietnamese Communist Party in 1986 legalized private ownership, abolished price control, withdrew support from loss-making state enterprises and opened the country to foreign investment. A trade embargo imposed by the United States was lifted in 1992.

By 2004 more than 4500 foreign investment projects were operating, with a combined capital of more than $42 billion. The Chu Lai free economic zone, which offers generous tax and land rent concessions, had attracted more than 100 foreign businesses a year after its opening in 2003. About a third of these were Chinese. Almost a billion dollars of foreign investment went into Vietnam in the first three months of 2004.

Nevertheless, Vietnam's human rights record has been criticized in recent years, especially towards the Montagnard hill tribe minority in the central highlands, many of whom have fled into neighbouring Cambodia. A report by Amnesty International in 2004 stated that 'the civil and political rights situation did not improve in 2003'. According to official figures 103 people were sentenced to death in 2003, mostly for drug offences and murder, and 64 were executed, often publicly before large crowds at the Thu Duc execution grounds near Ho Chi Minh City (formerly Saigon).

Amnesty's report commented that the true figures would be much higher, and noted official persecution and imprisonment of people advocating democracy, and religious personages, both Christian and Buddhist.

The extensive use by the United States of Agent Orange, a defoliant containing a dangerous dioxin – both a poison and a teratogenic agent – created what has been described as 'a genetic time bomb'. As late as 2004 Western observers were describing the continuing occurrence generation after generation of birth defects, at times amounting to the most horrendous malformations of foetuses and infants. In a conversation with a Vietnamese doctor in that year, she told me of 'many fourth generation cases . . . some poor families try to have a normal child, they end up with four, five, all malformed, or with mental problems or leukemia. The worst are like beasts, they have to be kept in cages.' This continuing tragedy is happening almost entirely in the south of Vietnam, where Agent Orange was used extensively, rather than in the north, where the defoliant was not used.

Development of oil and gas fields assisted the economy, with exports of 130 million barrels of oil a year providing about a third of the country's export income. Timber exports were limited in 1992, in order to preserve forests which still cover about 40 per cent of Vietnam. A considerable recovery in the rice industry has made her the world's third largest exporter, and has resulted from redistribution of land to poor farmers. Vietnam has one of Asia's best performing economies, growing an average of 7.4 per cent annually for the decade to 2004. Export income reached $20 billion in 2003, although much of this came from large industries backed by foreign investment. More than 50,000 locally owned small businesses opened in the two years after the government encouraged such initiatives in 2000.

Tourism is an industry of growing importance in Vietnam. Almost three million foreigners visited the country in 2004, spending about $700 million. Tourist numbers are growing at around ten per cent a year. More than 500 graduates in tourism are now working in the industry, with 100 more training students. The government is committed to major spending to develop more tourist destinations.

A population of 27 million in 1957 had grown to 80 million in 2004, with a disturbing annual increase rate of more than two per cent, and a considerable unemployment problem, especially among young people. Nevertheless most social indicators are good, with a literacy rate of more than 90 per cent and a UN assessment that poverty had declined from 58 per cent of the population to 29 per cent in the decade to 2002. An active poverty reduction programme is in place, with international donors pledging $3.4 billion in 2005.

Among the great buildings of Angkor, early in the fourteenth century, a marriage took place between a princess of the Khmer royal line and the 16-year-old son of an exiled chief from the region now called Laos. This youth, Fa Ngum, was educated at the court of Angkor by Buddhist monks and scholars, and subsequently led a Khmer army of 10,000 back to recapture his father's lands. The kingdom thus established was based on the town of Luang Prabang in the mountainous north of Laos, and was called Lane Xang – the Land of the Million Elephants and One White Parasol.

The transference of Khmer methods and culture to this remote hill country allowed the new kingdom to develop rapidly. There was considerable territorial expansion. What is now Isan – north-east Thailand – became part of Lane Xang, hence the strong Laotian influence still evident in its language and culture. After almost four centuries of continuous existence Lane Xang was replaced by three principalities based on the main towns, Luang Prabang, the present capital, Vientiane, and Champassak in the south. All were subject to constant interference, and at times long periods of occupation, by either Vietnam or Thailand. Vientiane, the most vulnerable, on the fertile plain of the Mekong River, was conquered by Siam (Thailand) in 1778. It was not until 1896 that French pressure forced the return of these Vientiane lands to Laos.

As with Afghanistan, it can be argued that Laos does not exist as a national entity, but is merely a group of tribes artificially welded into a 'nation' by the French colonial administration. This view is supported by the considerable autonomy of the provinces, which, from the establishment of the Communist government in 1975, have collected their own taxes and conducted independent trade with the outside world. These provinces are often dominated by local 'strong men' who have considerable authority. Difficult communications also encourage regionalism – barely 20 per cent of the roads are sealed and many are almost untrafficable. Most of Laos consists of high rugged mountains that march across the country, range after range, to form an almost complete barrier to easy communication. These are clothed in dense forest, and all but the larger towns can be approached only by footpaths. Again like Afghanistan, Laos has many different ethnic groups and dialects. Many of these minorities are in border areas, and consist of peoples also living in neighbouring countries – the Lao people are considered to make up less than half the total population. There is no industry of consequence other than the illegal export of opium, which is grown by the Meo (Hmong) hill tribes.

However, like many south-east Asian countries, Laos has begun to market its considerable timber resources to feed the increasing world hunger for wood. The extent of this logging of some of the world's largest and most beautiful rainforest has attracted considerable criticism. Three 'development' companies run by the military have been given the right to exploit the forests. This appears to be largely for the benefit of Thai interests, especially the military who dominate government and business in that country.

French colonial dominion over Laos was unprogressive, but not onerous. A few French scholars became interested in the region's past and resurrected and rationalized the history of Lane Xang, by that time almost lost in obscurity. This permitted Laos to acquire at least the theoretical basis of a national identity. Nevertheless, nationalist feeling scarcely existed until the 1930s, when a Marxist group was established in northern Laos. This, the Pathet Lao, was probably the mildest and most eclectic Communism in the world until in 1954 it was stiffened by cadres from the Vietminh, at that time locked in their final struggle with the French. A shadowy, slow-moving war ensued until, at the end of the Vietnam War, the Communists controlled most of Laos, subsequently forming the government. In 1975 the Lao monarchy was dissolved, and replaced by the Communist People's Democratic Republic. With this the long-drawn-out war also ended.

Among its less attractive aspects was heavy American B52 bombing of many parts of Laos, including a remote and beautiful upland, the Plain of the Jars. Over two million tons of bombs were dropped on Laos, as much as the United States used in the Second World War. A major feature of the war was recruitment by both the Americans and the Communists of Meo hill tribesmen, who were thus compelled to fight against each other. By 1964 7000 Meo volunteers were being provided with rice, weapons and pay by a CIA operation based on Udorn Thani, in north-east Thailand. More than 400,000 people fled the country in 1975 – about half to the United States – and the Australian and US governments agreed to accept more in 2004.

The new government was considerably influenced in its policies and actions by Communist Vietnam, which itself had embraced a Leninist philosophy derived from the former USSR. It undertook a purge of its former antagonists, directed with particular ferocity against the remaining Meo hill tribesmen, who were now to be largely abandoned by the United States. As many as 30,000 people were consigned to re-education camps, under harsh conditions. The king, queen and crown prince, all of whom had tried to stand aside from the conflict, died in one of these places – the king reportedly from starvation. A peaceful student demonstration in Vientiane in 1999 was severely repressed.

Laos is an almost universally poor country. Survey results released in 1995 indicated that almost three-quarters of households were poor, with nearly half very poor. Average income fell during the 1990s to under a dollar a day. The economy is weak, with inflation above 100 per cent in 1999, 12 per cent in 2004. Population growth is an alarming 2.4 per cent a year.

Opposition political parties are not tolerated and the media are strictly controlled. The government – effectively a central committee of 53 of whom only three are women – has a reputation for being reclusive, corrupt and at times brutal. An Australian woman, Kerry Danes, wrongly imprisoned in Laos, subsequently publicized details about the Phonthong Detention Centre, 'where prisoners, male and female, were kept in tiny sweltering cells and had to kneel in order to address their guards. Many were suffering malnutrition and severe dehydration, others had gone mad. Torture during interrogations, conducted by special police from outside the prison, was routine, including the infamous wooden leg blocks, which interrogators stood on, rolling them back and forth along prisoners' legs, caused excruciating pain.'

The opening of the first bridge across the lower Mekong in 1994 made possible road traffic between Thailand and Vientiane for the first time. A network of roads into China, Cambodia, Vietnam and Burma, and the first railways in Laos, planned under the proposed Greater Mekong Sub-region Scheme, would further reduce the country's isolation, perhaps making it an entrepôt for the whole region. There is also a 18,000 megawatt hydro-electricity potential along the rapidly flowing Mekong River, which Thailand is anxious to exploit. Foreign aid to Laos, mainly from Japan and Denmark, has been among the highest in the world, but, as elsewhere, the demands of Iraq and Afghanistan have resulted in a reduction.

The great natural beauty of Laos, its quietude and picturesque towns, attracted a growing tourist trade, peaking at 735,000 visitors in 1993, although numbers dropped sharply the following year. Sporadic terrorist attacks linked to the former regime have reduced the number of tourists, with a consequent general depression of the economy.

Although the French maintained the monarchy in Cambodia throughout the colonial period, they did little else for the country. Education and health services were minimal. Between the world wars roads and railways were built to service rubber plantations and to facilitate rice exports, to the benefit of French planters and an increasing number of Chinese businessmen. The Cambodian peasant was, however, heavily taxed – around a third of his income in direct tax and indirect taxes on rice, salt, opium and alcohol.

Cambodia was at this time almost the epitome of the decadent Asian state. The king maintained a harem of 400, spent money at will on all kinds of extravagances – Filipino bands, 250 elephants, yachts, boats, carriages – with the willing concurrence of the Cambodian peasantry. The king was seen as near divine, an indispensable link to the gods on high who condemn the crops to failure through flood or drought, or kill with lightning. The profligacy of his material possessions and apparently abundant virility were considered essential to his status.

In 1941 the French selected, from some 400 possible contenders for the throne, the 18-year-old Prince Norodom Sihanouk. He led the traditional life of leisure and luxury over the next decade, but even in this he displayed the restless energy that was to become characteristic. He interested himself in jazz music, wrote his own songs, learned to play the saxophone, and conducted his own band. He travelled widely, married four times and had 13 children.

France granted Cambodia a measure of self-government in 1949, but real independence did not come until after Dien Bien Phu in 1954. Sihanouk abdicated in favour of his parents, became leader of a political party that won a landslide victory in a general election and made a widely publicized transition from king to prime minister. He held this position until his father's death in 1960, when he again became head of state.

For several years Cambodia under Sihanouk became something of a model for south-east Asia. A large rice export surplus kept the economy in a healthy state and provided funds for development – schools, health clinics and irrigation works. A descendant of the Khmer kings, Sihanouk took a particular interest in the restoration of Angkor, which became a major tourist destination. Driving through Thailand to Angkor at about that time, I can recall being impressed at the succession of tidy, prosperous and placid villages in Cambodia. After living in north-east Thailand, with its sad-eyed children showing the tell-tale pot-bellies that betray malnutrition, it was a pleasure and a relief to see well-dressed and well-fed children and contented-looking communities.

Unfortunately this Arcadian situation was not to last. Sihanouk disagreed with American policies in Vietnam. He predicted that China would come to dominate the region, and based Cambodian policies on what he saw as an inevitable need for an accommodation with her. In 1960 the two countries signed a treaty of non-aggression and friendship. Sihanouk broke off diplomatic relations with Thailand and South Vietnam, and in 1963 demanded an end to all United States aid programmes, under which $65 million had been given to Cambodia during the previous eight years. He asserted that his reason was evidence of a United States Central Intelligence Agency plot to overthrow his government, in the same way, he claimed, as the CIA had engineered the downfall and murder of Ngo Dinh Diem in South Vietnam. Cambodia turned, not to the Communist world, but to France to replace the American projects.

The end to US aid, which, including funding of the army, probably amounted to a quarter of Cambodia's revenues, and declining income from the rice crop, caused considerable financial hardship. The army became particularly disgruntled and its leader, General Lon Nol, disenchanted with Sihanouk. The head of state himself had divorced himself almost completely from national affairs, and was almost completely preoccupied with his newest enthusiasm, making movies.

In spite of Cambodia's neutralism, she eventually became involved in the Vietnam War. The Vietnamese Communists used the wild eastern section of Cambodia, near the border, to move supplies and men, and this attracted heavy American bombing within Cambodia along what came to be known as the Ho Chi Minh Trail. A coup in 1970 by General Lon Nol, then prime minister, resulted in Sihanouk's downfall and exile. Lon Nol, who was strongly pro-American, committed Cambodia to a disastrous direct involvement in the war. Lon Nol's offensives against the Vietnamese in that and the following year were failures, in which the Cambodian army suffered severe losses. From this time on Vietnamese and local Communists, and disaffected peasants and hill tribesmen, continued to fight the Cambodian army.

Lon Nol was defeated, leaving the country in a state of virtual anarchy. It was then subjected to four nightmare years of Communist Khmer Rouge government from 1975 under the leadership of a former schoolteacher, Saloth Sar, who took the revolutionary name of Pol Pot. Mass killings justified as 'class struggle' destroyed 20 per cent of the Cambodian people, including nearly all of the educated and professional classes and the Vietnamese minority of about half a million, in brutal mass executions that shocked the world. People were executed on the flimsiest of pretexts – often simply because they wore glasses, this being considered the mark of an intellectual. Estimates of the dead are as high as 1.7 million. In an echo of China's 'great leap forward' Cambodians were driven to 12-hour work days in the interests of a Four Year Plan for the economy that had little hope of realization. Many more people died of overwork and malnutrition. Meanwhile relations with Vietnam became increasingly strained.

In 1979 a Vietnamese invasion was on the whole welcomed by most Cambodians. Nevertheless it brought more social disintegration and death, since the Khmer Rouge continued to fight. Although the Vietnamese had withdrawn from Cambodia by 1989, factional fighting continued and it was not until 1991 that an uneasy peace was signed. Hun Sen, a leading figure in the government imposed by the Vietnamese, emerged as the major focus of power, winning internationally supervised elections in 1998. The last Khmer Rouge gave themselves up later that year. But even now there was no

peace, with regular reports of killings by the Hun Sen government of political opponents, and savage police attacks on demonstrators.

The events of the past three decades have virtually destroyed what was
previously a prosperous and peaceful country, now oppressed by a major
cluster of endemic diseases, continuing malnutrition and one of the highest rates of infant mortality in the world. A United Nations food
programme statement early in 1999 estimated that 20 per cent of
Cambodia's children were in a state of acute malnutrition, due to shortfalls
in food production from subsistence farms. Families borrowing to feed
their children were being charged interest rates of up to 100 per cent. Per
capita GNP is about $225 a year, among the lowest in the world. Due to the
murder of so many teachers by the Khmer Rouge, few schools can now
operate effectively, and the literacy rate is under 50 per cent.

Cambodia has been especially cursed with landmines, estimated at
between two and six million, which will take at least a century to clear up.
So much of the agricultural land is seeded with these deadly devices that
they regularly kill at least 50 innocent civilians – often children – every
month and injure several times that number. It is claimed that Cambodia
has the world's highest number of amputees for its population. Landmine
contamination has also severely affected food production, making large
areas too dangerous to work.

29 Burma: Rule by the Gun

Of the countries of south-east Asia Burma (Myanmar) is perhaps the most varied and beautiful, ranging as it does from placid beaches in the south through broad and fertile river plains to snow-clad uplands in the wild border regions with China and Laos. Cherry trees, rhododendrons, magnolia and juniper grow wild in these mountains, in which bears, tigers, leopards and elephants can still be found. A romantic and timeless river life continues on and alongside the huge Irrawaddy, over a thousand miles long, that divides the country as it flows to a fertile delta, once the most prolific rice-growing region in the world. Bamboo and teak from the virgin forest that still covers much of the country are rafted down the river. It is the main highway of Burma, used by ancient river steamers, fishing boats and barges on which whole families live out their lives.

The people are equally varied. As in so much of Asia, Burma's boundaries were determined by the colonial power, and they include at least seven racial groups in a country that can be divided into four distinct regions. The majority are the Burmese, making up about 70 per cent of the population. Almost all of the inhabitants of Burma are Buddhist. They are friendly, tolerant and cultured people, conservative and bred from early childhood to a deep respect for established authority, politeness in social relationships, and education. They have a particular dislike of violence, both by virtue of a long-standing Buddhist influence but also due to an older animist belief which has it that those who die a violent death become evil though influential spirits called *nats*.

Burma's paradox is that it is ruled, absolutely against the declared intention of its people, by a violent, cruel, inept and self-seeking military government, which imprisons, kills or tortures its own people as a matter of routine if they offer even token opposition, or refuse to be driven into slave labour to the financial benefit of army officers. This sinister organization, which has brought Burma to its knees economically, and into world disrepute, is the State Law and Order Restoration Council, better known by the appropriately unpleasant acronym of SLORC. It appears not to have changed as a result of its cosmetic renaming as the State Peace and

Development Council in 1997. One of its actions was to rename the country Myanmar, but such is the disrepute in which the regime is held this name has been extensively disregarded.

Burma was governed as a province of India until 1937 – virtually the whole of the colonial period. The delta of the Irrawaddy, some 200 by 100 miles of flat plain, was largely jungle and tall grass when the British came. When they left it was a cultivated region of ten million acres, growing two-fifths of the world's rice – rice said to have been the best in the world. Largely because of this rapid expansion of agriculture Burma's population of four million in 1825 increased fourfold over the next 100 years. But this increase in productivity did not benefit the average Burmese, and the British only indirectly. Although the larger trading ventures were British, the rice-growing industry that was so large a factor in the country's sudden social and economic revolution was substantially controlled by Indian businessmen.

The diversion of such large areas of land to a rice monoculture severely damaged a placid self-sufficient village life previously typical of Burma. The agrarian problems which had reduced so many Burmese peasants to desti-tution by the 1930s were exacerbated by the rapacity of the money-lending class, the Chettiars, who lent the Burmese peasants money on the security of their ricefields, then foreclosed on the mortgages. Interest at 18 per cent was common, and rates up to 100 per cent not unusual. The situation was aggravated by the volume of indentured labour brought in annually from India to help plant and harvest the rice crop – almost half a million in 1927 alone. While many of these Indians returned home, probably a million stayed.

Britain, which, after all, governed Burma, could have imposed controls on immigration and the alienation of land. But she did not do so until it was too late. Hence she must be considered responsible for the almost universal poverty and unrest that afflicted the Burmese in the final decades before the Second World War. Violent anti-Indian rioting in the capital, Yangon (Rangoon), in 1930 was symptomatic: 120 Indians were killed and more than 1000 injured. Rioting continued on and off throughout the ensuing years. Often these disturbances seemed to have religious origins, but their intensity and duration were really due to increasing rural poverty as the world depression deepened. As yet the rebellions were regional and lacked specific direction. The factor common to most of them was a demand to separate Burma from the Indian administration.

During the stormy years of the 1930s a group of students at the univer-sity, founded in Yangon in 1920, banded together under the name of *thakins*, and it is in the activities of this group that a revolutionary nationalism can first be seen. The word *thakin* means 'master', and was customarily required of Burmese when addressing a European. The Burmese *thakins* adopted it as an assertion of their racial equality. They were to become very important to Burma, for among them were most of the leaders who would bring the country to independence.

As in India, internal self-government was granted in 1937, although Britain retained control of foreign policy, defence and finance, and the power to overrule the legislature in an emergency. However, this new constitution did separate Burma from India. In the light of later events, it is important to note that the new government had jurisdiction over little more than half the country. Important areas in the northern, eastern and western border regions, occupied by non-Burman racial groups, were outside its authority. The most important minority were the Shans, who are akin to the Thai and Lao peoples, and the warlike hill tribes called Karens, from among whom the British recruited most of the colonial police and militia.

The first years of internal self-government were stormy, as the communal problems worsened. In 1938, 200 Indians were killed and hundreds of their houses and shops looted and burned. Civil disobedience campaigns became common, with persistent strikes and demonstrations. At times the transport system of Yangon was disrupted by scores of women lying down across the tram lines. British goods, and the shops that sold them, were picketed and boycotted.

Matters did not improve with the coming of the Second World War. An opportunistic lawyer named U Saw, who became prime minister, arrested most of the *thakin* nationalists on the grounds of subversion. However, one of the more important, Aung San, escaped to Japan. U Saw was arrested and exiled when the British discovered that he too was negotiating with the Japanese.

However, when the Japanese occupied Burma in 1942 they brought with them a puppet government headed by Ba Maw and the *thakin* exile Aung San, at the head of a nucleus anti-British Burmese army called the Thirty, which had been organized in Bangkok. Although the Japanese were at first welcomed as liberators, their arrogance and brutality during the war years soon reversed public opinion. In August 1944 Aung San turned against them, operating a secret underground that was to become Burma's leading political party.

After the war the Labour government in Britain was willing to grant Burmese independence. Aung San did not live to see it. On a July morning in 1947 six hired gunmen assassinated him and six of his colleagues. The former prime minister, U Saw, who had been released from internment, was convicted of instigating this political massacre, and hanged early in 1948.

The astrologers, always consulted in Buddhist countries on the timing of events, decided that 4.20 a.m. on 4 January 1948, was the most auspicious moment for Burma's freedom. Accordingly, from that time she became an independent republic, outside the British Commonwealth, under the prime ministership of one of the surviving *thakins*, a gentle, devout Buddhist named U Nu. U Nu adhered so strictly to the Buddhist principle of taking no life it is said he made his Cabinet use a side entrance rather than step over a stream of ants crossing a corridor, and so risk killing one of them.

The country was immediately beset with problems – Communist, Shan and Karen insurrections among them. Within weeks U Nu had lost control of all of Burma outside Yangon. The rebels had no difficulty arming themselves, for both Japanese and Allied arms dumps remained open to any comer. There were many Communist cells in the army and they deserted practically en masse, leaving the Yangon government with only a few loyal battalions and provincial units. Forty-four members of the Constituent Assembly left it to become insurgents. For eight years Burma was the scene of an almost incredibly confused pattern of intrigue and violence. The main sufferers were the civilian population. The rebels blew up bridges, rail track and roads, and ambushed trains and river ferries. Passengers were held until their relatives paid ransoms.

The government moved closer to the Communist world in 1953, when it refused any further United States economic aid. At the end of 1954 Burma concluded barter agreements with China and Russia that committed a million tons of rice a year – rather more than half her export surplus – until 1960. Considerable disillusionment resulted from this, due to the slow delivery and poor quality of the Communist goods.

Matters reached a crisis in 1962, when the army commander, General Ne Win, who had been one of the Thirty, took over the government. A complex ideology, known as the Burmese Way to Socialism, was evolved, owing much to traditional customary law. Patterns for the present – and probably the future – were set by Ne Win's inception of a cadre system within the army, a special corps of army cadets trained at a centre near Rangoon. Recruitment was competitive and very selective – Ne Win plainly regarded them as a class of future leaders.

Burma was almost completely sealed off from the world. Ne Win's regime was reluctant to allow any foreigners into the country, and had a passion for keeping foreign influences to a minimum. Much of this was directed at Indians. Their businesses were steadily nationalized and the owners deported during the 1960s. This has not resulted in improvements.

Many factories and shops have been grossly mismanaged since they became government-owned.

While the origins of these policies should be obvious in the light of Burma's late colonial history, this is no way implies that they were desirable or useful. In spite of attempts to revive and reform agricultural practice, rice production continued to decline. Community health remained among the worst in the world, with high rates of infant mortality and almost a million registered lepers. Military rule took a turn for the worse in 1988 with the inception of SLORC and a declaration that the country was no longer on the socialist path. Repression of unrest and student riots now became brutal, the army using its weapons, torture and imprisonment to repress any opposition. At least 3000 people were killed by the army in 1988, including hundreds of students cut down by machine-gun fire in Yangon. SLORC committees were set up at local government levels to ensure its tight control over the community. These local LORCs also took over the judicial function under thinly disguised martial law. The Burmese media are heavily censored, and public assemblies of more than five people are illegal.

Following continued unrest, SLORC permitted elections in 1990. These were won by the National League for Democracy, led by Aung San's daughter, Aung San Suu Kyi, with a landslide victory, taking 392 seats of 485 contested. Parties supported by the army won only two per cent of the seats. Suu Kyi, after living and being educated abroad, had returned to Burma in 1988 to care for her ailing mother. She became a rallying point for democratic forces almost at once, and was placed under house arrest in 1989. SLORC refused to hand over power to the democratically elected party – it still has not done so – and Suu Kyi is again under house arrest. She was awarded the Nobel Prize for Peace in 1991, and has shown outstanding courage in maintaining an international profile while coming under persistent attack from SLORC. Her followers have suffered sustained and vicious persecution.

Meanwhile, social and economic conditions continue to deteriorate in what is now one of the world's poorest countries. Burma's export of more than three million tons of rice a year before the Second World War had fallen below a million tons in 1967, and is now about 600,000 tons. Production has not been assisted by the fact that growers are forced to sell any surplus rice to the government at very low prices. Exports of teak and other hardwoods make up around half of Burma's small export income. Probably Burma's most valuable export is a theoretically illegal one. Growing and selling of opium has virtually doubled in volume over the past decade to around 3000 tons a year, making it the world's largest producer after Afghanistan.

The United States and a number of other countries have applied trade sanctions in protest at the human rights record of the Burmese military. The American sanctions were strengthened in 1997 and again in 2003, restricting private investment in Burma. Burma's population is growing only very slowly, not because of effective birth control measures, but because of the almost universal poverty and ill health. HIV/AIDS is a major problem, partly due to the number of Burmese women who are driven by poverty into prostitution in neighbouring Thailand.

The sheer size of the military has become a millstone around Burma's neck. By 1997 SLORC had doubled the size of the army to almost half a million in order to continue its oppression of the nation's population of 43 million. Nearly 40 per cent of all government spending is devoted to it, compared with one per cent each devoted to public education and health care. The armed forces have emerged as a separate elite, provided with subsidized housing, health care, food and transport. A recent development has been the conscription of thousands of ordinary citizens, at gunpoint, as slave labourers on railways, pipelines and business ventures, such as tourist hotels, often owned by army officers and their families. The army is anxious to attract more tourists, who, however, may wish to consider the pain and distress that result from the accommodation they may use.

SLORC has orientated Burma towards China, with whom she has considerable trade and cultural contacts. China also provides much of the weaponry of the Burmese army. In 2003 China granted Burma a $200 million loan package – China is now the largest foreign investor in Burma. Beijing was recently granted access to one of the world's last major stands of teak timber, which is, reportedly, being milled unsustainably.

The year 2003 was not a good one for Burma or its military government. Early in the year Burma's private banks were in crisis, and were forced to severely limit cash withdrawals. While in reclusive Burma the facts about anything are hard to establish, it appears that one of the biggest banks was forced to underwrite gambling debts of some millions incurred by two members of the regime in Macao. It also seems certain that the financial position of many banks was precarious, with debts far exceeding their assets. Unprecedented measures were introduced to meet this crisis, with borrowers ordered to pay back up to 50 per cent of secured loans intended to be long term, and a restriction on cash withdrawals as low as $50 a week. The incident weakened confidence in the banking system and was also a blow to private businesses attempting to establish themselves in adverse conditions. The Burmese currency, the *kyat*, was further depressed, selling on the black market at much lower than the official rate. Inflation was reported to be 49 per cent in 2004.

On 30 May 2003, as Suu Kyi, briefly released from house arrest, and her supporters were travelling along a quiet road in northern Burma, their road convoy was attacked by government-recruited militia, who killed between 70 and 80 unarmed people brutally, using spears, stones and knives, and injured many others. Suu Kyi herself was fortunate to escape injury or worse. Although the government did its best to conceal the facts about this 'black Friday', it is alleged that 30 convicts were taken from Mandalay Prison to a nearby army camp, where they were ordered to make the attack in company with others similarly recruited. It is also claimed that this militia did not know who they were to attack. Adding to the bizarre nature of this violent and tragic incident, some of the attackers were reported to have been dressed as Buddhist monks.

Immediately after this Suu Kyi was returned to close house arrest, in which she was still confined early in 2005, in spite of an international outcry. Japan and the United States suspended their aid programmes and the USA banned all Burmese imports. However, the junta has elected to ignore international protests, apparently reassured by its firm relationship with China. Significantly, in 2004 an Association of South-east Asian Nations meeting in Jakarta backed off from reiterating an earlier demand that Aung San Suu Kyi be released, reportedly because of pressure from the Burmese delegation.

In spite of a cosmetic, so-called 'road map' to democracy in Burma sponsored by the military, an Amnesty International delegation to the country late in 2003 were denied access to Aung San Suu Kyi, and reported that human rights abuse in Burma showed no signs of improvement. The ironically renamed government – the State Peace and Development Council – now appears to be controlled by its chairman, Than Shwe, who, it is alleged, ordered the 'black Friday' attack. He is said to be relatively uneducated, stubborn, highly conservative, to have a profound dislike of Suu Kyi, and inclined to favour withdrawal to Burma's former isolationist stance, rather than any active engagement with the outside world. Repressive elements hardened further in 2004, with the dismissal of the prime minister, Khin Nyunt, and the foreign minister, Win Aung, both of whom had been regarded as relatively moderate. Soë Win, believed to have been involved in the 'black Friday' affair, became the new prime minister.

It is correspondingly indicative of parlous conditions in Burma that the government uncharacteristically appealed for international assistance when the worst typhoon for nearly half a century struck the coastal town of Myebon in 2004, killing 150 people and destroying the homes of 20,000 more. A further unknown number of casualties resulted from the loss of more than 80 ships and small craft at sea. The government appealed for donations of rice, plastic sheeting, water tanks, medical supplies, blankets and clothes.

A further attempt at a constitutional convention in May 2004 was indicted as a failure by UN observers, because it was composed only of delegates subservient to the junta. The convention was boycotted by Suu Kyi and her supporters in spite of an offer to free her from house arrest if she attended. The junta's response to criticism has been to refuse UN officials entry to Burma.

30 Asia – Today and Tomorrow

Continued poverty and rapid population growth in many of the Asian nations seem likely to remain major world problems. Already dangerous to the planet as a whole, they will become increasingly so unless they are remedied. While this need to improve the lot of the poor is obvious on compassionate grounds alone, the catastrophic economic, environmental and social consequences globally if remedies are delayed are no less important. Although it seems unlikely that world population will double again from the present 6.3 billion, because of minimally increasing or falling populations in the developed world and the severe mortality caused by disease and natural disasters in the developing countries, it is certain that there will be a considerable increase. The best estimates are for eight billion people by 2030.

Assuming this figure, virtually all resources – food, water, energy, arable soil, minerals, fisheries – will become scarcer, and ocean and air pollution will increase. Eight hundred million people are already on the verge of starvation; lakes and rivers everywhere are becoming polluted and depleted; and almost half of all humans lack access to safe and satisfactory drinking water. Per capita grain production in the world, after increasing steadily after the Second World War, actually began to decline in 1984. World grain production fell behind consumption for each of the five years to 2004.

One implication is that the billions of Asia will not be able to evolve into affluent consumerist societies like those of the West and Japan, because of the planet's finite resources and its limited tolerance for pollution. Consequently, the drive to emulate the material profligacy of the West evident in several Asian countries, and its encouragement by elements in the West, are terrible and potentially disastrous mistakes. One simple statistic makes this clear. The wealthiest 20 per cent of the world's people consume over 80 per cent of its resources, the poorest fifth less than two per cent. Even large surrenders of Western affluence could not permit significantly larger consumerism in the developing world.

It was fashionable until quite recently to speak of the 'Asian tigers' and 'Asia's economic miracle'. While both these terms could be applied to

China and Singapore, elsewhere they were inappropriate, as the financial catastrophes of 1997 and 1998 and the difficulties of recovery since have shown. The reality is that the so-called 'tiger' economies brought substantial wealth to a tiny minority in India, Korea and south-east Asia, low wages by Western standards to a somewhat larger but still small fraction of industrial workers, and did little to ease the massive problems of the majority of the people, who still live in villages and work on the land. The reality behind the 'miracle' was and remains the existence of a low-priced, compliant workforce ready for exploitation by Western and Japanese capital.

Hence much of this industry has been based on money borrowed or invested from abroad, low wages and bad, often dangerous and unhealthy, work conditions. Frequently the industry is subsidized by governments, at the initiative of officials who are themselves the main beneficiaries. Too often borrowed money has been spent on infrastructure of no real value to the bulk of the people, such as urban office towers and golf courses. This illusory prosperity created, for a time, work for peasants who left the villages and the fields to become labourers and factory workers, and who have now become unemployed. In most places pressure on rural land makes it difficult for these displaced workers to go back to where they came from. Discontented, desperately poor, with little hope for the future, they have become a dangerous idle class, forced into crime, driven to become social and political malcontents. Such people now number in the scores of millions.

None of this is to say that development in Asia over the last three decades has been uniformly bad. There have been innumerable innovative and useful projects, as the many examples in Japan and China and the advanced position of India in information technology demonstrate. It becomes a question of what form development should take in Asia as a whole. Plainly, if the almost two and a half billion people in China and India follow the consumerist models of the West, as Japan has already done, the consequences for the world will be disastrous.

Innovative forms of industry that conserve resources and use energy minimally could contribute significantly to a happy, fulfilling and healthy lifestyle for the millions now disadvantaged. Appropriate infrastructure built on the existing societies and economic structure – safe water supplies, fuel-conserving cooking stoves, better health services, cheap solar-powered or spring-wound computers with Internet capability, village access roads and bridges, rubber tyres for buffalo wagons, simple value-added industries – these are a few things that suggest themselves. Such objectives are consistent with the tradition of co-operation, the almost universal respect for education and the ambition, and the frugality and will to work typical of much of Asia. The 1997 financial crash destroyed many productive and basically sound enterprises because depreciated local currencies made it impossible for them to meet their loan obligations. Achievement of an innovative and conservational industry may well require a considerable diversity of ownership and direction, and a versatile workforce. Unfortunately the tendencies in many parts of Asia are in the opposite direction. These obstacles to free enterprise are therefore worth considering.

The cartel or monopoly system, during the 1930s characterized by the Japanese *zaibatsu*, is again prominent in several Asian countries. The modern name in Japan is *keiretsu*, but the system is much the same, and is dominated by much the same interests. *Keiretsu* are agglomerates which control whole areas of commerce, from manufacturing through wholesaling to retail shops. Among other things, they provide an effective method of eliminating competing products, especially foreign ones, and tend to discourage innovation. In South Korea the equivalent is the *chaebol*, large conglomerates like Samsung, Hyundai and Daewoo, which generally were fostered by government patronage during the Korean War from the billions of aid dollars poured in by the United States. Almost without exception they are owned or controlled by families from the country's traditional aristocracy.

In India, most of the capital and industry is controlled by a few families; in China the military and the Communist Party have huge business involvements. In Pakistan Bhutto campaigned against the 22 families he said dominated the national economy. Big business, the army and politics have been closely associated in Indonesia, where most large enterprises have been controlled by the generals and their immediate families. In both these countries, as well as in Thailand, Burma and North Korea, the army has come to dominate most lucrative business. Huge fortunes were accumulated by Filipino President Ferdinand Marcos from funds that should have been used for public welfare. This money, deviously transferred to foreign banks, is still being pursued by the present government.

The question that might well be asked is why the Asian peoples concerned tolerate their oppressors. Sometimes, of course, they do not, but where the usurping authority happens to be the armed forces, dissent becomes debatable when you are likely to be shot for it. Much of the blame for this situation must attach to the nations who make and supply arms, not for the purposes of defence, but to equip minorities to murder, oppress and terrorize their own people. Perhaps the most despicable are those who have made the millions of landmines which now litter several Asian countries, regularly killing or maiming thousands of the innocent, in many cases small children, and likely to go on doing so for many decades to come.

Part of the reason for acceptance of tyranny lies in the way children are educated and brought up, taught from their earliest years to be respectful to their elders and to established authority – a tradition of conservatism, a learned reluctance to question or interfere with established institutions. As a Cambodian proverb has it: 'Choose the path your ancestors have trod.' In many parts of Asia at least a minority are better educated and less likely to accept such ideas and constraints. But when this 'middle class' publicly seeks reforms, they encounter a powerful disincentive when they are shot down in the streets, as they have been in Burma, Thailand and Indonesia, by their own army or police.

The growth of industry in Asia has been associated with rapid and large rises in population, and the advent of mega-cities. Greater Tokyo is the biggest with 28 million people, but Shanghai, Chongqing, Calcutta, Jakarta, Mumbai, Beijing, Seoul, Karachi, Manila and Dhaka all have over ten million. Such large concentrations of humanity are a problem in themselves, but they are all the worse because of the nature of these cities. Most include overpopulated fringe areas of slums and shanty towns, in which people lead seriously deprived and difficult lives. Disease and shortened life spans are the norm.

They, and their environs, are also heavily polluting. According to a World Health Organization report in 1998 seven of the world's ten worst polluted cities are in China. This is due to massive use of coal, which produces more than two-thirds of China's energy. A Tsinghua University report in 2002 noted serious acid rain pollution and photochemical smog in the cities. Several researchers have warned that pollution levels could reduce crop yields by ten per cent or more and affect summer monsoon rains. The independent Tata Energy Research Institute in India, quoted in New Scientist (23 August 1997), described as a 'quiet crisis' soil erosion and depletion now affecting 57 per cent of India's productive land. The report predicted drops in the yields of 11 major food crops in India by as much as 26 per cent. The researchers said the area of critically eroded land had doubled over the previous 18 years, partly due to deforestation for fuel or to create new farmlands. Intensive farming and high use of fertilizers was also resulting in rapid depletion of soil nutrients. According to the UN Food and Agriculture Organization, 27 per cent of India's soil is badly degraded, with barely a third unaffected at all. But perhaps the most telling example of the pollutant effects of largely uncontrolled development is the huge forest fires of 1997, 1998, 1999 and 2004 in Sumatra and Kalimantan, which spread a pall of smoke over much of south-east Asia, inflicted respiratory illnesses on tens of thousands, and disrupted air and sea transport.

This seems a gloomy enough picture. Is the future, then, inevitably one of an increasingly urbanized and impoverished mass of oppressed people in Asia, limited only by the ancient scourges of hunger and disease, visiting increasingly large volumes of pollution on the world?

Not necessarily so. A concerted and sincere world effort to end poverty and ignorance is the best and most obvious answer. Beyond the merit of making people wealthier and better educated is another – the near certainty that they will eventually become more independent and able to govern themselves fairly. The modern revolution in news and information exchange must also help, because it has made it next to impossible for tyrant regimes to persecute their own people without some exposure. One example is the use of the Internet to expose the excesses of the Burmese military and to encourage trade boycotts against them, and to react against the heavy censorship of news in Malaysia. Another was the massive world news coverage of the suppression of the democracy movement in China's Tien An Men Square in 1989.

The problem of pollution in the mega-cities of Asia may also provide its own solutions. Already motor traffic has induced air pollution at dangerous levels, a situation which must become even worse if the number of internal combustion engines is allowed to increase. The incentives therefore exist for the large-scale development of economical and low-polluting fuel-cell, compressed air and hybrid vehicles in Asia, which could be exported and compete effectively in Western markets. It is not without significance that the first two mass-produced petrol-electric hybrids were developed and marketed in Japan.

Such promising but often fragile twigs of progress need encouragement and assistance from the Western world to grow. However, foreign aid budgets are dwindling and many Asian countries are crippled by vast mountains of debt, usually incurred by unscrupulous dictators and military regimes. Industry, driven by Western capital and Western ideas, mostly produces what Western consumers want, not what Asia needs. The yawning gap between rich and poor will only be bridged when there is understanding that genuine progress in the Asian nations can come most easily and naturally upwards from the village structure, and that such developments, like the proliferation of solar cookers in India, are the most likely to be sustainable. The simplest solutions, such as higher-bearing fruit trees, efficient fish-farms, safe water supplies made possible by impervious roofing on houses and rainwater tanks, local industries at least initially labour-intensive, simple farm and irrigation machinery, reliable grain seed, are necessary to encourage a modest overall growth in prosperity. Appropriate and immediately useful small industry would grow naturally from that. There is plenty of evidence that aid funds would be better channelled by Western governments to non-government organizations, which are more experienced and have a far better track record in the field than governments.

None of the above is suggested on purely charitable or altruistic grounds. The world economy can expect huge opportunities if and when the average income and security of the billions of Asian people can be steadily improved, if only slowly. Conversely, with the Asian peoples becoming the greater part of world population, sheer lack of markets must increasingly cripple the world economy if a practical and major effort to remedy poverty is not made. Imagination and innovation are needed in this cause. For instance, there is potential for a vast industry in the countries with desert or semi-desert and abundant sunlight to provide the metropolitan powers with hydrogen made from dissociating water or ammonia through the use of solar power, or through the use of catalysts. Research into this technology is well advanced in Israel and elsewhere. Fuel cells run on hydrogen. This example is quoted because it is of a nature that would provide the Asian countries with a permanently renewable, non-polluting source of industrial income. Liquid hydrogen could be carried by existing tanker fleets or pipelines to the metropolitan powers.

World assistance to Asia will need to be based on a proper understanding and acceptance of Asian traditions. Unpalatable though this conclusion may be, control of whole peoples by authoritarian regimes is likely to continue because, failing some potent new influence, the tradition favours them. If they are progressive, as the Singapore government has been, 'controlled' democracies may have their values. However, world indifference to plainly bad regimes – or worse, support for them for muddled political or unscrupulous economic reasons – ought not to continue.

On the other hand, the West, having taken the trouble to understand the Asian traditions, must also accept that it would be naïve, dangerous and inappropriate to promote Asian governments and economies which are clones of Western models. New solutions, based on existing Asian social patterns, minimal pollution, the best possible use of resources and permanently renewable energy, are, then, not only desirable but essential. Given encouragement and support in the right direction, these solutions may well be devised by the Asian peoples themselves, with the potential to offer new models to the world. This presents a remarkable opportunity, a third millennium challenge well worth meeting.

The West ought also to recognize the rejection in Asia of the Western political style in favour of new forms consciously based on past traditions. This is evident in the growth of Hindu nationalism in India, the recent adaptations of Chinese Communism, the resurgence of Shinto in Japanese political rhetoric, the persistence of autocratic governments in south-east Asia, and a turning towards traditional Islam in Pakistan, Bangladesh and Afghanistan. Why are these things happening? Where will they lead? Can an informed Western interest influence these institutions for good or ill?

This gives further, and not the least, importance to an intelligent general knowledge of the Asian traditions. If this book has assisted the reader towards a beginning of that process it will have served its purpose.

Suggested Further Reading

The following are books the reader or student might look at if they wish to go further into areas this book has touched on. This is not intended as a bibliography, but rather as readily approachable and readable material that will advance the interested reader's knowledge of the region.

The Cambridge Histories and Encyclopedias of South-east Asia, South Asia, China and Japan, all issued over the last decade or so, offer useful and reliable sources, and should be available in most public libraries. However, they are organized to approach the subject from many differing angles and by many authors, and so are suggested as references rather than reading *in toto* by all but the most enthusiastic. J. Keegan's *The Second World War* (1997) is one book providing more detail of the Pacific war.

China

See J. A. G. Roberts, *A History of China* (2000); C. Dietrich, *People's China* (1994); and C. P. Fitzgerald, *China: A Short Cultural History* (1986).

For those who want more detailed studies:

J. Gernet's *A History of Chinese Civilisation* (1972) is a readable classic account, which could profitably be followed by Jonathan D. Spence's *The Search for Modern China* (1990), an excellent background from the beginning of the Ming Dynasty on, and a thorough and detailed account of the growth of Chinese nationalism and the modern Communist state.

D. S. Goodman and G. Segal's *China without Deng* (1995) offers interesting insights into recent Chinese history, as also do J. Myrdal's *Return to a Chinese Village* (1984) and P. Hessler, *River Town* (2001). *Tremble and Obey* by T. Watson (1990) is an eyewitness account of the clashes between students and the government in Beijing in 1989. *Dragon Bone Hill* by N. T. Boaz and R. L. Ciochon (2004) is a modern view of Chinese prehistory. See also A. Waley, *The Opium War through Chinese Eyes* (1958) and C. Martin, *The Boxer Rebellion* (1968). Iris Chang's *The Rape of Nanking: The Forgotten Holocaust of World War Two* (1998) gives a graphic and horrifying account of Japanese atrocities in Nanking (Nanjing), although some Japanese claim it is overstated. Chris Patten's *East and West* (1998) comments broadly on modern China, and has interesting chapters on Asian values and the 'tiger' economies. *Treasures of China* by Michael Ridley (1973) is a manageable, well-illustrated paperback that deals mainly with Chinese art of all periods, but also has some good historical sections which help to bring the two fields into focus.

See also M. Loewe, *Everyday Life in Early Imperial China* (1973); G. W. Skinner, *The City in Late Imperial China* (1977); and V. Purcell, *The Chinese in South-east Asia* (1951).

See the following books on Tibet: D. Snellgrove and H. Richardson, *A Cultural History of Tibet* (1995); P. Levy, *Tibet* (1996); and P. French, *Tibet, Tibet* (2003).

Japan

There are numerous books dealing with Japanese history. Among them see: D. McCargo, *Contemporary Japan* (2004), M. Hane, *Japan: A Short History* (2000); W. G. Beasley, *The Japanese Experience* (1999); R. Buckley, *Japan Today* (1998); G. Allinson, *Japan's Post-war History* (1997); K. Pyle, *The Making of Modern Japan* (1996); M. Kennedy, *A History of Japan* (1963); R. Storry, *A History of Modern Japan* (1960); and G. B. Sansom, *Japan: A Short Cultural History* (1931). Rather broader but illuminating, and concerned with trends in modern Japan, are R. Harvey, *The Undefeated* (1994); G. McCormack, *The Emptiness of Japanese Affluence* (1996); David Suzuki and Keibo Oiwa, *The Japan We Never Knew* (1998); L.D. Hayes, *Introduction to Japanese Politics* (2005); D. T. Suzuki, *An Introduction to Zen Buddhism* (1949); H. Conroy, *The Japanese Seizure of Korea* (1960); W. G. Beasley, *The Meiji Restoration* (1972); C. R. Boxer, *The Christian Century in Japan* (1967); and J. Stanley-Baker, *Japanese Art* (2000). S. Murasaki's *The Tale of Genji* should be read for its own merits – I found the 1933 translation by Arthur Waley very readable. H. Kahn and T. Pepper's *The Japanese Challenge: The Success and Failure of Economic Success* (1979) deals mainly with postwar economic matters but relates these well with other aspects of Japanese society; it is an interesting harbinger of later Japanese economic problems. D. Keene (ed.), *Anthology of Japanese Literature* (1955) is an early anthology, a UNESCO production and claiming to be the first such anthology in English, is still a good start to the area. Fosco Maraini's *Meeting with Japan* (1959), by a respected observer and beautifully written and illustrated, is still worth a look. Pico Iyer's *The Lady and the Monk: Four Seasons in Kyoto* (1992) is a sensitive and illuminating picture of contact with modern Japanese on a one-to-one basis; not a history, more a wide-ranging personal view, which nevertheless makes points not to be found elsewhere.

John Hersey, *Hiroshima* (1946), first published in the *New Yorker*, is still the outstanding report of the atomic bombing.

Korea

See: R. T. Oliver, *A History of the Korean People in Modern Times* (1993), W. E. Henthorn, *A History of Korea* (1971), M. Breen, *Kim Jong-il* (2004), C. Osgood, *The Koreans and Their Culture* (1951) and E. McCune, *The Arts of Korea* (1961). *Korea's Place in the Sun*, by B. Cumings (1997), is penetrating and interesting.

South Asia

There are two short histories covering the whole area: H. Tinker, *South Asia: A Short History* (1989), and B. H. Farmer, *An Introduction to South Asia* (1993).

Shorter histories of India include: P. Robb, *A History of India* (2002); J. Keay, *India* (2000); S. Wolpert, *India* (1991); J. M. Brown, *Modern India* (1993); S. Khilnani, *The Idea of India* (1998); Z. Masani and M. Tully, *India: Forty Years of Independence* (1988); B. Chandler et al., *India's Struggle for Independence* (1988); F. Watson, *A Concise History of India* (1974); T. G. P. Spear, *India: A Modern History* (1961); D. P. Singhal, *A History of the Indian People* (1983); and L. James, *Raj – The Making and Unmaking of British India* (1997).

S. Brata's *India: Labyrinths in the Lotus Land* (1985) gives a personal insight by an expatriate Indian into the complexities and problems of the modern society. *Autobiography of an Unknown Indian*, by N. C. Chaudhuri (1951), does much the same for the independence struggle. C. Hibbert's *The Great Mutiny* (1978) gives a readable account of the 'Indian Mutiny', researched from contemporary documents. John Masters's *The Ravi Lancers* (1981) is a novel that gives a vivid picture of the effects of the First World War on Indian society.

See also: V. A. Smith, *Akbar: The Great Mogul* (1928); S. M. Ikram, *Muslim Civilisation in India* (1964); and R. Whitehouse, *The First Cities* (1973), a brief clear account of the Harappa, but now somewhat dated – there are several good Internet sites outlining the most recent research. Other books include: A. L. Basham, *The Wonder That Was India* (1954); J. Auboyer, *Daily Life in Ancient India* (1965); and J. M. Brown, *Modern India: The Origins of an Asian Democracy* (1994).

Other books on specific areas include:

- V. McClure, *Bangladesh* (1989); C. Baxter, *Bangladesh* (1984); and A. Mascarenhas, *Bangladesh: A Legacy of Blood* (1986).
- R. Zimmerman, *Sri Lanka* (1992); and S. Arasaratnam, *Ceylon* (1964).

- J. Yusufali, *Pakistan* (1990).
- G. Arney, *Afghanistan* (1989); and P. Marsden, *The Taliban: War and Religion in Afghanistan* (2002).

South-east Asia

Introductory histories of South-east Asia include: D. R. Sardesai, *South-east Asia, Past and Present* (1989); D. G. E. Hall, *A History of South-east Asia* (1981); B. Harrison, *South-east Asia* (1963); G. Coedes, *The Making of South-east Asia* (1966); N. A. Tarling, *A Concise History of South-east Asia* (1966). Wide ranging, interesting and not too massive is the *Cambridge History of South-east Asia* (1992).

Indonesia

See M. C. Ricklefs, *A History of Modern Indonesia* (2001); A. Schwarz, *Indonesia: A Nation in Waiting* (1999); G. Forrester (ed.), *Post-Suharto Indonesia* (1999); M. Maher, *Indonesia: An Eye-witness Account* (2000); R. E. Elson, *Suharto* (2002); B. Grant, *Indonesia* (1964); and J. D. Legge, *Indonesia* (1964) are all good general histories up to that date. B. H. M. Vlekke, *Nusantara: A History of Indonesia* (1959) gives a detailed account from the earliest times and considerable treatment to the colonial phase. E. Douwes Dekker's, *Max Havelaar* was the first exposé and protest at the excesses of Dutch colonialism. My edition, the first in English, is dated 1868.

Of more specialized interest are: D. Wehl, *The Birth of Indonesia* (1948); L. H. Palmier, *Dutch Java* (1960); J. Ramos-Horta, *Funu: The Unfinished Saga of East Timor* (1987); D. Ball and H. McDonald, *Death at Balibo* (2000); J. Martinkus, *A Dirty Little War* (2001); and T. Vittachi, *The Fall of Sukarno* (1967).

Burma

See: S. M. Yin, *Burma* (1990); Aung San Su-kyi, *Freedom from Fear* (1995); D. G. E. Hall, *Burma* (1960); D. Woodman, *The Making of Burma* (1962); A. Selth, *Burma's Armed Forces* (2002); and A. Marshall, *The Trouser People* (2002).

Thailand

See: C. Baker and P. Phongpaichit, *Thailand: Economy and Politics* (2002); J. Girling, *Thailand: Society and Politics* (2002); D. Bowden, *Thailand: Society and Politics* (1997); D. K. Wyatt, *Thailand: A Short History* (2003); W. Blanchard (ed.), *Thailand* (1958); and G. Young, *The Hill Tribes of Northern Thailand* (1962).

Vietnam, Cambodia and Laos

See: S. Karnow, *Vietnam* (1991); P. J. Griffiths, *Agent Orange: Collateral Damage in Vietnam* (2003); M. F. Herz, *A Short History of Cambodia* (1968); D. P. Chandler, *A History of Cambodia* (1992); M. Osborne, *Sihanouk* (1994); G. Coedes, *Angkor: An Introduction* (1963); Malcolm MacDonald, *Angkor* (1960) (illustrated by Loke Wan Tho); Chou Ta Kuan (ed.), J. G. Paul, *The Customs of Cambodia* (1997); G. Evans (ed.), *Laos* (2000); Rene de Berval, *Kingdom of Laos* (1956), written with the collaboration of the Laotian Royal family; and O. Meeker, *The Little World of Laos* (1995).

Malaysia and Singapore

See: B. W. and L. Y. Andaya, *A History of Malaysia* (2001); V. M. Hooker, *A Short History of Malaysia* (2003); J. Baker, *Crossroads: A Popular History of Malaysia and Singapore* (1999); J. Kennedy, *A History of Malaya* (1962); and R. Vasil, *Governing Singapore* (2000).

Index